The Tale of Genji

[Translated into English by Suyematz Kenchio]

MURASAKI SHIKIB

[ZHINGOORA BOOKS]

CONTENTS

GENJI MONOGATARI (The Tale of Genji)

Introduction

CHAPTER

I.	—The Chamber of Kiri
II.	—The Broom-like Tree
III.	—Beautiful Cicada
IV.	—Evening Glory
V.	—Young Violet
VI.	—Saffron Flower
VII.	—Maple Fête
VIII.	—Flower-Feast
IX.	—Hollyhock
X.	—Divine Tree
XI.	—Villa of Falling Flowers
XII.	—Exile at Suma
XIII.	—Exile at Akashi
XIV.	—The Beacon

XV. —Overgrown Mugwort

XVI. —Barrier House

XVII. —Competitive Show of Pictures

GENJI MONOGATARI

BY

MURASAKI SHIKIB

[*Translated into English by Suyematz Kenchio*]

INTRODUCTION

BY THE TRANSLATOR

Genji Monogatari,[1] the original of this translation, is one of the standard works of Japanese literature. It has been regarded for centuries as a national treasure. The title of the work is by no means unknown to those Europeans who take an interest in Japanese matters, for it is mentioned or alluded to in almost every European work relating to our country. It was written by a lady, who, from her writings, is considered one of the most talented women that Japan has ever produced.

She was the daughter of Fujiwara Tametoki, a petty Court noble, remotely connected with the great family of Fujiwara, in the tenth century after Christ, and was generally called Murasaki Shikib. About these names a few remarks are necessary. The word "Shikib" means "ceremonies," and is more properly a name adopted, with the addition of certain suffixes, to designate special Court offices. Thus the term "Shikib-Kiô" is synonymous with "master of the ceremonies," and "Shikib-no-Jiô" with "secretary to the master of the ceremonies." Hence it might at first sight appear rather peculiar if such an appellation should happen to be used as the name of a woman. It was, however, a custom of the period for noble ladies and their attendants to be often called after such offices, generally with the suffix "No-Kata," indicating the female sex, and somewhat corresponding to the word "madam." This probably originated in the same way as the practice in America of calling ladies by their husbands' official titles, such as Mrs. Captain, Mrs. Judge, etc., only that in the case of the Japanese custom the official title came in time to be used without any immediate association with the offices themselves, and often even as a maiden name. From this custom our authoress came to be called "Shikib," a name which did not originally apply to a person. To this another name, Murasaki, was added, in order to distinguish her from other ladies who may also have been called Shikib. "Murasaki" means "violet," whether the flower or the color. Concerning the origin of this appellation there exist two different opinions. Those holding one, derive it from her family name, Fujiwara; for "Fujiwara" literally means "the field of Wistaria," and the color of the Wistaria blossom is violet. Those holding the other, trace it to the fact that out of several persons introduced into the story, Violet (Murasaki in the text) is a most modest and gentle woman, whence it is thought that the admirers of the work transferred the name to the authoress herself. In her youth she was maid of honor to a daughter of the then prime minister, who became eventually the wife of the Emperor Ichijiô, better known by her surname, Jiôtô-Monin, and who is especially famous as having been the patroness of our authoress. Murasaki Shikib married a noble, named Nobtaka, to whom she bore a daughter, who, herself, wrote a work of fiction, called "Sagoromo" (narrow sleeves). She survived her husband, Nobtaka, some years, and spent her latter days in quiet retirement, dying in the year 992 after Christ. The diary which she wrote during her retirement is still in existence, and her tomb may yet be seen in a Buddhist temple in Kiôto, the old capital where the principal scenes of her story are laid.

The exact date when her story was written is not given in the work, but her diary proves that it was evidently composed before she arrived at old age.

The traditional account given of the circumstances which preceded the writing of the story is this: when the above-mentioned Empress was asked by the Saigû (the sacred virgin of the temple of Ise) if her Majesty could not procure an interesting romance for her, because the older fictions had become too familiar, she requested Shikib to write a new one, and the result of this request was this story.

The tradition goes on to say that when this request was made Shikib retired to the Buddhist temple in Ishiyama, situated on hilly ground at the head of the picturesque river Wooji, looking down on Lake Biwa. There she betook herself to undergo the "Tooya" (confinement in a temple throughout the night), a solemn religious observance for the purpose of obtaining divine help and good success in her undertaking. It was the evening of the fifteenth of August. Before her eyes the view extended for miles. In the silver lake below, the pale face of the full moon was reflected in the calm, mirror-like waters, displaying itself in indescribable beauty. Her mind became more and more serene as she gazed on the prospect before her, while her imagination became more and more lively as she grew calmer and calmer. The ideas and incidents of the story, which she was about to write, stole into her mind as if by divine influence. The first topic which struck her most strongly was that given in the chapters on exile. These she wrote down immediately, in order not to allow the inspiration of the moment to be lost, on the back of a roll of Daihannia (the Chinese translation of Mahâprajñâpâramitâ, one of the Buddhist Sûtras), and formed subsequently two chapters in the text, the Suma and Akashi, all the remaining parts of the work having been added one by one. It is said that this idea of exile came naturally to her mind, because a prince who had been known to her from her childhood had been an exile at Kiûsiû, a little before this period.

It is also said that the authoress afterwards copied the roll of Daihannia with her own hand, in expiation of her having profanely used it as a notebook, and that she dedicated it to the Temple, in which there is still a room where she is alleged to have written down the story. A roll of Daihannia is there also, which is asserted to be the very same one copied by her.

How far these traditions are in accordance with fact may be a matter of question, but thus they have come down to us, and are popularly believed.

Many Europeans, I daresay, have noticed on our lacquer work and other art objects, the representation of a lady seated at a writing-desk, with a pen held in her tiny fingers, gazing at the moon reflected in a lake. This lady is no other than our authoress.

The number of chapters in the modern text of the story is fifty-four, one of these having the title only and nothing else. There is some reason to believe that there might have existed a few additional chapters.

Of these fifty-four chapters, the first forty-one relate to the life and adventures of Prince Genji; and those which come after refer principally to one of his sons. The last ten are supposed to have been added by another hand, generally presumed to have been that of her daughter. This is conjectured because the style of these final chapters is somewhat dissimilar to that of those which precede. The period of time covered by the entire story is some sixty years, and this volume of translation comprises the first seventeen chapters.

The aims which the authoress seems always to have kept in view are revealed to us at some length by the mouth of her hero: "ordinary histories," he is made to say, "are the mere records of events, and are generally treated in a one-sided manner. They give no insight into the true state of society. This, however, is the very sphere on which romances principally dwell. Romances," he continues, "are indeed fictions, but they are by no means always pure inventions; their only peculiarities being these, that in them the writers often trace out, among numerous real characters, the best, when they wish to represent the good, and the oddest, when they wish to amuse."

From these remarks we can plainly see that our authoress fully understood the true vocation of a romance writer, and has successfully realized the conception in her writings.

The period to which her story relates is supposed to be the earlier part of the tenth century after Christ, a time contemporary with her own life. For some centuries before this period, our country had made a signal progress in civilization by its own internal development, and by the external influence of the enlightenment of China, with whom we had had for some time considerable intercourse. No country could have been happier than was ours at this epoch. It enjoyed perfect tranquillity, being alike free from all fears of foreign invasion and domestic commotions. Such a state of things, however, could not continue long without producing some evils; and we can hardly be surprised to find that the Imperial capital became a sort of centre of comparative luxury and idleness. Society lost sight, to a great extent, of true morality, and the effeminacy of the people constituted the chief feature of the age. Men were ever ready to carry on sentimental adventures whenever they found opportunities, and the ladies of the time were not disposed to disencourage them altogether. The Court was the focus of society, and the utmost ambition of ladies of some birth was to be introduced there. As to the state of politics, the Emperor, it is true, reigned; but all the real power was monopolized by members of the Fujiwara families. These, again, vied among themselves for the possession of this power, and their daughters were generally used as political instruments, since almost all the Royal consorts were taken from some of these families. The abdication of an emperor was a common event, and arose chiefly from the intrigues of these same families, although partly from the prevailing influence of Buddhism over the public mind.

Such, then, was the condition of society at the time when the authoress, Murasaki Shikib, lived; and such was the sphere of her labors, a description of which she was destined to hand down to posterity by her writings. In fact, there is no better history than her story, which so vividly illustrates the society of her time. True it is that she openly declares in one passage of her story that politics are not matters which women are supposed to understand; yet, when we carefully study her writings, we can scarcely fail to recognize her work as a partly political one. This fact becomes more vividly interesting when we consider that the unsatisfactory conditions of both the state and society soon brought about a grievous weakening of the Imperial authority, and opened wide the gate for the ascendency of the military class. This was followed by the systematic formation of feudalism, which, for some seven centuries, totally changed the face of Japan. For from the first ascendency of this military system down to our own days everything in society—ambitions, honors, the very temperament and daily pursuits of men, and political institutes themselves— became thoroughly unlike those of which our authoress was an eye-witness. I may almost say that for several centuries Japan never recovered the ancient civilization which she had once attained and lost.

Another merit of the work consists in its having been written in pure classical Japanese; and here it may be mentioned that we had once made a remarkable progress in our own language quite independently of any foreign influence, and that when the native literature was at first founded, its language was identical with that spoken. Though the predominance of Chinese studies had arrested the progress of the native literature, it was still extant at the time, and even for some time after the date of our authoress. But with the ascendency of the military class, the neglect of all literature became for centuries universal. The little that has been preserved is an almost unreadable chaos of mixed Chinese and Japanese. Thus a gulf gradually opened between the spoken and the written language. It has been only during the last two hundred and fifty years that our country has once more enjoyed a long continuance of peace, and has once more renewed its interest in literature. Still Chinese has occupied the front rank, and almost monopolized attention. It is true that within the last sixty or seventy years numerous works of fiction of different schools have been produced, mostly in the native language, and that these, when judged as stories, generally excel in their plots those of the classical period. The status, however, of these writers has never been recognized by the public, nor have they enjoyed the same degree of honor as scholars of a different description. Their style of composition, moreover, has never reached the same degree of refinement which distinguished the ancient works. This last is a strong reason for our appreciation of true classical works such as that of our authoress.

Again, the concise description of scenery, the elegance of which it is almost impossible to render with due force in another language, and the true and delicate touches of human nature which everywhere abound in the work, especially in the long dialogue in Chapter II, are almost marvellous when we consider the sex of the writer, and the early period when she wrote.

Yet this work affords fair ground for criticism. The thread of her story is often diffuse and somewhat disjointed, a fault probably due to the fact that she had more flights of imagination than power of equal and systematic condensation: she having been often carried away by that imagination from points where she ought to have rested. But, on the other hand, in most parts the dialogue is scanty, which might have been prolonged to considerable advantage, if it had been framed on models of modern composition. The work, also, is too voluminous.

In translating I have cut out several passages which appeared superfluous, though nothing has been added to the original.

The authoress has been by no means exact in following the order of dates, though this appears to have proceeded from her endeavor to complete each distinctive group of ideas in each particular chapter. In fact she had even left the chapters unnumbered, simply contenting herself with a brief heading, after which each is now called, such as "Chapter Kiri-Tsubo," etc., so that the numbering has been undertaken by the translator for the convenience of the reader. It has no extraordinarily intricate plot like those which excite the readers of the sensational romances of the modern western style. It has many heroines, but only one hero, and this comes no doubt from the peculiar purpose of the writer to portray different varieties and shades of female characters at once, as is shadowed in Chapter II, and also to display the intense fickleness and selfishness of man.

I notice these points beforehand in order to prepare the reader for the more salient faults of the work. On the whole my principal object is not so much to amuse my readers as to present them with a study of human nature, and to give them information on the history of the social and political condition of my native country nearly a thousand years ago. They will be able to compare it with the condition of mediæval and modern Europe.

Another peculiarity of the work to which I would draw attention is that, with few exceptions, it does not give proper names to the personages introduced; for the male characters official titles are generally employed, and to the principal female ones some appellation taken from an incident belonging to the history of each; for instance, a girl is named Violet because the hero once compared her to that flower, while another is called Yûgao because she was found in a humble dwelling where the flowers of the Yûgao covered the hedges with a mantle of blossom.

I have now only to add that the translation is, perhaps, not always idiomatic, though in this matter I have availed myself of some valuable assistance, for which I feel most thankful.

Suyematz Kenchio.

Tokyo, Japan.

FOOTNOTES:

[1]Which means, "The Romance of Genji."

GENJI MONOGATARI

CHAPTER I

THE CHAMBER OF KIRI[2]

I

n the reign of a certain Emperor, whose name is unknown to us, there was, among the Niogo[76] and Kôyi[3] of the Imperial Court, one who, though she was not of high birth, enjoyed the full tide of Royal favor. Hence her superiors, each one of whom had always been thinking—"I shall be the *one*," gazed upon her disdainfully with malignant eyes, and her equals and inferiors were more indignant still.

Such being the state of affairs, the anxiety which she had to endure was great and constant, and this was probably the reason why her health was at last so much affected, that she was often compelled to absent herself from Court, and to retire to the residence of her mother.

Her father, who was a Dainagon,[4] was dead; but her mother, being a woman of good sense, gave her every possible guidance in the due performance of Court ceremony, so that in this respect she seemed but little different from those whose fathers and mothers were still alive to bring them before public notice, yet, nevertheless, her friendliness made her oftentimes feel very diffident from the want of any patron of influence.

These circumstances, however, only tended to make the favor shown to her by the Emperor wax warmer and warmer, and it was even shown to such an extent as to become a warning to after-generations. There had been instances in China in which favoritism such as this had caused national disturbance and disaster; and thus the matter became a subject of public animadversion, and it seemed not improbable that people would begin to allude even to the example of Yô-ki-hi.[5]

In due course, and in consequence, we may suppose, of the Divine blessing on the sincerity of their affection, a jewel of a little prince was born to her. The first prince who had been born to the Emperor was the child of Koki-den-Niogo,[6] the daughter of the Udaijin (a great officer of State). Not only was he first in point of age, but his influence on his mother's side was so great that public opinion had almost unanimously fixed upon him as heir-apparent. Of this the Emperor was fully conscious, and he only regarded the new-born child with that affection which one lavishes on a domestic favorite. Nevertheless, the mother of the first prince had, not unnaturally, a foreboding that unless matters were managed adroitly her child might be superseded by the younger one. She, we may observe, had been established at Court before any other lady, and had more children than one. The Emperor, therefore, was obliged to treat her with due respect, and reproaches from her always affected him more keenly than those of any others.

To return to her rival. Her constitution was extremely delicate, as we have seen already, and she was surrounded by those who would fain lay bare, so to say, her hidden scars. Her apartments in the palace were Kiri-Tsubo (the chamber of Kiri); so called from the trees that were planted around. In visiting her there the Emperor had to pass before several other chambers, whose occupants universally chafed when they saw it. And again, when it was her turn to attend upon the Emperor, it often happened that they played off mischievous pranks upon her, at different points in the corridor, which leads to the Imperial quarters. Sometimes they would soil the skirts of her attendants, sometimes they would shut against her the door of the covered portico, where no other passage existed; and thus, in every possible way, they one and all combined to annoy her.

The Emperor at length became aware of this, and gave her, for her special chamber, another apartment, which was in the Kôrô-Den, and which was quite close to those in which he himself resided. It had been originally occupied by another lady who was now removed, and thus fresh resentment was aroused.

When the young Prince was three years old the Hakamagi[7] took place. It was celebrated with a pomp scarcely inferior to that which adorned the investiture of the first Prince. In fact, all available treasures were exhausted on the occasion. And again the public manifested its disapprobation. In the summer of the same year the Kiri-Tsubo-Kôyi became ill, and wished to retire from the palace. The Emperor, however, who was accustomed to see her indisposed, strove to induce her to remain. But her illness increased day by day; and she had drooped and pined away until she was now but a shadow of her former self. She made scarcely any response to the affectionate words and expressions of tenderness which her Royal lover caressingly bestowed upon her. Her eyes were half-closed: she lay like a fading flower in the last stage of exhaustion, and she became so much enfeebled that her mother appeared before the Emperor and entreated with tears that she might be allowed to leave. Distracted by his vain endeavors to devise means to aid her, the Emperor at length ordered a Te-gruma[8] to be in readiness to convey her to her own home, but even then he went to her apartment and cried despairingly: "Did not we vow that we would neither of us be either before or after the other even in travelling the last long journey of life? And can you find it in your heart to leave me now?" Sadly and tenderly looking up, she thus replied, with almost failing breath:—

"Since my departure for this dark journey,Makes you so sad and lonely,Fain would I stay though weak and weary,And live for your sake only!"

"Had I but known this before—"

She appeared to have much more to say, but was too weak to continue. Overpowered with grief, the Emperor at one moment would fain accompany her himself, and at another moment would have her remain to the end where she then was.

At the last, her departure was hurried, because the exorcism for the sick had been appointed to take place on that evening at her home, and she went. The child Prince, however, had been left in the Palace, as his mother wished, even at that time, to make her withdrawal as privately as possible, so as to avoid any invidious observations on the part of her rivals. To the Emperor the night now became black with gloom. He sent messenger after messenger to make inquiries, and could not await their return with patience. Midnight came, and with it the sound of lamentation. The messenger, who could do nothing else, hurried back with the sad tidings of the truth. From that moment the mind of the Emperor was darkened, and he confined himself to his private apartments.

He would still have kept with himself the young Prince now motherless, but there was no precedent for this, and it was arranged that he should be sent to his grandmother for the mourning. The child, who understood nothing, looked with amazement at the sad countenances of the Emperor, and of those around him. All separations have their sting, but sharp indeed was the sting in a case like this.

Now the funeral took place. The weeping and wailing mother, who might have longed to mingle in the same flames,[9] entered a carriage, accompanied by female mourners. The procession arrived at the cemetery of Otagi, and the solemn rites commenced. What were then the thoughts of the desolate mother? The image of her dead daughter was still vividly present to her—still seemed animated with life. She must see her remains become ashes to convince herself that she was really dead. During the ceremony, an Imperial messenger came from the Palace, and invested the dead with the title of Sammi. The letters patent were read, and listened to in solemn silence. The Emperor conferred this title now in regret that during her lifetime he had not even promoted her position from a Kôyi to a Niogo, and wishing at this last moment to raise her title at least one step higher. Once more several tokens of disapprobation were manifested against the proceeding. But, in other respects, the beauty of the departed, and her gracious bearing, which had ever commanded admiration, made people begin to think of her with sympathy. It was the excess of the Emperor's favor which had created so many detractors during her lifetime; but now even rivals felt pity for her; and if any did not, it was in the Koki-den. "When one is no more, the memory becomes so dear," may be an illustration of a case such as this.

Some days passed, and due requiem services were carefully performed. The Emperor was still plunged in thought, and no society had attractions for him. His constant consolation was to send messengers to the grandmother of the child, and to make inquiries after them. It was now autumn, and the evening winds blew chill and cold. The Emperor—who, when he saw the first Prince, could not refrain from thinking of the younger one—

became more thoughtful than ever; and, on this evening, he sent Yugei-no Miôbu[10] to repeat his inquiries. She went as the new moon just rose, and the Emperor stood and contemplated from his veranda the prospect spread before him. At such moments he had usually been surrounded by a few chosen friends, one of whom was almost invariably his lost love. Now she was no more. The thrilling notes of her music, the touching strains of her melodies, stole over him in his dark and dreary reverie.

The Miôbu arrived at her destination; and, as she drove in, a sense of sadness seized upon her.

The owner of the house had long been a widow; but the residence, in former times, had been made beautiful for the pleasure of her only daughter. Now, bereaved of this daughter, she dwelt alone; and the grounds were overgrown with weeds, which here and there lay prostrated by the violence of the winds; while over them, fair as elsewhere, gleamed the mild lustre of the impartial moon. The Miôbu entered, and was led into a front room in the southern part of the building. At first the hostess and the messenger were equally at a loss for words. At length the silence was broken by the hostess, who said:—

"Already have I felt that I have lived too long, but doubly do I feel it now that I am visited by such a messenger as you." Here she paused, and seemed unable to contend with her emotion.

"When Naishi-no-Ske returned from you," said the Miôbu, "she reported to the Emperor that when she saw you, face to face, her sympathy for you was irresistible. I, too, see now[16] how true it is!" A moment's hesitation, and she proceeded to deliver the Imperial message:—

"The Emperor commanded me to say that for some time he had wandered in his fancy, and imagined he was but in a dream; and that, though he was now more tranquil, he could not find that it was only a dream. Again, that there is no one who can really sympathize with him; and he hopes that you will come to the Palace, and talk with him. His Majesty said also that the absence of the Prince made him anxious, and that he is desirous that you should speedily make up your mind. In giving me this message, he did not speak with readiness. He seemed to fear to be considered unmanly, and strove to exercise reserve. I could not help experiencing sympathy with him, and hurried away here, almost fearing that, perhaps, I had not quite caught his full meaning."

So saying, she presented to her a letter from the Emperor. The lady's sight was dim and indistinct. Taking it, therefore, to the lamp, she said, "Perhaps the light will help me to decipher," and then read as follows, much in unison with the oral message: "I thought that time only would assuage my grief; but time only brings before me more vividly my recollection of the lost one. Yet, it is inevitable. How is my boy? Of him, too, I am always thinking. Time once was when we both hoped to bring him up together. May he still be to you a memento of his mother!"

Such was the brief outline of the letter, and it contained the following:—

"The sound of the wind is dull and drearAcross Miyagi's[11] dewy lea,And makes me mourn for the motherless deerThat sleeps beneath the Hagi tree."

She put gently the letter aside, and said, "Life and the world are irksome to me; and you can see, then, how reluctantly I should present myself at the Palace. I cannot go myself, though it is painful to me to seem to neglect the honored command. As for the little

Prince, I know not why he thought of it, but he seems quite willing to go. This is very natural. Please to inform his Majesty that this is our position. Very possibly, when one remembers the birth of the young Prince, it would not be well for him to spend too much of his time as he does now."

Then she wrote quickly a short answer, and handed it to the Miôbu. At this time her grandson was sleeping soundly.

"I should like to see the boy awake, and to tell the Emperor all about him, but he will already be impatiently awaiting my return," said the messenger. And she prepared to depart.

"It would be a relief to me to tell you how a mother laments over her departed child. Visit me, then, sometimes, if you can, as a friend, when you are not engaged or pressed for time. Formerly, when you came here, your visit was ever glad and welcome; now I see in you the messenger of woe. More and more my life seems aimless to me. From the time of my child's birth, her father always looked forward to her being presented at Court, and when dying he repeatedly enjoined me to carry out that wish. You know that my daughter had no patron to watch over her, and I well knew how difficult would be her position among her fellow-maidens. Yet, I did not disobey her father's request, and she went to Court. There the Emperor showed her a kindness beyond our hopes. For the sake of that kindness she uncomplainingly endured all the cruel taunts of envious companions. But their envy ever deepening, and her troubles ever increasing, at last she passed away, worn out, as it were, with care. When I think of the matter in that light, the kindest favors seem to me fraught with misfortune. Ah! that the blind affection of a mother should make me talk in this way!"

"The thoughts of his Majesty may be even as your own," said the Miôbu. "Often when he alluded to his overpowering affection for her, he said that perhaps all this might have been because their love was destined not to last long. And that though he ever strove not to injure any subject, yet for Kiri-Tsubo, and for her alone, he had sometimes caused the ill-will of others; that when all this has been done, she was no more! All this he told me in deep gloom, and added that it made him ponder on their previous existence."

The night was now far advanced, and again the Miôbu rose to take leave. The moon was sailing down westward and the cool breeze was waving the herbage to and fro, in which numerous *mushi* were plaintively singing.[12] The messenger, being still somehow unready to start, hummed—

"Fain would one weep the whole night long,As weeps the Sudu-Mushi's song,Who chants her melancholy lay,Till night and darkness pass away."

As she still lingered, the lady took up the refrain—

"To the heath where the Sudu-Mushi sings,From beyond the clouds[13] one comes from on highAnd more dews on the grass around she flings,And adds her own, to the night wind's sigh."

A Court dress and a set of beautiful ornamental hairpins, which had belonged to Kiri-Tsubo, were presented to the Miôbu by her hostess, who thought that these things, which her daughter had left to be available on such occasions, would be a more suitable gift, under present circumstances, than any other.

On the return of the Miôbu she found that the Emperor had not yet retired to rest. He was really awaiting her return, but was apparently engaged in admiring the Tsubo-Senzai—or stands of flowers—which were placed in front of the palaces, and in which the flowers were in full bloom. With him were four or five ladies, his intimate friends, with whom he was conversing. In these days his favorite topic of conversation was the "Long Regret."[14] Nothing pleased him more than to gaze upon the picture of that poem, which had been painted by Prince Teishi-In, or to talk about the native poems on the same subject, which had been composed, at the Royal command, by Ise, the poetess, and by Tsurayuki, the poet. And it was in this way that he was engaged on this particular evening.

To him the Miôbu now went immediately, and she faithfully reported to him all that she had seen, and she gave to him also[19] the answer to his letter. That letter stated that the mother of Kiri-Tsubo felt honored by his gracious inquiries, and that she was so truly grateful that she scarcely knew how to express herself. She proceeded to say that his condescension made her feel at liberty to offer to him the following:—

"Since now no fostering love is found,And the Hagi tree is dead and sere,The motherless deer lies on the ground,Helpless and weak, no shelter near."

The Emperor strove in vain to repress his own emotion; and old memories, dating from the time when he first saw his favorite, rose up before him fast and thick. "How precious has been each moment to me, but yet what a long time has elapsed since then," thought he, and he said to the Miôbu, "How often have I, too, desired to see the daughter of the Dainagon in such a position as her father would have desired to see her. 'Tis in vain to speak of that now!"

A pause, and he continued, "The child, however, may survive, and fortune may have some boon in store for him; and his grandmother's prayer should rather be for long life."

The presents were then shown to him. "Ah," thought he, "could they be the souvenirs sent by the once lost love," as he murmured—

"Oh, could I find some wizard sprite,To bear my words to her I love,Beyond the shades of envious night,To where she dwells in realms above!"

Now the picture of beautiful Yô-ki-hi, however skilful the painter may have been, is after all only a picture. It lacks life and animation. Her features may have been worthily compared to the lotus and to the willow of the Imperial gardens, but the style after all was Chinese, and to the Emperor his lost love was all in all, nor, in his eyes, was any other object comparable to her. Who doubts that they, too, had vowed to unite wings, and intertwine branches! But to what end? The murmur of winds, the music of insects, now only served to cause him melancholy.

In the meantime, in the Koki-Den was heard the sound of music. She who dwelt there, and who had not now for a long time been with the Emperor, was heedlessly protracting her strains until this late hour of the evening.

How painfully must these have sounded to the Emperor!

"Moonlight is gone, and darkness reignsE'en in the realms 'above the clouds,'Ah! how can light, or tranquil peace,Shine o'er that lone and lowly home!"

Thus thought the Emperor, and he did not retire until "the lamps were trimmed to the end!" The sound of the night watch of the right guard[15] was now heard. It was five o'clock in the morning. So, to avoid notice, he withdrew to his bedroom, but calm slumber hardly visited his eyes. This now became a common occurrence.

When he rose in the morning he would reflect on the time gone by when "they knew not even that the casement was bright." But now, too, he would neglect "Morning Court." His appetite failed him. The delicacies of the so-called "great table" had no temptation for him. Men pitied him much. "There must have been some divine mystery that predetermined the course of their love," said they, "for in matters in which she is concerned he is powerless to reason, and wisdom deserts him. The welfare of the State ceases to interest him." And now people actually began to quote instances that had occurred in a foreign Court.

Weeks and months had elapsed, and the son of Kiri-Tsubo was again at the Palace. In the spring of the following year the first Prince was proclaimed heir-apparent to the throne. Had the Emperor consulted his private feelings, he would have substituted the younger Prince for the elder one. But this was not possible, and, especially for this reason:—There was no influential party to support him, and, moreover, public opinion would also have been strongly opposed to such a measure, which, if effected by arbitrary power, would have become a source of danger. The Emperor, therefore, betrayed no such desire, and repressed all outward appearance of it. And now the public expressed its satisfaction at the self-restraint of the Emperor, and the mother of the first Prince felt at ease.

In this year, the mother of Kiri-Tsubo departed this life. She may not improbably have longed to follow her daughter at an earlier period; and the only regret to which she gave utterance, was that she was forced to leave her grandson, whom she had so tenderly loved.

From this time the young Prince took up his residence in the Imperial palace; and next year, at the age of seven, he began to learn to read and write under the personal superintendence of the

Emperor. He now began to take him into the private apartments, among others, of the Koki-den, saying, "The mother is gone! now at least, let the child be received with better feeling." And if even stony-hearted warriors, or bitter enemies, if any such there were, smiled when they saw the boy, the mother of the heir-apparent, too, could not entirely exclude him from her sympathies. This lady had two daughters, and they found in their half-brother a pleasant playmate. Every one was pleased to greet him, and there was already a winning coquetry in his manners, which amused people, and made them like to play with him. We need not allude to his studies in detail, but on musical instruments, such as the flute and the koto,[16] he also showed great proficiency.

About this time there arrived an embassy from Corea, and among them was an excellent physiognomist. When the Emperor heard of this, he wished to have the Prince examined by him. It was, however, contrary to the warnings of the Emperor Wuda, to call in foreigners to the Palace. The Prince was, therefore, disguised as the son of one Udaiben, his instructor, with whom he was sent to the Kôro-Kwan, where foreign embassies are entertained.

When the physiognomist saw him, he was amazed, and, turning his own head from side to side, seemed at first to be unable to comprehend the lines of his features, and then said, "His physiognomy argues that he might ascend to the highest position in the State, but, in that case, his reign will be disturbed, and many misfortunes will ensue. If, however, his position should only be that of a great personage in the country, his fortune may be different."

This Udaiben was a clever scholar. He had with the Corean pleasant conversations, and they also interchanged with one another some Chinese poems, in one of which the Corean said what great pleasure it had given him to have seen before his departure, which was now imminent, a youth of such remarkable promise. The Coreans made some valuable presents to the Prince, who had also composed a few lines, and to them, too, many costly gifts were offered from the Imperial treasures.

In spite of all the precautions which were taken to keep all this rigidly secret, it did, somehow or other, become known to others, and among those to the Udaijin, who, not unnaturally, viewed it with suspicion, and began to entertain doubts of the Emperor's intentions. The latter, however, acted with great prudence. It must be remembered that, as yet, he had not even created the boy a Royal Prince. He now sent for a native physiognomist, who approved of his delay in doing so, and whose observations to this effect, the Emperor did not receive unfavorably. He wisely thought to be a Royal Prince, without having any influential support on the mother's side, would be of no real advantage to his son. Moreover, his own tenure of power seemed precarious, and he, therefore, thought it better for his own dynasty, as well as for the Prince, to keep him in a private station, and to constitute him an outside supporter of the Royal cause.

And now he took more and more pains with his education in different branches of learning; and the more the boy studied, the more talent did he evince—talent almost too great for one destined to remain in a private station. Nevertheless, as we have said, suspicions would have been aroused had Royal rank been conferred upon him, and the astrologists, whom also the Emperor consulted, having expressed their disapproval of such a measure, the Emperor finally made up his mind to create a new family. To this family he assigned the name of Gen, and he made the young Prince the founder of it.[17]

Some time had now elapsed since the death of the Emperor's favorite, but he was still often haunted by her image. Ladies were introduced into his presence, in order, if possible, to divert his attention, but without success.

There was, however, living at this time a young Princess, the fourth child of a late Emperor. She had great promise of beauty, and was guarded with jealous care by her mother, the Empress-Dowager. The Naishi-no-Ske, who had been at the Court from the time of the said Emperor, was intimately acquainted with the Empress and familiar with the Princess, her daughter, from her very childhood. This person now recommended the Emperor to see the Princess, because her features closely resembled those of Kiri-Tsubo.

"I have now fulfilled," she said, "the duties of my office under three reigns, and, as yet, I have seen but one person who resembles the departed. The daughter of the Empress-Dowager does resemble her, and she is singularly beautiful."

"There may be some truth in this," thought the Emperor, and he began to regard her with awakening interest.

This was related to the Empress-Dowager. She, however, gave no encouragement whatever to the idea, "How terrible!" she said. "Do we not remember the cruel harshness of the mother of the Heir-apparent, which hastened the fate of Kiri-Tsubo!"

While thus discountenancing any intimacy between her daughter and the Emperor, she too died, and the princess was left parentless. The Emperor acted with great kindness, and intimated his wish to regard her as his own daughter. In consequence of this her guardian, and her brother, Prince Hiôb-Kiô, considering that life at Court would be better for her and more attractive for her than the quiet of her own home, obtained for her an introduction there.

She was styled the Princess Fuji-Tsubo (of the Chamber of Wistaria), from the name of the chamber which was assigned to her.

There was, indeed, both in features and manners a strange resemblance between her and Kiri-Tsubo. The rivals of the latter constantly caused pain both to herself and to the Emperor; but the illustrious birth of the Princess prevented any one from ever daring to humiliate her, and she uniformly maintained the dignity of her position. And to her alas! the Emperor's thoughts were now gradually drawn, though he could not yet be said to have forgotten Kiri-Tsubo.

The young Prince, whom we now style Genji (the Gen), was still with the Emperor, and passed his time pleasantly enough in visiting the various apartments where the inmates of the palace resided. He found the companionship of all of them sufficiently agreeable; but beside the many who were now of maturer years, there was one who was still in the bloom of her youthful beauty, and who more particularly caught his fancy, the Princess Wistaria. He had no recollection of his mother, but he had been told by Naishi-no-Ske that this lady was exceedingly like her; and for this reason he often yearned to see her and to be with her.

The Emperor showed equal affection to both of them, and he sometimes told her that he hoped she would not treat the boy with coldness or think him forward. He said that his affection for the one made him feel the same for the other too, and that the mutual resemblance of her own and of his mother's face easily accounted for Genji's partiality to her. And thus as a result of this generous feeling on the part of the Emperor, a warmer tinge was gradually imparted both to the boyish humor and to the awakening sentiment of the young Prince.

The mother of the Heir-apparent was not unnaturally averse to the Princess, and this revived her old antipathy to Genji also. The beauty of her son, the Heir-apparent, though remarkable, could not be compared to his, and so bright and radiant was his face that Genji was called by the public Hikal-Genji-no-Kimi (the shining Prince Gen).

When he attained the age of twelve the ceremony of Gembuk[18] (or crowning) took place. This was also performed with all possible magnificence. Various *fêtes*, which were to take place in public, were arranged by special order by responsible officers of the Household. The Royal chair was placed in the Eastern wing of the Seiriô-Den, where the Emperor dwells, and in front of it were the seats of the hero of the ceremony and of the Sadaijin, who was to crown him and to regulate the ceremonial.

About ten o'clock in the forenoon Genji appeared on the scene. The boyish style of his hair and dress excellently became his features; and it almost seemed matter for regret that it should be altered. The Okura-Kiô-Kurahito, whose office it was to rearrange the hair of Genji, faltered as he did so. As to the Emperor, a sudden thought stole into his mind. "Ah! could his mother but have lived to have seen him now!"This thought, however, he at once suppressed. After he had been crowned the Prince withdrew to a dressing-room, where he attired himself in the full robes of manhood. Then descending to the Court-yard he performed a measured dance in grateful acknowledgment. This he did with so much grace and skill that all present were filled with admiration; and his beauty, which some feared might be lessened, seemed only more remarkable from the change. And the Emperor, who had before tried to resist them, now found old memories irresistible.

Sadaijin had by his wife, who was a Royal Princess, an only daughter. The Heir-apparent had taken some notice of her, but her father did not encourage him. He had, on the other hand, some idea of Genji, and had sounded the Emperor on the subject. He regarded the idea with favor, and especially on the ground that such a union would be of advantage to Genji, who had not yet any influential supporters.

Now all the Court and the distinguished visitors were assembled in the palace, where a great festival was held; Genji occupied a seat next to that of the Royal Princess. During the entertainment Sadaijin whispered something several times into his ear, but he was too young and diffident to make any answer.

Sadaijin was now summoned before the daïs of the Emperor, and, according to custom, an Imperial gift, a white Ô-Uchiki (grand robe), and a suit of silk vestments were presented to him by a lady. Then proffering his own wine-cup, the Emperor addressed him thus:—

"In the first hair-knot[19] of youth,Let love that lasts for age be bound!"

This evidently implied an idea of matrimony. Sadaijin feigned surprise and responded:—

"Aye! if the purple[20] of the cord,I bound so anxiously, endure!"

He then descended into the Court-yard, and gave expression to his thanks in the same manner in which Genji had previously done. A horse from the Imperial stables and a falcon from the Kurand-Dokoro[21] were on view in the yard, and were now presented to him. The princes and nobles were all gathered together in front of the grand staircase, and appropriate gifts were also presented to each one of them. Among the crowd baskets and trays of fruits and delicacies were distributed by the Emperor's order, under the direction of Udaiben; and more rice-cakes and other things were given away now than at the Gembuk of the Heir-apparent.

In the evening the young Prince went to the mansion of the Sadaijin, where the espousal with the young daughter of the latter was celebrated with much splendor. The youthfulness of the beautiful boy was well pleasing to Sadaijin; but the bride, who was some years older than he was, and who considered the disparity in their age to be unsuitable, blushed when she thought of it.

Not only was this Sadaijin himself a distinguished personage in the State, but his wife was also the sister of the Emperor by the same mother, the late Empress; and her rank therefore was unequivocal. When to this we add the union of their daughter with Genji, it was easy to understand that the influence of Udaijin, the grandfather of the Heir-apparent, and who therefore seemed likely to attain great power, was not after all of very much moment.

Sadaijin had several children. One of them, who was the issue of his Royal wife, was the Kurand Shiôshiô.

Udaijin was not, for political reasons, on good terms with this family; but nevertheless he did not wish to estrange the youthful Kurand. On the contrary, he endeavored to establish friendly relations with him, as was indeed desirable, and he went so far as to introduce him to his fourth daughter, the younger sister of the Koki-Den.

Genji still resided in the palace, where his society was a source of much pleasure to the Emperor, and he did not take up his abode in a private house. Indeed, his bride, Lady Aoi (Lady Hollyhock), though her position insured her every attention from others, had few charms for him, and the Princess Wistaria much more frequently occupied his thoughts. "How pleasant her society, and how few like her!" he was always thinking; and a hidden bitterness blended with his constant reveries.

The years rolled on, and Genji being now older was no longer allowed to continue his visits to the private rooms of the Princess as before. But the pleasure of overhearing her sweet voice, as its strains flowed occasionally through the curtained casement, and blended with the music of the flute and *koto*, made him still glad to reside in the Palace. Under these circumstances he seldom visited the home of his bride, sometimes only for a day or two after an absence of five or six at Court.

His father-in-law, however, did not attach much importance to this, on account of his youth; and whenever they did receive a visit from him, pleasant companions were invited to meet him, and various games likely to suit his taste were provided for his entertainment.

In the Palace, Shigeisa, his late mother's quarters, was allotted to him, and those who had waited on her waited on him. The private house, where his grandmother had resided, was beautifully repaired for him by the Shuri Takmi—the Imperial Repairing Committee—in obedience to the wishes of the Emperor. In addition to the original loveliness of the landscape and the noble forest ranges, the basin of the lake was now enlarged, and similar improvements were effected throughout with the greatest pains. "Oh, how delightful would it not be to be in a place like that which such an one as one might choose!" thought Genji within himself.

We may here also note that the name Hikal Genji is said to have been originated by the Corean who examined his physiognomy.

FOOTNOTES:

[2]The beautiful tree, called Kiri, has been named Paulownia Imperialis, by botanists.

[3]Official titles held by Court ladies.

[4]The name of a Court office.

[5]A celebrated and beautiful favorite of an Emperor of the Thang dynasty in China, whose administration was disturbed by a rebellion, said to have been caused by the neglect of his duties for her sake.

[6]A Niogo who resided in a part of the Imperial palace called "Koki-den."

[7]The Hakamagi is the investiture of boys with trousers, when they pass from childhood to boyhood. In ordinary cases, this is done when about five years old, but in the Royal Family, it usually takes place earlier.

[8]A carriage drawn by hands. Its use in the Court-yard of the Palace was only allowed to persons of distinction.

[9]Cremation was very common in these days.

[10]A Court lady, whose name was Yugei, holding an office called "Miôbu."

[11]Miyagi is the name of a field which is famous for the Hagi or Lespedeza, a small and pretty shrub, which blooms in the Autumn. In poetry it is associated with deer, and a male and female deer are often compared to a lover and his love, and their young to their children.

[12]In Japan there is a great number of "mushi" or insects, which sing in herbage grass, especially in the evenings of Autumn. They are constantly alluded to in poetry.

[13]In Japanese poetry, persons connected with the Court, are spoken of as "the people above the clouds."

[14]A famous Chinese poem, by Hak-rak-ten. The heroine of the poem was Yô-ki-hi, to whom we have made reference before. The story is, that after death she became a fairy, and the Emperor sent a magician to find her. The works of the poet Peh-lo-tien, as it is pronounced by modern Chinese, were the only poems in vogue at that time. Hence, perhaps, the reason of its being frequently quoted.

[15]There were two divisions of the Imperial guard, right and left.

[16]The general name for a species of musical instrument resembling the zither, but longer.

[17]In these days Imperial Princes were often created founders of new families, and with some given name, the Gen being one most frequently used. These Princes had no longer a claim to the throne.

[18]The ceremony of placing a crown or coronet upon the head of a boy. This was an ancient custom observed by the upper and middle classes both in Japan and China, to mark the transition from boyhood to youth.

[19]Before the crown was placed upon the head at the Gembuk, the hair was gathered up in a conical form from all sides of the head, and then fastened securely in that form with a knot of silken cords of which the color was always purple.

[20]The color of purple typifies, and is emblematical of, love.

[21]A body of men who resembled "Gentlemen-at-arms," and a part of whose duty it was to attend to the falcons.

CHAPTER II

THE BROOM-LIKE TREE

Hikal Genji—the name is singularly well known, and is the subject of innumerable remarks and censures. Indeed, he had many intrigues in his lifetime, and most of them are vividly preserved in our memories. He had always striven to keep all these intrigues in the utmost secrecy, and had to appear constantly virtuous. This caution was observed to such an extent that he scarcely accomplished anything really romantic, a fact which Katano-no-Shiôshiô[22] would have ridiculed.

Even with such jealous watchfulness, secrets easily transpire from one to another; so loquacious is man! Moreover, he had unfortunately from nature a disposition of not appreciating anything within easy reach, but of directing his thought in undesirable quarters, hence sundry improprieties in his career.

Now, it was the season of continuous rain (namely, the month of May), and the Court was keeping a strict Monoimi.[23] Genji, who had now been made a Chiûjiô,[24] and who was still continuing his residence in the Imperial Palace, was also confined to his apartments for a considerable length of time. His father-in-law naturally felt for him, and his sons were sent to bear him company. Among these, Kurand Shiôshiô, who was now elevated to the post of Tô-no-Chiûjiô, proved to be the most intimate and interesting companion. He was married to the fourth daughter of the Udaijin, but being a man of lively disposition, he, too, like Genji, did not often resort to the mansion of the bride. When Genji went to the

Sadaijin's he was always his favorite associate; they were together in their studies and in their sports, and accompanied each other everywhere. And so all stiffness and formality were dispensed with, and they did not scruple to reveal their secrets to each other.

It was on an evening in the above-mentioned season. Rain was falling drearily. The inhabitants of the Palace had almost all retired, and the apartment of Genji was more than usually still. He was engaged in reading near a lamp, but at length mechanically put his book aside, and began to take out some letters and writings from a bureau which stood on one side of the room. Tô-no-Chiûjiô happened to be present, and Genji soon gathered from his countenance that he was anxious to look over them.

"Yes," said Genji; "some you may see, but there may be others!"

"Those others," retorted Tô-no-Chiûjiô, "are precisely those which I wish to see; ordinary ones, even your humble servant may have received. I only long to look upon those which may have been written by fair hands, when the tender writer had something to complain of, or when in twilight hour she was outpouring all her yearning!"

Being so pressed, Genji allowed his brother-in-law to see them all. It is, however, highly probable that any very sacred letters would not have been loosely deposited in an ordinary bureau; and these would therefore seem, after all, to have been of second-rate importance.

"What a variety," said Tô-no-Chiûjiô, as he turned them over, and he asked several questions guessingly about this or that. About some he guessed correctly, about others he was puzzled and suspicious.[25] Genji smiled and spoke little, only making some obscure remark, and continuing as he took the letters: "but *you*, surely, must have collected many. Will not you show me some? And then my bureau also may open more easily."

"You do not suppose that I have any worth reading, do you?" replied Tô-no-Chiûjiô. "I have only just now discovered," continued he, "how difficult it is to meet with a fair creature, of whom one can say, 'This is, indeed, *the* one; here is, at last, perfection.' There are, indeed, many who fascinate; many who are ready with their pens, and who, when occasion may require, are quick at repartee. But how often such girls as these are conceited about their own accomplishments, and endeavor unduly to disparage those of others! There are again some who are special pets of their parents, and most jealously watched over at home. Often, no doubt, they are pretty, often graceful; and frequently they will apply themselves with effect to music and to poetry, in which they may even attain to special excellence. But then, their friends will keep their drawbacks in the dark, and eulogize their merits to the utmost. If we were to give full credence to this exaggerated praise, we could not but fail in every single instance to be more or less disappointed."

So saying Tô-no-Chiûjiô paused, and appeared as if he were ashamed of having such an experience, when Genji smilingly remarked, "Can any one of them, however, exist without at least one good point?"

"Nay, were there any so little favored as that, no one would ever be misled at all!" replied Tô-no-Chiûjiô, and he continued, "In my opinion, the most and the least favored are in the same proportion. I mean, they are both not many. Their birth, also, divides them into three classes. Those, however, who are especially well born, are often too jealously guarded, and are, for the most part, kept secluded from the outside gaze, which frequently tends to make their deportment shy and timid. It is those of the middle class, who are much more frequently seen by us, who afford us most chance of studying their character. As for the lower class, it would be almost useless to trouble ourselves with them."

Thus Tô-no-Chiûjiô appeared to be thoroughly at home in his description of the merits of the fair sex, which made Genji amused, and he said: "But how do you define the classes you have referred to, and classify them into three? Those who are of high birth sink sometimes in the social scale until the distinction of their rank is forgotten in the abjectness of their present position. Others, again, of low origin, rise to a high position, and, with self-important faces and in ostentatious residences, regard themselves as inferior to none. Into what class will you allot *these*?"

Just at this moment the Sama-no-Kami[26] and Tô Shikib-no-Jiô[27] joined the party. They came to pay their respects to Genji, and both of them were gay and light-hearted talkers. So Tô-no-Chiûjiô now made over the discussion to them, and it was carried to rather questionable lengths.

"However exalted a lady's position may be," said Sama-no-Kami, "if her origin is an unenviable one, the estimation of the public for her would be widely different from that which it shows to those who are naturally entitled to it. If, again, adverse fortune assails one whose birth is high, so that she becomes friendless and helpless, degradation here will meet our eyes, though her heart may still remain as noble as ever. Examples of both of these are very common. After much reflection, I can only come to the conclusion that both of them should be included in the middle class. In this class, too, must be included many daughters of the Duriô,[28] who occupy themselves with local administration. These ladies are often very attractive, and are not seldom introduced at Court and enjoy high favor."

"And successes depend pretty much upon the state of one's fortune, I fancy," interrupted Genji, with a placid smile.

"That is a remark very unlikely to fall from the lips of a champion of romance," chimed in Tô-no-Chiûjiô.

"There may be some," resumed Sama-no-Kami, "who are of high birth, and to whom public respect is duly paid, yet whose domestic education has been much neglected. Of a lady such as this we may simply remark, 'Why, and how, is it that she is so brought up?' and she would only cause discredit to her class. There are, of course, some who combine in themselves every perfection befitting their position. These best of the best are, however, not within every one's reach. But, listen! Within an old dilapidated gateway, almost unknown to the world, and overgrown with wild vegetation, perchance we might find, shut up, a maiden charming beyond imagination. Her father might be an aged man, corpulent in person, and stern in mien, and her brothers of repulsive countenance; but there, in an uninviting room, she lives, full of delicacy and sentiment, and fairly skilled in the arts of poetry or music, which she may have acquired by her own exertions alone, unaided. If there were such a case, surely she deserves our attention, save that of those of us who themselves are highly exalted in position."

So saying, Sama-no-Kami winked slyly at Shikib-no-Jiô. The latter was silent: perhaps he fancied that Sama-no-Kami was speaking in the above strain, with a hidden reference to his (Shikib's) sisters, who, he imagined, answered the description.

Meantime, Genji may have thought, "If it is so difficult to choose one even from the best class, how can—Ah!" and he began to close his eyes and doze. His dress was of soft white silk, partly covered by the *naoshi*,[29] worn carelessly, with its cord left loose and untied. His appearance and bearing formed quite a picture.

Meanwhile, the conversation went on about different persons and characters, and Sama-no-Kami proceeded: "It is unquestionable that though at first glance many women appear to be without defects, yet when we come to the actual selection of any one of them, we should seriously hesitate in our choice.

"Let me illustrate my meaning by reference to the numerous public men who may be aspiring to fulfil the duties of several important posts. You will at once recognize the great difficulty there would be in fixing upon the individual statesman under whose guardianship the empire could best repose. And supposing that, if at last, by good fortune, the most able man were designated, even then we must bear in mind that it is not in the power of one or two individuals, however gifted they may be, to carry on the whole administration of the kingdom alone. Public business can only be tranquilly conducted when the superior receives the assistance of subordinates, and when the subordinate yields a becoming respect and loyalty to his superior, and affairs are thus conducted in a spirit of mutual conciliation. So, too, it is in the narrow range of the domestic circle. To make a good mistress of that circle, one must possess, if our ideal is to be fully realized, many important qualifications. Were we to be constantly indulging in the severity of criticism, always objecting to this or that, a perfect character would be almost unattainable. Men should therefore bear with patience any trifling dissatisfaction which they may feel, and strive constantly to keep alive, to augment, and to cherish, the warmth of their early love. Only such a man as this can be called faithful, and the partner of such a man alone can enjoy the real happiness of affection. How unsatisfactory to us, however, seems the actual world if we look round upon it. Still more difficult must it be to satisfy such as you who seek your companions but from among the best!

"How varied are the characters and the dispositions of women! Some who are youthful and favored by Nature strive almost selfishly to keep themselves with the utmost reserve. If they write, they write harmlessly and innocently; yet, at the same time, they are choice in their expressions, which have delicate touches of bewitching sentiment. This might possibly make us entertain a suddenly conceived fancy for them; yet they would give us but slight encouragement. They may allow us just to hear their voices, but when we approach them they will speak with subdued breath, and almost inaudibly. Beware, however, lest among these you chance to encounter some astute artiste, who, under a surface that is smooth, conceals a current that is deep. This sort of lady, it is true, generally appears quite modest; but often proves, when we come closer, to be of a very different temperament from what we anticipated. Here is one drawback to be guarded against.

"Among characters differing from the above, some are too full of sentimental sweetness—whenever occasion offers them romance they become spoilt. Such would be decidedly better if they had less sentiment, and more sense.

"Others, again, are singularly earnest—too earnest, indeed—in the performance of their domestic duty; and such, with their hair pushed back,[30] devote themselves like household drudges to household affairs. Man, whose duties generally call him from home all the day, naturally hears and sees the social movements both of public and private life, and notices different things, both good and bad. Of such things he would not like to talk freely with strangers, but only with some one closely allied to him. Indeed, a man may have many things in his mind which cause him to smile or to grieve. Occasionally something of a political nature may irritate him beyond endurance. These matters he would like to talk over with his fair companion, that she might soothe him, and sympathize with him. But a woman as above described is often unable to understand him, or does not endeavor to do so; and this only makes him more miserable. At another time he may brood over his hopes and aspirations; but he has no hope of solace. She is not only incapable of sharing these with him, but might carelessly remark, 'What ails you?' How severely would this try the temper of a man!

"If, then, we clearly see all these, the only suggestion I can make is that the best thing to do is to choose one who is gentle and modest, and strive to guide and educate her according to the best ideal we may think of. This is the best plan; and why should we not do so? Our efforts would not be surely all in vain. But no! A girl whom we thus educate, and who proves to be competent to bear us company, often disappoints us when she is left alone. She may then show her incapability, and her occasional actions may be done in such an unbecoming manner that both good and bad are equally displeasing. Are not all these against us men?—Remember, however, that there are some who may not be very agreeable at ordinary times, yet who flash occasionally upon us with a potent and almost irresistible charm."

Thus Sama-no-Kami, though eloquent, not having come to one point or another, remained thoughtful for some minutes, and again resumed:—

"After all, as I have once observed, I can only make this suggestion: That we should not too much consider either birth or beauty, but select one who is gentle and tranquil, and consider her to be best suited for our last haven of rest. If, in addition, she is of fair position, and is blessed with sweetness of temper, we should be delighted with her, and not trouble ourselves to search or notice any trifling deficiency. And the more so as, if her conscience is clear and pure, calmness and serenity of features can naturally be looked for.

"There are women who are too diffident, and too reserved, and carry their generosity to such an extent as to pretend not to be aware even of such annoyances as afford them just grounds of complaint. A time arrives when their sorrows and anxieties become greater than they can bear. Even then, however, they cannot resort to plain speaking, and complain. But, instead thereof, they will fly away to some remote retreat among the mountain hamlets, or to some secluded spot by the seaside, leaving behind them some painful letter or despairing verses, and making themselves mere sad memories of the past. Often when a boy I heard such stories read by ladies, and the sad pathos of them even caused my tears to flow; but now I can only declare such deeds to be acts of mere folly. For what does it all amount to? Simply to this: That the woman, in spite of the pain which it causes her, and discarding a heart which may be still lingering towards her, takes to flight, regardless of the feelings of others—of the anguish, and of the anxiety, which those who are dearest to her suffer with her. Nay, this act of folly may even be committed simply to test the sincerity of her lover's affection for her. What pitiable subtlety!

"Worse than this, the woman thus led astray, perhaps by ill advice, may even be beguiled into more serious errors. In the depth of her despairing melancholy she will become a nun. Her conscience, when she takes the fatal vow, may be pure and unsullied, and nothing may seem able to call her back again to the world which she forsook. But, as time rolls on, some household servant or aged nurse brings her tidings of the lover who has been unable to cast her out of his heart, and whose tears drop silently when he hears aught about her. Then, when she hears of his affections still living, and his heart still yearning, and thinks of the uselessness of the sacrifice she has made voluntarily, she touches the hair[31] on her forehead, and she becomes regretful. She may, indeed, do her best to persevere in her resolve, but if one single tear bedews her cheek, she is no longer strong in the sanctity of her vow. Weakness of this kind would be in the eyes of Buddha more sinful than those offences which are committed by those who never leave the lay circle at all, and she would eventually wander about in the 'wrong passage.'[32]

"But there are also women, who are too self-confident and obtrusive. These, if they discover some slight inconsistency in men, fiercely betray their indignation and behave with arrogance. A man may show a little inconsistency occasionally, but yet his affection may remain; then matters will in time become right again, and they will pass their lives happily together. If, therefore, the woman cannot show a tolerable amount of patience, this will but add to her unhappiness. She should, above all things, strive not to give way to excitement; and when she experiences any unpleasantness, she should speak of it frankly but with moderation. And if there should be anything worse than unpleasantness she should even then complain of it in such a way as not to irritate the men. If she guides her conduct on principles such as these, even her very words, her very demeanor, may in all probability increase his sympathy and consideration for her. One's self-denial and the restraint which one imposes upon one's self, often depend on the way in which another behaves to us. The woman who is too indifferent and too forgiving is also inconsiderate. Remember 'the unmoored boat floats about.' Is it not so?"

Tô-no-Chiûjiô quickly nodded assent, as he said, "Quite true! A woman who has no strength of emotion, no passion of sorrow or of joy, can never be holders of us. Nay even jealousy, if not carried to the extent of undue suspicion, is not undesirable. If we ourselves are not in fault, and leave the matter alone, such jealousy may easily be kept within due bounds. But stop"—added he suddenly—

"Some women have to bear, and do bear, every grief that they may encounter with unmurmuring and suffering patience."

So said Tô-no-Chiûjiô, who implied by this allusion that his sister was a woman so circumstanced. But Genji was still dozing, and no remark came from his lips.

Sama-no-Kami had been recently made a doctor of literature, and (like a bird) was inflating his feathers, so Tô-no-Chiûjiô, willing to draw him out as much as possible, gave him every encouragement to proceed with his discourse.

Again, therefore, he took up the conversation, and said, "Call to your mind affairs in general, and judge of them. Is it not always true that reality and sincerity are to be preferred to merely artificial excellence? Artisans, for instance, make different sorts of articles, as their talents serve them. Some of them are keen and expert, and cleverly manufacture objects of temporary fashion, which have no fixed or traditional style, and which are only intended to strike the momentary fancy. These, however, are not the true artisans. The real excellence of the true artisan is tested by those who make, without defects or sensational peculiarities, articles to decorate, we will say, some particular building, in conformity with correct taste and high æsthetic principles. Look for another instance at the eminence which has been attained by several of the artists of the Imperial College of Painting. Take the case of draughtsmen in black ink. Pictures, indeed, such as those of Mount Horai,[33] which has never been beheld by mortal eye, or of some raging monstrous fish in a rough sea, or of a wild animal of some far-off country, or of the imaginary face of the demon, are often drawn with such striking vividness that people are startled at the sight of them. These pictures, however, are neither real nor true. On the other hand, ordinary scenery, of familiar mountains, of calm streams of water, and of dwellings just before our eyes, may be sketched with an irregularity so charming, and with such excellent skill, as almost to rival Nature. In pictures such as these, the perspective of gentle mountain slopes, and sequestered nooks surrounded by leafy trees, are drawn with such admirable fidelity to Nature that they carry the spectator in imagination to something beyond them. These are the pictures in which is mostly evinced the spirit and effectiveness of the superior hand of a master; and in these an inferior artist would only show dulness and inefficiency.

"Similar observations are applicable to handwriting.[34] Some people boldly dash away with great freedom and endless flourishes, and appear at the first glance to be elegant and skilful. But that which is written with scrupulous neatness, in accordance with the true rules of penmanship, constitutes a very different handwriting from the above. If perchance the upstrokes and downstrokes do not, at first sight, appear to be fully formed, yet when we take it up and critically compare it with writing in which dashes and flourishes predominate, we shall at once see how much more of real and sterling merit it possesses.

"Such then is the nature of the case in painting, in penmanship, and in the arts generally. And how much more then are those women undeserving of our admiration, who though they are rich in outward and in fashionable display, attempting to dazzle our eyes, are yet lacking in the solid foundations of reality, fidelity, and truth! Do not, my friends, consider me going too far, but let me proceed to illustrate these observations by my own experience."

So saying, Sama-no-Kami advanced his seat, and Genji awoke. Tô-no-Chiûjiô was quite interested in the conversation, and was keeping his eye upon the speaker, leaning his cheek upon his hand. This long discourse of Sama-no-Kami reminds us of the preacher's sermon, and amuses us. And it seems that, on occasions like these, one may easily be carried away by circumstances, until he is willing to communicate even his own private affairs.

"It was at a time," continued Sama-no-Kami, "when I was in a still more humble position, that there was a girl to whom I had taken a fancy. She was like one of those whom I described in the process of my discourse; not a regular beauty. Although for this reason my youthful vanity did not allow me to pledge myself to her forever, I still considered her a pleasant companion. Nevertheless, from occasional fits of restlessness, I roamed often here and there. This she always resented fiercely, and with so much indignation that I sighed for a sweeter temper and more moderation. Indeed, there were times when her suspicion and spitefulness were more than I could endure. But my irritation was generally calmed down, and I even felt sorry myself, when I reflected how strong and devoted her affection for me was, in spite of the mean state of my circumstances. As to her general character, her only endeavor seemed to be to do everything for my sake, even what was beyond her powers, while she struggled to perfect herself in anything in which she might be deficient, and took the most faithful care of all my interests, striving constantly and earnestly to please me. She appeared at first even too zealous, but in time became more moderate. She seemed as if she felt uneasy lest her plain face should cause me displeasure, and she even denied herself the sight of other people, in order to avoid unbecoming comment.

"As time went by, the more I became accustomed to observe how really simple-hearted she was, the more I sympathized with her. The one thing that I could not bear, however, was that jealousy of hers. Sincere and devoted as she is, thought I, is there no means of ridding her of this jealous weakness? Could I but do that, it would not matter even if I were to alarm her a little. And I also thought that since she was devoted to me, if I showed any symptoms of getting tired of her, she would, in all probability, be warned by it. Therefore, I purposely behaved to her with great coolness and heartlessness. This she resented as usual. I then said to her, that though our affection had been of old date, I should not see her again; 'if you wish to sever from me you may suspect me as much as you like. If you prefer to enjoy long happiness with me in future, be modest and patient in trifling matters. If you can only be so, how can I do otherwise than love you? My position also may in time be improved, and then we may enjoy greater happiness!'

"In saying this, I thought I had managed matters very ingeniously. Without meaning it, however, I had in fact spoken a little too harshly. She replied, with a bitter smile, that 'to put up with a life of undistinguished condition, even though with faint hopes of future promotion, was not a thing about which we ought to trouble ourselves, but that it was indeed a hard task to pass long wearisome days in waiting until a man's mind should be restored to a sense of propriety. And that for this reason we had, perhaps, better separate at once.'

"This she said with such sarcastic bitterness that I was irritated and stung to the quick, and overwhelmed her with a fresh torrent of reproaches. At this juncture she gave way to an uncontrollable fit of passion, and snatching up my hand, she thrust my little finger into her mouth and bit off the end of it. Then, notwithstanding my pain, I became quite cool and collected, and calmly said, 'insulted and maimed as I have now been, it is most fitting that I should absent myself for the future from polite society. Office and title would ill become me now. Your spite has now left me without spirit to face the world in which I should be ridiculed, and has left me no alternative but to withdraw my maimed person from the public gaze!' After I had alarmed her by speaking in this exalted strain, I added, 'to-day we meet for the last time,' and bending these fingers (pointing to them as she spoke) I made the farewell remark:—

When on my fingers, I must sayI count the hours I spent with thee,Is this, and this alone, I prayThe only pang you've caused to me?

You are now quits with me,' At the instant I said so, she burst into tears and without premeditation, poured forth the following:—

'From me, who long bore grievous harms,From that cold hand and wandering heart,You now withdraw your sheltering arms,And coolly tell me, we must part.'

"To speak the truth, I had no real intention of separating from her altogether. For some time, however, I sent her no communication, and was passing rather an unsettled life. Well! I was once returning from the palace late one evening in November, after an experimental practice of music for a special festival in the Temple of Kamo. Sleet was falling heavily. The wind blew cold, and my road was dark and muddy. There was no house near where I could make myself at home. To return and spend a lonely night in the palace was not to be thought of. At this moment a reflection flashed across my mind. 'How cold must she feel whom I have treated so coldly,' thought I, and suddenly became very anxious to know what she felt and what she was about. This made me turn my steps towards her dwelling, and brushing away the snow that had gathered on my shoulders I trudged on: at one moment shyly biting my nails, at another thinking that on such a night at least all her enmity towards me might be all melted away. I approached the house. The curtains were not drawn, and I saw the dim light of a lamp reflected on the windows. It was even perceivable that a soft quilt was being warmed and thrown over the large couch. The scene was such as to give you the notion that she was really anticipating that I might come at least on such an evening. This gave me encouragement, but alas! she whom I hoped to see was not at home. I was told she had gone to her parents that very evening. Previous to that time, she had sent me no sad verses, no conciliatory letter, and this had already given birth to unpleasant feelings on my part. And at this moment, when I was told that she had gone away, all these things seemed to have been done almost purposely, and I involuntarily began to suspect that her very jealousy had only been assumed by her on purpose to cause me to become tired of her.

"As I reflected what our future might be after such an estrangement as this, I was truly depressed. I did not, however, give up all hope, thinking that she would not be so determined as to abandon me forever. I had even carefully selected some stuff for a dress for her. Some time, however, passed away without anything particularly occurring. She neither accepted nor refused the offers of reconciliation which I made to her. She did not, it is true, hide herself away like any of those of whom I have spoken before. But, nevertheless, she did not evince the slightest symptom of regret for her previous conduct.

"At last, after a considerable interval, she intimated to me that her final resolve was not to forgive me any more if I intended in future to behave as I had done before; but that, on the other hand, she should be glad to see me again if I would thoroughly change my habits, and treat her with the kindness which was her due. From this I became more convinced that she still entertained longings for me. Hence, with the hope of warning her a little more, I made no expressions of any intention to make a change in my habits, and I tried to find out which of us had the most patience.

"While matters were in this state, she, to my great surprise, suddenly died, perhaps broken-hearted.

"I must now frankly confess that she certainly was a woman in whom a man might place his confidence. Often, too, I had talked with her on music and on poetry, as well as on the more important business of life, and I found her to be by no means wanting in intellect and capability. She had too the clever hands of Tatyta-himè[35] and Tanabata.[36]

"When I recall these pleasant memories my heart still clings to her endearingly."

"Clever in weaving, she may have been like Tanabata, that is but a small matter," interposed Tô-no-Chiûjiô, "we should have preferred to have seen your love as enduring as Tanabata's.[37] Nothing is so beautiful as the brilliant dyes spread over the face of Nature, yet the red tints of autumn are often not dyed to a color so deep as we desire, because of the early drying of the dew, so we say, 'such is the uncertain fate of this world,'" and so saying, he made a sign to Sama-no-Kami to go on with his story. He went on accordingly.

"About that time I knew another lady. She was on the whole a superior kind of person. A fair poetess, a good musician, and a fluent speaker, with good enunciation, and graceful in her movements. All these admirable qualities I noticed myself, and heard them spoken of by others. As my acquaintance with her commenced at the time when I was not on the best of terms with my former companion, I was glad to enjoy her society. The more I associated with her the more fascinating she became.

"Meanwhile my first friend died, at which I felt truly sorry, still I could not help it, and I therefore paid frequent visits to this one. In the course of my attentions to her, however, I discovered many unpleasant traits. She was not very modest, and did not appear to be one whom a man could trust. On this account, I became somewhat disappointed, and visited her less often. While matters were on this footing I accidentally found out that she had another lover to whom she gave a share of her heart.

"It happened that one inviting moonlight evening in October, I was driving out from home on my way to a certain Dainagon. On the road I met with a young noble who was going in the same direction. We therefore drove together, and as we were journeying on, he told me that 'some one might be waiting for him, and he was anxious to see her'; well! by and by we arrived at the house of my lady-love. The bright reflection of the waters of an ornamental lake was seen through crevices in the walls; and the pale moon, as she shed her full radiance over the shimmering waves, seemed to be charmed with the beauty of the scene. It would have been heartless to pass by with indifference, and we both descended from the carriage, without knowing each other's intention.

"This youth seems to have been 'the other one'; he was rather shy. He sat down on a mat of reeds that was spread beside a corridor near the gateway; and, gazing up at the sky, meditated for some moments in silence. The chrysanthemums in the gardens were in full bloom, whose sweet perfume soothed us with its gentle influence; and round about us the scarlet leaves of the maple were falling, as ever and anon they were shaken by the breeze. The scene was altogether romantic.

"Presently, he took a flute out of his bosom and played. He then whispered, 'Its shade is refreshing.'

"In a few minutes the fair one struck up responsively on a sweet-toned *wagon* (a species of *koto*).

"The melody was soft and exquisite, in charming strains of modern music, and admirably adapted to the lovely evening. No wonder that he was fascinated; he advanced towards the casement from which the sounds proceeded, and glancing at the leaves scattered on the ground, whispered in invidious tones, 'Sure no strange footsteps would ever dare to press these leaves.' He then culled a chrysanthemum, humming, as he did so:—

'Even this spot, so fair to viewWith moon, and Koto's gentle strain,Could make no other lover true,As me, thy fond, thy only swain.'

"'Wretched!' he exclaimed, alluding to his poetry; and then added, 'One tune more! Stay not your hand when one is near, who so ardently longs to hear you.' Thus he began to flatter the lady, who, having heard his whispers, replied thus, in a tender, hesitating voice:—

'Sorry I am my voice too lowTo match thy flute's far sweeter sound;Which mingles with the winds that blowThe Autumn leaves upon the ground.'

"Ah! she little thought I was a silent and vexed spectator of all this flirtation. She then took up a *soh* (another kind of *koto* with thirteen strings) and tuned it to a Banjiki key (a winter tune), and played on it still more excellently. Though an admirer of music, I cannot say that these bewitching melodies gave me any pleasure under the peculiar circumstances I stood in.

"Now, romantic interludes, such as this, might be pleasant enough in the case of maidens who are kept strictly in Court service, and whom we have very little opportunity of meeting with, but even there we should hesitate to make such a one our life companion. How much less could one ever entertain such an idea in a case like my own? Making, therefore, that evening's experience a ground of dissatisfaction I never saw her more.

"Now, gentlemen, let us take into consideration these two instances which have occurred to myself and see how equally unsatisfactory they are. The one too jealous, the other too forward. Thus, early in life, I found out how little reliance was to be placed on such characters. And now I think so still more; and this opinion applies more especially to the latter of the two. Dewdrops on the 'Hagi flower' of beauty so delicate that they disappear as soon as we touch them—hailstones on the bamboo grass that melt in our hand as soon as we prick them—appear at a distance extremely tempting and attractive. Take my humble advice, however, and go not near them. If you do not appreciate this advice now, the lapse of another seven years will render you well able to understand that such adventures will only bring a tarnished fame."

Thus Sama-no-Kami admonished them, and Tô-no-Chiûjiô nodded as usual. Genji slightly smiled; perhaps he thought it was all very true, and he said, "Your twofold experience was indeed disastrous and irritating!"

"Now," said Tô-no-Chiûjiô, "I will tell you a story concerning myself. It was the evil fortune of Sama-no-Kami to meet with too much jealousy in one of the ladies to whom he might otherwise have given his heart; while he could feel no confidence in another owing to flirtations. It was my hard lot to encounter an instance of excessive diffidence. I once knew a girl whose person was altogether pleasing, and although I, too, had no intention, as Sama-no-Kami said, of forming an everlasting connection with her, I nevertheless took a great fancy to her. As our acquaintance was prolonged, our mutual affection grew warmer. My thoughts were always of her, and she placed entire confidence in me. Now, when complete confidence is placed by one person in another, does not Nature teach us to expect resentment when that confidence is abused? No such resentment, however, seemed under any circumstances to trouble her. When I very seldom visited her, she showed no excitement or indignation, but behaved and looked as if we had never been separated from each other. This patient silence was more trying to me than reproaches. She was parentless and friendless. For this reason responsibility weighed more heavily on me. Abusing her gentle nature, however, I frequently neglected her. About this time, moreover, a certain person who lived near her, discovered our friendship, and frightened her by sending, through some channel, mischief-making messages to her. This I did not become aware of till afterwards, and, it seems, she was quite cast down and helpless. She had a little one for whose sake, it appears, she was additionally sad. One day I unexpectedly received a bunch of Nadeshiko[38] flowers. They were from her."

At this point Tô-no-Chiûjiô became gloomy.

"And what," inquired Genji, "were the words of her message?"

"Sir! nothing but the verse,

Forgot may be the lowly bedFrom which these darling flowerets spring,Still let a kindly dew be shed,Upon their early nurturing.

"No sooner had I read this than I went to her at once. She was gentle and sedate as usual, but evidently absent and preoccupied. Her eyes rested on the dew lying on the grass in the garden, and her ears were intent upon the melancholy singing of the autumn insects. It was as if we were in a real romance. I said to her:—

When with confused gaze we viewThe mingled flowers on gay parterre,Amid their blooms of radiant hueThe Tokonatz,[39] my love, is there.

And avoiding all allusion to the Nadeshiko flowers, I repeatedly endeavored to comfort the mother's heart. She murmured in reply:—

'Ah! Flower already bent with dew,The winds of autumn cold and chillWill wither all thy beauteous hue,And soon, alas, unpitying kill.'

Thus she spoke sadly. But she reproached me no further. The tears came involuntarily into her eyes. She was, however, apparently sorry for this, and tried to conceal them. On the whole she behaved as if she meant to show that she was quite accustomed to such sorrows. I certainly deeply sympathized with her, yet still further abusing her patience. I did not visit her again for some time; but I was punished. When I did so she had flown, leaving no traces behind her. If she is still living she must needs be passing a miserable existence.

"Now, if she had been free from this excessive diffidence, this apathy of calmness, if she had complained when it was necessary, with becoming warmth and spirit, she need never have been a wanderer, and I would never have abused her confidence. But, as I said before, a woman who has no strength of emotion, no passionate bursts of sorrow or of joy, can never retain a dominion over us.

"I loved this woman without understanding her nature; and I am constantly, but in vain, trying to find her and her little darling, who was also very lovely; and often I think with grief and pain that, though I may succeed in forgetting her, she may possibly not be able to forget me, and, surely, there must be many an evening when she is disquieted by sad memories of the past.

"Let us now sum up our experiences, and reflect on the lessons which they teach us. One who bites your finger will easily estrange your affection by her violence. Falseness and forwardness will be the reproach of some other, in spite of her melodious music and the sweetness of her songs. A third, too self-contained and too gentle, is open to the charge of a cold silence, which oppresses one, and cannot be understood.

"Whom, then, are we to choose? All this variety, and this perplexing difficulty of choice, seems to be the common lot of humanity. Where, again, I say, are we to go to find the one who will realize our desires? Shall we fix our aspirations on the beautiful goddess, the heavenly Kichijiô?[40] Ah! this would be but superstitious and impracticable."

So mournfully finished Tô-no-Chiûjiô; and all his companions, who had been attentively listening, burst simultaneously into laughter at his last allusion.

"And now, Shikib, it is your turn. Tell us your story," exclaimed Tô-no-Chiûjiô, turning to him.

"What worth hearing can your humble servant tell you?"

"Go on; be quick; don't be shy; let us hear!"

Shikib-no-Jiô, after a little meditation, thus began:—

"When I was a student at the University, I met there with a woman of very unusual intelligence. She was in every respect one with whom, as Sama-no-Kami has said, you could discuss affairs, both public and private. Her dashing genius and eloquence were such that all ordinary scholars would find themselves unable to cope with her, and would be at once reduced to silence. Now, my story is as follows:—

"I was taking lessons from a certain professor, who had several daughters, and she was one of them. It happened by some chance or other I fell much into her society. The professor, who noticed this, once took up a wine-cup in his hand, and said to me, 'Hear what I sing about two choices.'[41]

"This was a plain offer put before me, and thenceforward I endeavored, for the sake of his tuition, to make myself as agreeable as possible to his daughter. I tell you frankly, however, that I had no particular affection for her, though she seemed already to regard me as her victim. She seized every opportunity of pointing out to me the way in which we should have to steer, both in public and private life. When she wrote to me she never employed the effeminate style of the Kana,[42] but wrote, oh! so magnificently! The great interest which she took in me induced me to pay frequent visits to her; and, by making her my tutor, I learned how to compose ordinary Chinese poems. However, though I do not forget all these benefits, and though it is no doubt true that our wife or daughter should not lack intelligence, yet, for the life of me, I cannot bring myself to approve of a woman like this. And still less likely is it that such could be of any use to the wives of high personages like yourselves. Give me a lovable nature in lieu of sharpness! I quite agree with Sama-no-Kami on this point."

"What an interesting woman she must have been," exclaimed Tô-no-Chiûjiô, with the intention of making Shikib go on with his story.

This he fully understood, and, making a grimace, he thus proceeded:—

"Once when I went to her after a long absence—a way we all have, you know—she did not receive me openly as usual, but spoke to me from behind a screen. I surmised that this arose from chagrin at my negligence, and I intended to avail myself of this opportunity to break with her. But the sagacious woman was a woman of the world, and not like those who easily lose their temper or keep silence about their grief. She was quite as open and frank as Sama-no-Kami would approve of. She told me, in a low clear voice, 'I am suffering from heartburn, and I cannot, therefore, see you face to face; yet, if you have anything important to say to me, I will listen to you.' This was, no doubt, a plain truth; but what answer could I give to such a terribly frank avowal? 'Thank you,' said I, simply; and I was just on the point of leaving, when, relenting, perhaps, a little, she said aloud, 'Come again soon, and I shall be all right.' To pass this unnoticed would have been impolite; yet I did not like to remain there any longer, especially under such circumstances: so, looking askance, I said—

Here I am, then why excuse me, is my visit all in vain: And my consolation is, you tell me, come again?

No sooner had I said this than she dashed out as follows with a brilliancy of repartee which became a woman of her genius:—

'If we fond lovers were, and meeting every night, I should not be ashamed, were it even in the light!'

"Nonsense, nonsense!" cried Genji and the others, who either were, or pretended to be, quite shocked. "Where can there be such a woman as that? She must have been a devil! Fearful! fearful!" And, snapping their fingers with disapproving glances, they said, "Do tell us something better—do give us a better story than that."

Shikib-no-Jiô, however, quietly remarked: "I have nothing else to relate," and remained silent.

Hereupon a conversation took place to the following effect:—

"It is a characteristic of thoughtless people—and that, without distinction of sex—that they try to show off their small accomplishments. This is, in the highest degree, unpleasant. As for ladies, it may not, indeed, be necessary to be thorough master of the three great histories, and the five classical texts; yet they ought not to be destitute of some knowledge of both public and private affairs, and this knowledge can be imperceptibly acquired without any regular study of them, which, though superficial, will yet be amply sufficient to enable them to talk pleasantly about them with their friends. But how contemptible they would seem if this made them vain of it! The Manna[43] style and pedantic phrases were not meant for them; and, if they use them, the public will only say, 'would that they would remember that they are women and not men,' and they would only incur the reproach of being pedants, as many ladies, especially among the aristocracy, do. Again, while they should not be altogether unversed in poetical compositions, they should never be slaves to them, or allow themselves to be betrayed into using strange quotations, the only consequence of which would be that they would appear to be bold when they ought to be reserved, and abstracted when very likely they have practical duties to attend to. How utterly inappropriate, for instance, it would be on the May festival[44] if, while the attention of all present was concentrated on the solemnity of the occasion, the thoughts of these ladies were wandering on their own poetical imaginations about 'sweet flags;' or if, again, on the Ninth-day festival,[45] when all the nobles present were exercising their inventive faculties on the subject of Chinese poems, they were to volunteer to pour forth their grand ideas on the dew-laid flowers of the chrysanthemum, thus endeavoring to rival their opponents of the stronger sex. There is a time for everything; and all people, but more especially women, should be constantly careful to watch circumstances, and not to air their accomplishments at a time when nobody cares for them. They should practise a sparing economy in displaying their learning and eloquence, and should even, if circumstances require, plead ignorance on subjects with which they are familiar."

As to Genji, even these last observations seemed only to encourage his reverie still to run upon a certain one, whom he considered to be the happy medium between the too much and the too little; and, no definite conclusion having been arrived at through the conversation, the evening passed away.

The long-continued rainy weather had now cleared up bright and fine, and the Prince Genji proceeded to the mansion of his father-in-law, where Lady Aoi, his bride, still resided with him. She was in her private suite of apartments, and he soon joined her there. She was dignified and stately, both in manners and demeanor, and everything about her bore traces of scrupulous neatness.

"Such may be one of those described by Sama-no-Kami, in whom we may place confidence," he thought, as he approached her. At the same time, her lofty queenliness caused him to feel a momentary embarrassment, which he at once tried to hide by chatting with the attendant maid. The air was close and heavy, and he was somewhat oppressed by it. His father-in-law happened to pass by the apartment. He stopped and uttered a few words from behind the curtain which overhung the door. "In this hot weather," said Genji, in a low tone, "what makes him come here?" and did not give the slightest encouragement to induce his father-in-law to enter the room; so he passed along. All present smiled significantly, and tittered. "How indiscreet!" exclaimed Genji, glancing at them reprovingly, and throwing himself back on *akiô-sok* (arm-stool), where he remained calm and silent.

It was, by no means, becoming behavior on the part of the Prince.

The day was drawing to an end when it was announced that the mansion was closed in the certain celestial direction of the Naka-gami (central God).[46] His own mansion in Nijiô (the one mentioned as being repaired in a previous chapter) was also in the same line of direction.

"Where shall I go then?" said Genji, and without troubling himself any further, went off into a doze. All present expressed in different words their surprise at his unusual apathy. Thereupon some one reported that the residence of Ki-no-Kami, who was in waiting on the Prince, on the banks of the middle river (the River Kiôgok) had lately been irrigated by bringing the stream into its gardens, making them cool and refreshing.

"That's very good, especially on such a close evening," exclaimed Genji, rousing himself, and he at once intimated to Ki-no-Kami his desire of visiting his house. To which the latter answered simply, "Yes." He did not, however, really like the Prince's visit, and was reluctantly telling his fellow attendants that, owing to a certain circumstance which had taken place at Iyo-no-Kami's[47] residence, his wife (Ki-no-Kami's stepmother) had taken up her abode with him that very evening, and that the rooms were all in confusion.

Genji heard all this distinctly, but he would not change his mind, and said, "That is all the better! I don't care to stay in a place where no fair statue dwells; it is slow work."

Being thus pressed, no alternative remained for the Ki-no-Kami, and a messenger was despatched to order the preparation of apartments for the Prince. Not long after this messenger had gone, Genji started on his way to the house of Ki-no-Kami, whose mild objections against this quick proceeding were not listened to.

He left the mansion as quietly as possible, even without taking formal leave of its master, and his escort consisted of a few favorite attendants.

The "eastern front room" in the "dwelling quarters" was wide open, and a temporary arrangement was made for the reception of the Prince, who arrived there very quickly. The scene of the garden struck him before anything else. The surface of the lake sparkled with its glittering waters. The hedges surrounded it in rustic beauty, and luxuriant shrubs grew in pleasing order. Over all the fair scene the breeze of evening swept softly, summer insects sang distinctly here and there, and the fireflies hovered about in mazy dances.

The escort took up its quarters in a position which overlooked the stream of water which ran beneath the corridor, and here began to take cups of *saké*. The host hastened to order also some refreshment to be prepared for Genji.

The latter was meanwhile gazing abstractedly about him, thinking such a place might belong to the class which Sama-no-Kami fairly placed in the middle category. He knew that the lady who was under the same roof was a young beauty of whom he had heard something before, and he was looking forward to a chance of seeing her.

He then noticed the rustling of a silken dress escaping from a small boudoir to the right, and some youthful voices, not without charm, were also heard, mingled with occasional sounds of suppressed laughter. The casement of the boudoir had been, until a short time before, open, but was pulled down by order of Ki-no-Kami, who, perhaps, doubted the propriety of its being as it was, and now only allowed a struggling light to issue through the paper of the "sliding screen!" He proceeded to one side of his room that he might see what could be seen, but there was no chance. He still stood there that he might be able, at least, to catch some part of the conversation. It seems that this boudoir adjoined the general family room of the female inmates, and his ears were greeted by some faint talking. He inclined his head attentively, and heard them whispering probably about himself.

"Is it not a pity that the fate of so fine a prince should be already fixed?" said one voice.

"Yet he loses no opportunity of availing himself of the favors of fortune," added another.

These remarks may have been made with no serious intention, but as to Genji, he, even in hearing them, could not help thinking of a certain fair image of which he so fondly dreamt. At the same time feeling a thrill on reflecting that, if this kind of secret were to be discovered and discussed in such a manner, what could be done.

He then heard an observation in delicate allusion to his verse which he had presented to the Princess Momo-zono (peach-gardens) with the flowers of Asagao (morning-glory, or convolvulus).

"What *cautious* beauties they are to talk in that way! But I wonder if their forms when seen will answer to the pictures of my fancy," thought Genji, as he retired to his original position, for he could hear nothing more interesting.

Ki-no-Kami presently entered the room, brought in some fruits, trimmed the lamp, and the visitor and host now began to enjoy a pleasant leisure.

"What has become of the ladies? Without some of them no society is cheerful," observed Genji.

"Who can there be to meet such wishes?" said the Ki-no-Kami to himself, but took no notice of Genji's remark.

There were several boys in the house who had followed Ki-no-Kami into the room. They were the sons and brothers of Ki-no-Kami. Among them there was one about twelve or thirteen, who was nicer-looking than the others. Genji, of course, did not know who they all were, and accordingly made inquiries. When he came to the last-mentioned boy, Ki-no-Kami replied:—

"He is the youngest son of the late Lord Yemon, now an orphan, and, from his sister's connections, he is now staying here. He is shrewd and unlike ordinary boys. His desire is to take Court service, but he has as yet no patron."

"What a pity! Is, then, the sister you mentioned your stepmother?"

"Yes, sir, it is so."

"What a good mother you have got. I once overheard the Emperor, to whom, I believe, a private application had been some time made in her behalf, referring to her, said, 'What has become of her?' Is she here now?" said Genji; and lowering his voice, added, "How changeable are the fortunes of the world!"

"It is her present state, sir. But, as you may perceive, it differs from her original expectation. Changeable indeed are the fortunes of this world, especially so the fortunes of women!"

"Does Iyo respect her? Perhaps he idolizes her, as his master."

"That is a question, perhaps, as a *private* master. I am the foremost to disapprove of this infatuation on his part."

"Are you? Nevertheless he trusts her to such a one as you. He is a kind father! But where are they all?"

"All in their private apartments."

Genji by this time apparently desired to be alone, and Ki-no-Kami now retired with the boys. All the escort were already slumbering comfortably, each on his own cool rush mat, under the pleasant persuasion of *saké*.

Genji was now alone. He tried to doze, but could not. It was late in the evening, and all was still around. His sharpened senses made him aware that the room next but one to his own was occupied, which led him to imagine that the lady of whom he had been speaking might be there. He rose softly, and once more proceeded to the other side of the room to listen to what he might overhear. He heard a tender voice, probably that of Kokimi, the boy spoken of before, who appeared to have just entered the room, saying:—

"Are you here?"

To which a female voice replied, "Yes, dear, but has the visitor yet retired?" And the same voice added—

"Ah! so near, and yet so far!"

"Yes, I should think so, he is so nice-looking, as they say."

"Were it daytime I would see him, too," said the lady in a drowsy voice.

"I shall go to bed, too! But what a bad light," said the boy, and Genji conjectured that he had been trimming the lamp.

The lady presently clapped her hands for a servant, and said, "Where is Chiûjiô, I feel lonely, I wish to see her."

"Madam, she is in the bath now, she will be here soon," replied the servant.

"Suppose I pay my visit to her, too? What harm! no harm, perhaps," said Genji to himself. He withdrew the fastening of the intervening door, on the other side there was none, and it opened. The entrance to the room where the lady was sitting was only screened by a curtain, with a glimmering light inside. By the reflection of this light he saw travelling trunks and bags all scattered about; through these he groped his way and approached the curtain. He saw, leaning on a cushion, the small and pretty figure of a lady, who did not seem to notice his approach, probably thinking it was Chiûjiô, for whom she had sent. Genji felt nervous, but struggling against the feeling, startled the lady by saying:—

"Chiûjiô was called for, I thought it might mean myself, and I come to offer you my devoted services."

This was really an unexpected surprise, and the lady was at a loss.

"It is, of course, natural," he said, "you should be astonished at my boldness, but pray excuse me. It is solely from my earnest desire to show at such an opportunity the great respect for you which I have felt for a very long time."

He was clever enough to know how to speak, and what to say, under all circumstances, and made the above speech in such an extremely humble and insinuating manner that the demon himself could not have taken offence, so she forbore to show any sudden resentment. She had, however, grave doubts as to the propriety of his conduct, and felt somewhat uncomfortable, saying shyly, "Perhaps you have made a mistake!"

"No, certainly not," he replied. "What mistake can I have made? On the other hand, I have no wish to offend you. The evening, however, is very irksome, and I should feel obliged if you would permit me to converse with you." Then gently taking her hand he pressed her to return with him to his lonely apartment.

She was still young and weak, and did not know what was most proper to do under these circumstances, so half yielding, half reluctantly was induced to be led there by him.

At this juncture Chiûjiô, for whom she had sent previously, entered the room. Upon which Genji exclaimed "Ha!"

Chiûjiô stared with astonishment at him, whom she at once recognized as the Prince, by the rich perfume which he carried about him.

"What does this mean?" thought Chiûjiô. She could still do nothing. Had he been an ordinary personage she would have immediately seized him. Even in that case, however, there was enough room to doubt whether it would not have been better to avoid any violent steps lest it might have given rise to a disagreeable family scandal, hence Chiûjiô was completely perplexed and mechanically followed them.

Genji was too bold to fear bystanders, a common fault with high personages, and coolly closed the door upon her saying, "She will soon return to you."

The lady being placed in such an awkward position, and not knowing what Chiûjiô might imagine, became, as it were, bewildered. Genji was, however, as artful and insinuating as might be expected in consoling her, though we do not know where he had learnt his eloquence. This was really trying for her, and she said,

"Your condescension is beyond my merit. I cannot disregard it. It is, however, absolutely necessary to know 'Who is who.'"

"But such ignorance," he a little abashed, rejoined "as not to know 'Who is who,' is the very proof of my inexperience. Were I supposed to understand too well, I should indeed be sorry. You have very likely heard how little I mix in the world. This perhaps is the very reason why you distrust me. The excess of the blindness of my mind seems strange even to myself."

He spoke thus insinuatingly. She, on her part, feared that if his fascinating address should assume a warmer tone it would be still more trying for her and more difficult to withstand, so she determined, however hard she might appear, not to give any encouragement to his feelings, and showed therefore a coolness of manner. To her meek character there was thus added a firm resolution, and it seemed like a young bamboo reed with its strength and tenderness combined, difficult to bend! Still she felt the struggle very keenly, and tears moistened her eyes.

Genji could not help feeling touched. Not knowing exactly how to soothe her, he exclaimed, "What makes you treat me so coolly? It is true we are not old acquaintances, but it does not follow that this should prevent us from becoming good friends. Please don't discompose yourself like one who does not know the world at all: it pierces my heart."

This speech touched her, and her firmness began to waver.

"Were my position what it once was," said she, "and I received such attention, I might, however unworthy, have been moved by your affection, but as my position in life is now changed, its unsatisfactory condition often makes me dream of a happiness I cannot hope to enjoy." Hereupon she remained silent for some moments, and looked as if she meant to say that she could no longer help thinking of the line:—

Don't tell anyone you've seen my home.

But these few moments of silence agitated the pure waters of her virtuous mind, and the sudden recollection of her aged husband, whom she did not generally think much about, occurred tenderly to her memory. She shuddered at the idea of his seeing her in such a dilemma as this, even in a dream, and without a word fled back to her apartment, and Genji was once more alone.

Now the chanticleer began to proclaim the coming day, and the attendants rose from their couches, some exclaiming "How soundly we have slept," others, "Let us get the carriage ready."

Ki-no-Kami also came out saying, "Why so early, no need of such hurry for the Prince."

Genji also arose, and putting on his *naoshi*, went out on a balcony on the southern side of the house, where he leaned upon the wooden balustrade and meditated as he looked round him.

It appears that people were peeping out of the casement on the western side, probably being anxious to catch a glimpse of the Prince, whose figure was indistinctly to be seen by them from the top of a short screen standing within the trellis. Among these spectators there was one who perhaps might have felt a thrill run through her frame as she beheld him. It was the very moment when the sky was being tinted by the glowing streaks of morn, and the moon's pale light was still lingering in the far distance. The aspect of the passionless heavens becomes radiant or gloomy in response to the heart of him who looks upon it. And to Genji, whose thoughts were secretly occupied with the events of the evening, the scene could only have given rise to sorrowful emotions.

Reflecting how he might on some future occasion convey a message to the lady, and looking back several times, he presently quitted the house and returned to the mansion of his father-in-law.

During some days succeeding the above events, he was staying at the mansion with his bride. His thoughts, however, were now constantly turning to the lady on the bank of the middle river. He therefore summoned Ki-no-Kami before him, and thus addressed him:—

"Cannot you let me have the boy, the son of the late Chiûnagon[48] whom I saw the other day? He is a nice lad, and I wish to have him near at hand. I will also introduce him to the Emperor."

"I receive your commands. I will talk with his *sister*, and see if she consents to it," replied Ki-no-Kami with a bow.

These last words alluding to the object which occupied his thoughts caused Genji to start, but he said with apparent calmness—

"Has the lady presented you yet with a brother or a sister?"

"No, sir, not yet; she has been married now these two years, but it seems she is always thinking she is not settled in the way her parents desired, and is not quite contented with her position."

"What a pity! I heard, however, she was a very good lady. Is it so?"

"Yes, I quite believe so; but hitherto we have lived separately, and were not very cordial, which, as all the world knows, is usual in such relationship."

After the lapse of five or six days the boy Kokimi was brought to him. He was not tall or handsome but very intelligent, and in manners perfectly well-bred. Genji treated him with the greatest kindness, at which, in his boyish mind, he was highly delighted. Genji now asked him many questions about his sister, to which he gave such answers as he could, but often with shyness and diffidence. Hence Genji was unable to take him into his confidence, but by skilfully coaxing and pleasing him, he ventured to hand him a letter to be taken to his sister. The boy, though he possibly guessed at its meaning, did not trouble himself much, but taking it, duly delivered it to his sister. She became confused and thoughtful as she took it, and fearing what the boy might think, opened the letter and held it before her face as she read, in order to conceal the expression of her countenance.

It was a long one, and among other things contained the following lines:—

I had a dream, a dream so sweet,Ah! would that I could dream again;Alas, no sleep these eyes will greet,And so I strive to dream in vain!

It was beautifully written, and as her eyes fell upon the passionate words, a mist gathered over them, and a momentary thought of her own life and position once more flashed over her mind, and without a word of comment to the boy, she retired to rest.

A few days afterwards Kokimi was again invited to join the Prince. Thereupon he asked his sister to give him an answer to the Prince's letter.

"Tell the Prince," she said, "there is no one *here* who reads such letters."

"But," said the boy, "he does not expect such an answer as this! How can I tell him so?"

At first, she half-resolved to explain everything to Kokimi, and to make him thoroughly understand why she ought not to receive such letters, but the effort was too painful, so she simply said, "It is all the better for you not to talk in that way. If you think it so serious why should you go to him at all?"

"Yet, how can I disobey his commands to go back?" exclaimed the boy, and so he returned to Genji without any written answer to him.

"I was weary of waiting for you. Perhaps you, too, had forgotten me," said Genji, when he saw the boy, who was, however, silent and blushed. "And what answer have you brought me?" continued Genji, and then the boy replied in the exact words which his sister had used.

"What?" cried Genji: and continued, "Perhaps you may not know, so I will tell you. I knew your sister before she knew Iyo. But she likes to treat me so because she thinks she has got a very good friend in Iyo; but do you be like a brother to me. The days of Iyo will be probably fewer than mine."

He now returned to the Palace taking Komini with him, and, going to his dressing-room, attired him nicely in the Court style; in a word, he treated him as a parent would do.

By the boy's assistance several more letters were conveyed to his sister. Her resolution, however, remained unshaken.

"If one's heart were once to deviate from the path," she reflected, "the only end we could expect would be a damaged reputation and misery for life: the good and the bad result from one's self!"

Thus thinking, she resolved to return no answer. She might, indeed, have admired the person of Genji, and probably did so, yet, whenever such feelings came into her mind, the next thought that suggested itself was, "What is the use of such idle admiration?"

Meanwhile, Genji was often thinking of paying a visit to the house where she was staying, but he did not consider it becoming to do so, without some reasonable pretext, more especially as he would have been sorry, and for her sake more than his own, to draw a suspicion upon her.

It happened, however, after a prolonged residence at the Court, that another occasion of closing the Palace in the certain celestial line of direction arrived. Catching at this opportunity he left the Palace, and suddenly turning out of his road, went straight to Ki-no-Kami's residence, with the excuse that he had just discovered the above fact on his way. Ki-no-Kami surprised at this unexpected visit, had only to bow before him, and acknowledge the honor of his presence. The boy, Kokimi, was already there before him, having been secretly informed of his intention beforehand, and he attended on him as usual in his apartment on his arrival.

The lady, who had been told by her brother that the Prince earnestly desired to see her, knew well how dangerous it was to approach an inviting flower growing on the edge of a precipice. She was not, of course, insensible to his coming in such a manner, with an excuse for the sake of seeing her, but she did not wish to increase her dreamlike inquietude by seeing him. And again, if he ventured to visit her apartment, as he did before, it might be a serious compromise for her.

For these reasons she retired while her brother was with Genji, to a private chamber of Chiûjiô, her companion, in the rear of the main building, under the pretence that her own room was too near that of the Prince, besides she was indisposed and required "Tataki,"[49] which she desired to have done in a retired part of the house.

Genji sent his attendants very early to their own quarters, and then, through Kokimi, requested an interview with the lady. Kokimi at first was unable to find her, till after searching everywhere, he, at last, came to the apartment of Chiûjiô, and with great earnestness endeavored to persuade her to see Genji, in an anxious and half trembling voice, while she replied in a tone slightly angry, "What makes you so busy? Why do you trouble yourself? Boys carrying such messages are highly blamable."

After thus daunting him, she added, more mildly, "Tell the Prince I am somewhat indisposed, and also that some friends are with me, and I cannot well leave them now." And she again cautioned the boy not to be too officious, and sent him away from her at once.

Yet, at the bottom of her heart, different feelings might have been struggling from those which her words seemed to express, and some such thoughts as these shaped themselves to her mind: "Were I still a maiden in the home of my beloved parents, and occasionally received his visits there, how happy might I not be? How trying to act as if no romantic sentiment belonged to my heart!"

Genji, who was anxiously waiting to know how the boy would succeed in persuading his sister, was soon told that all his efforts were in vain. Upon hearing this he remained for some moments silent, and then relieved his feelings with a long-drawn sigh, and hummed:—

"The Hahaki-gi[50] distant treeSpreads broom-like o'er the silent waste;Approach, how changed its shape we see,In vain we try its shade to taste."

The lady was unable to sleep, and her thoughts also took the following poetic shape:—

Too like the Hahaki-gi tree,Lonely and humble, I must dwell,Nor dare to give a thought to thee,But only sigh a long farewell.

All the other inmates of the house were now in a sound slumber, but sleep came not to Genji's eyes. He did, indeed, admire her immovable and chaste nature, but this only drew his heart more towards her. He was agitated. At one moment he cried, "Well, then!" at another, "However!" "Still!" At last, turning to the boy, he passionately exclaimed, "Lead me to her at once!"

Kokimi calmly replied, "It is impossible, too many eyes are around us!"

Genji with a sigh then threw himself back on the cushion, saying to Kokimi, "You, at least, will be my friend, and shall share my apartment!"

FOOTNOTES:

[22]A hero of an older fiction, who is represented as the perfect ideal of a gallant.

[23]A fast observed when some remarkable or supernatural event took place, or on the anniversary of days of domestic misfortune.

[24]A general of the Imperial Guards.

[25]Love letters generally are not signed or are signed with a fancy name.

[26]Left Master of the Horse.

[27]Secretary to the Master of Ceremonies.

[28]Deputy-governors of provinces. In those days these functionaries were greatly looked down upon by the Court nobles, and this became one of the causes of the feudal system.

[29]The naoshi is an outer attire. It formed part of a loose and unceremonious Court dress.

[30]This alludes to a common habit of women, who push back their hair before commencing any task.

[31]Some kinds of nuns did not shave their heads, and this remark seems to allude to the common practice of women who often involuntarily smooth their hair before they see people, which practice comes, no doubt, from the idea that the beauty of women often depends on the tidiness of their hair.

[32]This means that her soul, which was sinful, would not go at once to its final resting-place, but wander about in unknown paths.

[33]A mountain spoken of in Chinese literature. It was said to be in the Eastern Ocean, and people of extraordinary long lives, called Sennin, were supposed to dwell there.

[34]In China and Japan handwriting is considered no less an art than painting.

[35]An ideal woman patroness of the art of dyeing.

[36]The weaver, or star Vega. In the Chinese legend she is personified as a woman always engaged in weaving.

[37]In the same legend, it is said that this weaver, who dwells on one side of the Milky Way in the heavens, meets her lover—another star called Hikoboshi, or the bull-driver—once every year, on the evening of the seventh day of the seventh month. He dwelt on the other side of the Milky Way, and their meeting took place on a bridge, made by birds (jays), by the intertwining of their wings. It was this which gave rise to the popular festival, which takes place on this day, both in China and Japan.

[38]Little darlings—a kind of pink.

[39]The Tokonatz (everlasting summer) is another name for the pink, and it is poetically applied to the lady whom we love.

[40]A female divinity in Indian mythology.

[41]From the Chinese poet Hak-rak-ten, who was mentioned before. He says in one of his poems: "Once upon a time a certain host invited to his abode a clever match-maker. When the guests were assembled he poured forth wine into a beautiful jar, and said to all present, 'drink not for a moment, but hear what I say about the two choices, daughters of the rich get married soon, but snub

their husbands, daughters of the poor get married with difficulty but dearly love their mothers-in-law.'"

[42]A soft style of Japanese writing commonly used by ladies.

[43]A stiff and formal style of Japanese writing.

[44]The fifth of May is one of the five important national festivals. A solemn celebration of this fête used to be performed at Court. It is sometimes called the festival of the "Sweet Flags,"—*calami aromatici*—because it was held at the season when those beautiful water-plants were in the height of perfection.

[45]Another of the five above-mentioned. It was held on the ninth of September, and it was customary on the occasion for rhymes to be given out to those present, wherewith to compose Chinese poems. It was sometimes called the "Chrysanthemum Festival," for the same reason that the celebration of the fifth of May was termed the "Sweet Flag Festival."

[46]This is an astrological superstition. It is said that when this God is in any part of the compass, at the time being, it is most unlucky to proceed towards it, and to remain in the same line of its direction.

[47]The deputy governor of the province Iyo; he is supposed to be in the province at this time, leaving his young wife and family behind.

[48]The father of Kokimi seems to have been holding the office Yemon-no-Kami as well as Chiûnagon.

[49]Tataki, or Amma, a sort of shampooing, a very common medical treatment in Japan.

[50]Hahaki-gi, the broom-like tree, is said to have been a certain tree growing in the plain of Sonohara, so called from its shape, which, at a distance, looked like a spreading broom, but when one comes near, its appearance was totally changed.

CHAPTER III

BEAUTIFUL CICADA

Genji was still sleepless! "Never have I been so badly treated. I have now discovered what the disappointment of the world means," he murmured, while the boy Kokimi lay down beside him fast asleep. The smallness of his stature, and the graceful waving of his short hair, could not but recall to Genji the beautiful tresses of his sister, and bring her image vividly before him; and, long before the daylight appeared, he rose up, and returned to his residence with all speed. For some time after this no communication took place between the lady and himself. He could not, however, banish her from his thoughts, and he said to Kokimi that "he felt his former experience too painful, and that he strove to drive away his care; yet in vain; his thoughts would not obey his wish, and he begged him, therefore, to seek some favorable opportunity for him to see her." Kokimi, though he did not quite like the task, felt proud of being made his confidant, and thenceforward looked incessantly, with keen boyish eyes, for a chance of obliging him.

Now, it happened that Ki-no-Kami went down to his official residence in his province, and only the female members of his family were left at home. "This is the time," said Kokimi to himself, and went to Genji, and persuaded him to come with him. "What can the boy do?" thought Genji; "I fear not very much, but I must not expect too much"; and they started at once, in Kokimi's carriage, so as to arrive in good time.

The evening was darkening round them, and they drew up on one side of the house, where few persons were likely to observe them. As it happened to be Kokimi who had come, no fuss was made about his arrival, nor any notice taken of it. He entered the house; and, leaving the Prince in the Eastern Hall, proceeded first into the inner room. The casement was closed.

"How is it the casement is closed?" he demanded of the servants. They told him "That the Lady of the West (Ki-no-Kami's sister, so called by the domestics from her living to the westward of the house) was there on a visit since noon, and was playing Go with his sister." The door by which the boy had entered the room was not entirely closed. Genji softly came up to it, and the whole interior of the apartment was visible. He stood facing the west. On one side of the room was a folding screen, one end of which was pushed back, and there was nothing besides to obstruct his view. His first glance fell on the fair figure of her of whom he had so fondly dreamt, sitting by a lamp near a central pillar. She wore a dress of dark purple, and a kind of scarf thrown over her shoulders; her figure was slight and delicate, and her face was partly turned aside, as if she did not like to expose it even to her companions. Her hands were prettily shaped and tiny, and she used them with a gentle reserve, half covering them. Another lady, younger than herself, sat facing the east—that is, just opposite Genji—and was, therefore, entirely visible to him. She was dressed in a thin white silk, with a Ko-uchiki (outer vestment), worked with red and blue flowers, thrown loosely over it, and a crimson sash round her waist. Her bosom was partly revealed; her complexion very fair; her figure rather stout and tall; the head and neck in good proportions, and the lips and eyelids lovely. The hair was not very long, but reached in wavy lines to her shoulders.

"If a man had such a daughter, he might be satisfied," thought Genji. "But perhaps she may be a little deficient in quietness. No matter how this may be, she has sufficient attractions."

The game was drawing to a close, and they paid very little attention to Kokimi on his entrance. The principal interest in it was over; they were hurrying to finish it. One was looking quietly at the board, and said, "Let me see, that point must be Ji. Let me play the Kôh[51] of this spot." The other saying, "I am beaten; let me calculate," began to count on her fingers the number of spaces at each corner, at the same time saying "Ten! twenty! thirty! forty!" When Genji came in this way to see them together, he perceived that his idol, in the matter of personal beauty, was somewhat inferior to her friend. He was not, indeed, able to behold the full face of the former; yet, when he shifted his position, and fixed his gaze steadfastly upon her, the profile became distinct. He observed that her eyelids were a little swollen, and the line of the nose was not very delicate. He still admired her, and said to himself, "But perhaps she is more sweet-tempered than the others"; but when he again turned his eyes to the younger one, strange to say the calm and cheerful smile which occasionally beamed in her face touched the heart of Genji; moreover, his usual interviews with ladies generally took place in full ceremony. He had never seen them in so familiar an attitude before, without restraint or reserve, as on the present occasion, which made him quite enjoy the scene. Kokimi now came out, and Genji retired stealthily to one side of the door along the corridor. The former, who saw him there, and supposed he had remained waiting in the place he had left him all the while, apologized for keeping him so long, and said: "A certain young lady is now staying here; I am sorry, but I did not dare mention your visit."

"Do you mean to send me away again disappointed? How inglorious it is," replied Genji.

"No; why so? The lady may leave shortly. I will then announce you."

Genji said no more. The ladies had by this time concluded their game, and the servants, who were about to retire to their own apartments, cried out, "Where is our young master? we must close this door."

"Now is the time; pray take me there; don't be too late. Go and ask," said Genji.

Kokimi knew very well how hard was his task to persuade his sister to see the Prince, and was meditating taking him into her room, without her permission, when she was alone. So he said, hesitatingly, "Please wait a little longer, till the other lady, Ki-no-Kami's sister, goes away."

"Is Ki-no's sister here? So much the better. Please introduce me to her before she leaves," said Genji.

"But!"

"But what? Do you mean that she is not worth seeing?" retorted Genji; and would fain have told the boy that he had already seen her, but thought it better not to do so, and continued: "Were we to wait for her to retire, it would become too late; we should have no chance."

Hereupon Kokimi determined to risk a little, and went back to his sister's room, rolling up a curtain which hung in his way. "It is too warm—let the air in!" he cried, as he passed through. After a few minutes he returned, and led Genji to the apartment on his own responsibility. The lady with the scarf (his sister), who had been for some time fondly supposing that Genji had given up thinking about her, appeared startled and embarrassed when she saw him; but, as a matter of course, the usual courtesies were paid. The younger lady, however (who was free from all such thoughts), was rather pleased at his appearance. It happened that, when the eyes of the younger were turned in another direction, Genji ventured to touch slightly the shoulder of his favorite, who, startled at the action rose suddenly and left the room, on pretence of seeking something she required, dropping her scarf in her haste, as a cicada casts off its tender wingy shell, and leaving her friend to converse with the Prince. He was chagrined, but did not betray his vexation either by words or looks, and now began to carry on a conversation with the lady who remained, whom he had already admired. Here his usual bold flirtation followed. The young lady, who was at first disturbed at his assurance, betrayed her youthful inexperience in such matters; yet for an innocent maiden, she was rather coquettish, and he went on flirting with her.

"Chance meetings like this," said he, "often arise from deeper causes than those which take place in the usual routine of things, so at least say the ancients. If I say I love you, you might not believe me; and yet, indeed, it is so. Do think of me! True, we are not yet quite free, and perhaps I might not be able to see you so often as I wish; but I hope you will wait with patience, and not forget me."

"Truly, I also fear what people might suspect; and, therefore, I may not be able to communicate with you at all," said she, innocently.

"Perhaps it might not be desirable to employ any other hand," he rejoined. "If you only send your message, say through Kokimi, there would not be any harm."

Genji now rose to depart, and slyly possessed himself of the scarf which had been dropped by the other lady. Kokimi, who had been dozing all the time, started up suddenly when Genji roused him. He then led the latter to the door. At this moment, the tremulous voice of an aged female domestic, who appeared quite unexpectedly, exclaimed—

"Who is there?"

To which Kokimi immediately replied, "It is I!"

"What brings you here so late?" asked the old woman, in a querulous tone.

"How inquisitive! I am now going out. What harm?" retorted the boy, rather scornfully; and, stepping up to the threshold, gave Genji a push over it, when all at once the shadow of his tall figure was projected on the moonlit floor.

"Who's that?" cried the old woman sharply, and in alarm; but the next moment, without waiting for any reply, mumbled on: "Ah, ah! 'tis Miss Mimb, no wonder so tall."

This remark seemed to allude to one of her fellow-servants, who must have been a stalwart maiden, and the subject of remarks among her companions. The old woman, quite satisfied in thinking that it was she who was with Kokimi, added: "You, my young master, will soon be as tall as she is; I will come out this way, too," and approached the door. Genji could do nothing but stand silent and motionless. When she came nearer she said, addressing the supposed Mimb, "Have you been waiting on the young mistress this evening? I have been ill since the day before yesterday, and kept myself to my room, but was sent for this evening because my services were required. I cannot stand it." So saying, and without waiting for any reply, she passed on, muttering as she went, "Oh! my pain! my pain!" Genji and the boy now went forth, and they drove back to the mansion in Nijiô. Talking over the events of the evening, Genji ironically said to his companion, "Ah! you are a nice boy!" and snapped his fingers with chagrin at the escape of his favorite and her indifference. Kokimi said nothing. Genji then murmured, "I was clearly slighted. Oh wretched me! I cannot rival the happy Iyo!" Shortly after, he retired to rest, taking with him, almost unconsciously, the scarf he had carried off, and again making Kokimi share his apartment, for company's sake. He had still some hope that the latter might be useful to him; and, with the intention of stirring up his energies, observed, "You are a nice boy; but I am afraid the coldness shown to me by your sister may at last weaken the friendship between you and me."

Kokimi still made no reply. Genji closed his eyes but could not sleep, so he started up and, taking writing materials, began to write, apparently without any fixed purpose, and indited the following distich:—

"Where the cicada casts her shellIn the shadows of the tree,There is one whom I love well,Though her heart is cold to me."

Casting away the piece of paper on which these words were written—purposely or not, who knows?—he again leaned his head on his hand. Kokimi slyly stretching out his hand, picked up the paper from the floor, and hid it quickly in his dress. Genji soon fell into profound slumber, in which he was speedily joined by Kokimi.

Some days passed away and Kokimi returned to his sister, who, on seeing him, chided him severely, saying:—

"Though I managed with some difficulty, we must not forget what people might say of us, *your* officiousness is most unpardonable. Do you know what the Prince himself will think of your childish trick?"

Thus was poor Kokimi, on the one hand, reproached by Genji for not doing enough, and on the other by his sister for being too officious! was he not in a very happy position! Yet, notwithstanding her words, he ventured to draw from his dress the paper he had picked up in Genji's apartment, and offered it to her. The lady hesitated a moment, though somewhat inclined to read it, holding it in her hand for some little time, undecided. At length she ventured to throw her eyes over its contents. At once the loss of her scarf floated upon her mind as she read, and, taking up her pen, wrote on part of the paper where Genji had written his verses, the words of a song:—

"Amidst dark shadows of the tree,Cicada's wing with dew is wet,So in mine eyes unknown to thee,Spring sweet tears of fond regret."

FOOTNOTES:

[51]Ji and Kôh are the names of certain positions in the game of "Go."

CHAPTER IV

EVENING GLORY

I t happened that when Genji was driving about in the Rokjiô quarter, he was informed that his old nurse, Daini, was ill, and had become a nun. Her residence was in Gojiô. He wished to visit her, and drove to the house. The main gate was closed, so that his carriage could not drive up; therefore, he sent in a servant to call out Koremitz, a son of the nurse.

Meantime, while awaiting him, he looked round on the deserted terrace. He noticed close by a small and rather dilapidated dwelling, with a wooden fence round a newly-made enclosure. The upper part, for eight or ten yards in length, was surrounded by a trellis-work, over which some white reed blinds—rude, but new—were thrown. Through these blinds the indistinct outline of some fair heads were faintly delineated, and the owners were evidently peeping down the roadway from their retreat. "Ah," thought Genji, "they can never be so tall as to look over the blind. They must be standing on something within. But whose residence is it? What sort of people are they?" His equipage was strictly private and unostentatious. There were, of course, no outriders; hence he had no fear of being recognized by them. And so he still watched the house. The gate was also constructed of something like trellis-work, and stood half open, revealing the loneliness of the interior. The line: "Where do we seek our home?" came first into his mind, and he then thought that "even this must be as comfortable as golden palaces to its inmates."

A long wooden rail, covered with luxuriant creepers, which, fresh and green, climbed over it in full vigor, arrested his eye; their white blossoms, one after another disclosing their smiling lips in unconscious beauty. Genji began humming to him[69]self: "Ah! stranger crossing there." When his attendant informed him that these lovely white flowers were called "Yûgao" (evening-glory), adding, and at the same time pointing to the flowers, "See the flowers *only*, flourishing in that glorious state."

"What beautiful flowers they are," exclaimed Genji. "Go and beg a bunch."

The attendant thereupon entered the half-opened gate and asked for some of them, on which a young girl, dressed in a long tunic, came out, taking an old fan in her hand, and saying, "Let us put them on this, those with strong stems," plucked off a few stalks and laid them on the fan.

These were given to the attendant, who walked slowly back. Just as he came near to Genji, the gate of Koremitz's courtyard opened and Koremitz himself appeared, who took the flowers from him and handed them to Genji, at the same moment saying, "I am very sorry I could not find the gate key, and that I made you wait so long in the public road, though there is no one hereabouts to stare at, or recognize you, I sincerely beg your pardon."

The carriage was now driven in, and Genji alighted. The Ajari,[52] elder brother of Koremitz; Mikawa-no-Kami, his brother-in-law; and the daughter of Daini, all assembled and greeted him. The nun also rose from her couch to welcome him.

"How pleased I am to see you," she said, "but you see I have quite altered, I have become a nun. I have given up the world. I had no reluctance in doing this. If I had any uneasiness, it was on your account alone. My health, however, is beginning to improve; evidently the divine blessing on this sacrifice."

"I was so sorry," replied Genji, "to hear you were ill, and now still more so to find you have given up the world. I hope that you may live to witness my success and prosperity. It grieves me to think you were compelled to make such a change; yet, I believe, this will secure your enjoyment of happiness hereafter. It is said that when one leaves this world without a single regret, one passes straight to Paradise." As he said these words his eyes became moistened.

Now, it is common for nurses to regard their foster children with blind affection, whatever may be their faults, thinking, so to speak, that what is crooked is straight. So in Genji's case, who, in Daini's eyes, was next door to perfection, this blindness was still more strongly apparent, and she always regarded her office as his nurse, as an honor, and while Genji was discoursing in the above manner, a tear began to trickle from her eyes.

"You know," he continued, "at what an early age I was deprived of my dearest ties; there were, indeed, several who looked after me, but you were the one to whom I was most attached. In due course, after I grew up, I ceased to see you regularly. I could not visit you as often as I thought of you, yet, when I did not see you for a long time, I often felt very lonely. Ah! if there were no such things as partings in the world!"

He then enjoined them earnestly to persevere in prayer for their mother's health, and said, "Good-by."

At the moment of quitting the house he remembered that something was written on the fan that held the flowers. It was already twilight, and he asked Koremitz to bring a taper, that he might see to read it. It seemed to him as if the fragrance of some fair hand that had used it still remained, and on it was written the following couplets:—

"The crystal dew at Evening's hourSleeps on the Yûgao's beauteous flower,Will this please him, whose glances bright,Gave to the flowers a dearer light?"

With apparent carelessness, without any indication to show who the writer was, it bore, however, the marks of a certain excellence. Genji thought, "this is singular, coming from whence it does," and turning to Koremitz, he asked, "Who lives in this house to your right?" "Ah," exclaimed Koremitz mentally, "as usual, I see," but replied with indifference, "Truly I have been here some days, but I have been so busy in attending my mother that I neither know nor have asked about the neighbors." "You may probably be surprised at my inquisitiveness," said Genji, "but I have reasons for asking this on account of this fan. I request you to call on them, and make inquiries what sort of people they are."

Koremitz thereupon proceeded to the house, and, calling out a servant, sought from him the information he wanted, when he was told that, "This is the house of Mr. Yômei-no-Ske. He is at present in the country; his lady is still young; her brothers are in the Court service, and often come here to see her. The whole history of the family I am not acquainted with." With this answer Koremitz returned, and repeated it to Genji, who thought, "Ah! the sending of this verse may be a trick of these conceited Court fellows!" but he could not entirely free his mind from the idea of its having been sent especially to himself. This was consistent with the characteristic vanity of his disposition. He, therefore, took out a paper, and disguising his handwriting (lest it should be identified), indited the following:—

"Were I the flower to see more near,Which once at dusky eve I saw,It might have charms for me more dear,And look more beauteous than before."

And this he sent to the house by his servant, and set off on his way. He saw a faint light through the chinks of the blinds of the house, like the glimmer of the firefly. It gave him, as he passed, a silent sort of longing. The mansion in Rokjiô, to which he was proceeding this evening, was a handsome building, standing amidst fine woods of rare growth and beauty, and all was of comfortable appearance. Its mistress was altogether in good circumstances, and here Genji spent the hours in full ease and comfort.

On his way home next morning he again passed the front of the house, where grew the Yûgao flowers, and the recollection of flowers which he had received the previous evening, made him anxious to ascertain who the people were who lived there.

After the lapse of some time Koremitz came to pay him a visit, excusing himself for not having come before, on account of his mother's health being more unsatisfactory. He said, "In obedience to your commands to make further inquiries, I called on some people who know about my neighbors, but could not get much information. I was told, however, that there is a lady who has been living there since last May, but who she is even the people in the house do not know. Sometimes I looked over the hedges between our gardens, and saw the youthful figure of a lady, and a maiden attending her, in a style of dress which betrayed a good origin. Yesterday evening, after sunset, I saw the lady writing a letter, her face was very calm in expression, but full of thought, and her attendant was often sobbing secretly, as she waited on her. These things I saw distinctly."

Genji smiled. He seemed more anxious than before to know something about them, and Koremitz continued: "Hoping to get some fuller information, I took an opportunity which presented itself of sending a communication to the house. To this a speedy answer was returned, written by a skilful hand. I concluded from this and other circumstances that there was something worth seeing and knowing enclosed within those walls." Genji immediately exclaimed, "Do! do! try again; not to be able to find out is too provoking," and he thought to himself, "If in lowly life, which is often left unnoticed, we find something attractive and fair, as Sama-no-Kami said, how delightful it will be, and I think, perhaps, this may be such a one."

In the meantime his thoughts were occasionally reverting to Cicada. His nature was not, perhaps, so perverted as to think about persons of such condition and position in life as Cicada; but since he had heard the discussion about women, and their several classifications, he had somehow become speculative in his sentiments, and ambitious of testing all those different varieties by his own experience. While matters were in this state Iyo-no-Kami returned to the capital, and came in haste to pay his respects to Genji. He was a swarthy, repulsive looking man, bearing the traces of a long journey in his appearance, and of advanced age. Still there was nothing unpleasant in his natural character and manners. Genji was about to converse with him freely, but somehow or another an awkward feeling arose in his mind, and threw a restraint upon his cordiality. "Iyo is such an honest old man," he reflected, "it is too bad to take advantage of him. What Sama-no-Kami said is true, 'that to strive to carry out wrong desires is man's evil failing!' Her hardheartedness to me is unpleasant, but from the other side this deserves praise!"

It was announced after this that Iyo-no-Kami would return to his province, and take his wife with him, and that his daughter would be left behind to be soon married.

This intelligence was far from pleasing to Genji, and he longed once more, only once more to behold the lady of the scarf, and he concerted with Kokimi how to arrange a plan for obtaining an interview. The lady, however, was quite deaf to such proposals, and the only concession she vouchsafed was that she occasionally received a letter, and sometimes answered it.

Autumn had now come; Genji was still thoughtful. Lady Aoi saw him but seldom, and was constantly disquieted by his protracted absence from her. There was, as we have before hinted, at Rokjiô, another person whom he had won with great difficulty, and it would have been a little inconsistent if he became too easily tired of her. He indeed had not become cool towards her, but the violence of his passion had somewhat abated. The cause of this seems to have been that this lady was rather too zealous, or, we may say, jealous; besides, her age exceeded that of Genji by some years. The following incident will illustrate the state of matters between them:—

One morning early Genji was about to take his departure, with sleepy eyes, listless and weary, from her mansion at Rokjiô. A slight mist spread over the scene. A maiden attendant of the mistress opened the door for his departure, and led him forth. The shrubbery of flowering trees struck refreshingly on the sight, with interlacing branches in rich confusion, among which was some Asagao in full blossom. Genji was tempted to dally, and looked contemplatively over them. The maiden still accompanied him. She wore a thin silk tunic of light green colors, showing off her graceful waist and figure, which it covered. Her appearance was attractive.

Genji looked at her tenderly, and led her to a seat in the garden, and sat down by her side. Her countenance was modest and quiet; her wavy hair was neatly and prettily arranged. Genji began humming in a low tone:—

"The heart that roams from flower to flower,Would fain its wanderings not betray,Yet 'Asagao,' in morning's hour,Impels my tender wish to stray."

So saying, he gently took her hand; she, however, without appearing to understand his real meaning, answered thus:—

"You stay not till the mist be o'er,But hurry to depart,Say can the flower you leave, no moreDetain your changeful heart?"

At this juncture a young attendant in Sasinuki[53] entered the garden, brushing away the dewy mist from the flowers, and began to gather some bunches of Asagao. The scene was one which we might desire to paint, so full of quiet beauty, and Genji rose from his seat, and slowly passed homeward. In those days Genji was becoming more and more an object of popular admiration in society, and we might even attribute the eccentricity of some of his adventures to the favor he enjoyed, combined with his great personal attractions. Where beautiful flowers expand their blossoms even the rugged mountaineer loves to rest under their shade, so wherever Genji showed himself people sought his notice.

Now with regard to the fair one about whom Koremitz was making inquiries. After some still further investigations, he came to Genji and told him that "there is some one who often visits there. Who he was I could not at first find out, for he comes with the utmost privacy. I made up my mind to discover him; so one evening I concealed myself outside the house, and waited. Presently the sound of an approaching carriage was heard, and the inmates of the house began to peep out. The lady I mentioned before was also to be seen; I could not see her very plainly, but I can tell you so much: she looked charming. The carriage itself was now seen approaching, and it apparently belonged to some one of rank. A little girl who was peeping out exclaimed, "Ukon, look here, quick, Chiûjiô is coming." Then one older came forward rubbing her hands and saying to the child, 'Don't be so foolish, don't be excited.' How could they tell, I wondered, that the carriage was a Chiûjiô's. I stole forth cautiously and reconnoitred. Near the house there is a small stream, over which a plank had been thrown by way of a bridge. The visitor was rapidly approaching this bridge when an amusing incident occurred: The elder girl came out in haste to meet him, and was passing the bridge, when the skirt of her dress caught in something, and she well-nigh fell into the water. 'Confound that bridge, what a bad Katzragi,'[54] she cried, and suddenly turned pale. How amusing it was, you may imagine. The visitor was dressed in plain style, he was followed by his page, whom I recognized as belonging to Tô-no-Chiûjiô."

"I should like to see that same carriage," interrupted Genji eagerly, as he thought to himself, "that house may be the home of the very girl whom he (Tô-no-Chiûjiô) spoke about, perhaps he has discovered her hiding-place."

"I have also made an acquaintance," Koremitz continued, "with a certain person in this house, and it was through these means that I made closer observations. The girl who nearly fell over the bridge is, no doubt, the lady's attendant, but they pretend to be all on an equality. Even when the little child said anything to betray them by its remarks, they immediately turned it off." Koremitz laughed as he told this, adding, "this was an amusing trick indeed."

"Oh," exclaimed Genji, "I must have a look at them when I go to visit your mother; you must manage this," and with the words the picture of the "Evening-Glory" rose pleasantly before his eyes.

Now Koremitz not only was always prompt in attending to the wishes of Prince Genji, but also was by his own temperament fond of carrying on such intrigues. He tried every means to favor his designs, and to ingratiate himself with the lady, and at last succeeded in bringing her and Genji together. The details of the plans by which all this was brought about are too long to be given here. Genji visited her often, but it was with the greatest caution and privacy; he never asked her when they met any particulars about her past life, nor did he reveal his own to her. He would not drive to her in his own carriage, and Koremitz often lent him his own horse to ride. He took no attendant with him except the one who had asked for the "Evening-Glory." He would not even call on the nurse, lest it might lead to discoveries. The lady was puzzled at his reticence. She would sometimes send her servant to ascertain, if possible, what road he took, and where he went. But somehow, by chance or design, he always became lost to her watchful eye. His dress, also, was of the most ordinary description, and his visits were always paid late in the evening. To her all this seemed like the mysteries of old legends. True, she conjectured from his demeanor and ways that he was a person of rank, but she never ascertained exactly who he was. She sometimes reproached Koremitz for bringing her into such strange circumstances. But he cunningly kept himself aloof from such taunts.

Be this as it may, Genji still frequently visited her, though at the same time he was not unmindful that this kind of adventure was scarcely consistent with his position. The girl was simple and modest in nature, not certainly manœuvring, neither was she stately or dignified in mien, but everything about her had a peculiar charm and interest, impossible to describe, and in the full charm of youth not altogether void of experience.

"But by what charm in her," thought Genji, "am I so strongly affected; no matter, I am so," and thus his passion continued.

Her residence was only temporary, and this Genji soon became aware of. "If she leaves this place," thought he, "and I lose sight of her—for when this may happen is uncertain—what shall I do?" He at last decided to carry her off secretly to his own mansion in Nijiô. True, if this became known it would be an awkward business; but such are love affairs; always some dangers to be risked! He therefore fondly entreated her to accompany him to some place where they could be freer.

Her answer, however, was "That such a proposal on his part only alarmed her." Genji was amused at her girlish mode of expression, and earnestly said, "Which of us is a fox?[55] I don't know, but anyhow be persuaded by me." And after repeated conversations of the same nature, she at last half-consented. He had much doubt of the propriety of inducing her to take this step, nevertheless her final compliance flattered his vanity. He recollected very well the Tokonatz (Pinks) which Tô-no-Chiûjiô spoke of, but never betrayed that he had any knowledge of that circumstance.

It was on the evening of the 15th of August when they were together. The moonlight streamed through the crevices of the broken wall. To Genji such a scene was novel and peculiar. The dawn at length began to break, and from the surrounding houses the voices of the farmers might be heard talking.

One remarked, "How cool it is." Another, "There is not much hope for our crops this year." "My carrying business I do not expect to answer," responded the first speaker. "But are our neighbors listening!" Conversing in this way they proceeded to their work.

Had the lady been one to whom surrounding appearances were important, she might have felt disturbed, but she was far from being so, and seemed as if no outward circumstances could trouble her equanimity, which appeared to him an admirable trait. The noise of the threshing of the corn came indistinctly to their ears like distant thunder. The beating of the bleacher's hammer was also heard faintly from afar off.

They were in the front of the house. They opened the window and looked out on the dawn. In the small garden before their eyes was a pretty bamboo grove; their leaves, wet with dew, shone brilliantly, even as bright as in the gardens of the palace. The cricket sang cheerfully in the old walls as if it was at their very ears, and the flight of wild geese in the air rustled overhead. Everything spoke of rural scenes and business, different from what Genji was in the habit of seeing and hearing round him.

To him all these sights and sounds, from their novelty and variety, combined with the affection he had for the girl beside him, had a delightful charm. She wore a light dress of clear purple, not very costly; her figure was slight and delicate; the tones of her voice soft and insinuating. "If she were only a little more cultivated," thought he, but, in any case, he was determined to carry her off.

"Now is the time," said he, "let us go together, the place is not very far off."

"Why so soon?" she replied, gently. As her implied consent to his proposal was thus given without much thought, he, on his part, became bolder. He summoned her maid, Ukon, and ordered the carriage to be got ready. Dawn now fairly broke; the cocks had ceased to crow, and the voice of an aged man was heard repeating his orisons, probably during his fast. "His days will not be many," thought Genji, "what is he praying for?" And while so thinking, the aged mortal muttered, "Nam Tôrai no Dôshi" (Oh! the Divine guide of the future). "Do listen to that prayer," said Genji, turning to the girl, "it shows our life is not limited to this world," and he hummed:—

"Let us together, bind our soulWith vows that Woobasok[56] has given,That when this world from sight shall rollUnparted we shall wake in heaven."

And added, "By Mirok,[57] let us bind ourselves in love forever."

The girl, doubtful of the future, thus replied in a melancholy tone:—

"When in my present lonely lot,I feel my past has not been freeFrom sins which I remember not,I dread more, what to come, may be."

In the meantime a passing cloud had suddenly covered the sky, and made its face quite gray. Availing himself of this obscurity, Genji hurried her away and led her to the carriage, where Ukon also accompanied her.

They drove to an isolated mansion on the Rokjiô embankment, which was at no great distance, and called out the steward who looked after it. The grounds were in great solitude, and over them lay a thick mist. The curtains of the carriage were not drawn close, so that the sleeves of their dresses were almost moistened. "I have never experienced this sort of trouble before," said Genji; "how painful are the sufferings of love."

"Oh! were the ancients, tell me pray,Thus led away, by love's keen smart,I ne'er such morning's misty rayHave felt before with beating heart.

Have you ever?"

The lady shyly averted her face and answered:—

"I, like the wandering moon, may roam,Who knows not if her mountain loveBe true or false, without a home,The mist below, the clouds above."

The steward presently came out and the carriage was driven inside the gates, and was brought close to the entrance, while the rooms were hurriedly prepared for their reception. They alighted just as the mist was clearing away.

This steward was in the habit of going to the mansion of Sadaijin, and was well acquainted with Genji.

"Oh!" he exclaimed, as they entered. "Without proper attendants!" And approaching near to Genji said, "Shall I call in some more servants?"

Genji replied at once and impressively, "I purposely chose a place where many people should not intrude. Don't trouble yourself, and be discreet."

Rice broth was served up for their breakfast, but no regular meal had been prepared.

The sun was now high in the heavens. Genji got up and opened the window. The gardens had been uncared for, and had run wild. The forest surrounding the mansion was dense and old, and the shrubberies were ravaged and torn by the autumn gales, and the bosom of the lake was hidden by rank weeds. The main part of the house had been for a long time uninhabited, except the servants' quarter, where there were only a few people living.

"How fearful the place looks; but let no demon molest us," thought Genji, and endeavored to direct the girl's attention by fond and caressing conversation. And now he began, little by little, to throw off the mask, and told her who he was, and then began humming:—

"The flower that bloomed in evening's dew,Was the bright guide that led to you."

She looked at him askance, replying:—

"The dew that on the Yûgao lay,Was a false guide and led astray."

Thus a faint allusion was made to the circumstances which were the cause of their acquaintance, and it became known that the verse and the fan had been sent by her attendant mistaking Genji for her mistress's former lover.

In the course of a few hours the girl became more at her ease, and later on in the afternoon Koremitz came and presented some fruits. The latter, however, stayed with them only a short time.

The mansion gradually became very quiet, and the evening rapidly approached. The inner room was somewhat dark and gloomy. Yûgao was nervous; she was too nervous to remain there alone, and Genji therefore drew back the curtains to let the twilight in, staying there with her. Here the lovers remained, enjoying each other's sight and company, yet the more the evening advanced, the more timid and restless she became, so he quickly closed the casement, and she drew by degrees closer and closer to his side. At these moments he also became distracted and thoughtful. How the Emperor would be asking after him, and know not where he might be! What would the lady, the jealous lady, in the neighboring mansion think or say if she discovered their secret? How painful it would be if her jealous rage should flash forth on him! Such were the reflections which made him melancholy; and as his eyes fell upon the girl affectionately sitting beside him, ignorant of all these matters, he could not but feel a kind of pity for her.

Night was now advancing, and they unconsciously dropped off to sleep, when suddenly over the pillow of Genji hovered the figure of a lady of threatening aspect. It said fiercely, "You faithless one, wandering astray with such a strange girl."

And then the apparition tried to pull away the sleeping girl near him. Genji awoke much agitated. The lamp had burnt itself out. He drew his sword, and placed it beside him, and called aloud for Ukon, and she came to him also quite alarmed.

"Do call up the servants and procure a light," said Genji.

"How can I go, 'tis too dark," she replied, shaking with fear.

"How childish!" he exclaimed, with a false laugh, and clapped his hands to call a servant. The sound echoed drearily through the empty rooms, but no servant came. At this moment he found the girl beside him was also strangely affected. Her brow was covered with great drops of cold perspiration, and she appeared rapidly sinking into a state of unconsciousness.

"Ah! she is often troubled with the nightmare," said Ukon, "and perhaps this disturbs her now; but let us try and rouse her."

"Yes, very likely," said Genji; "she was very much fatigued, and since noon her eyes have often been riveted upwards, like one suffering from some inward malady. I will go myself and call the servants"—he continued, "clapping one's hands is useless, besides it echoes fearfully. Do come here, Ukon, for a little while, and look after your mistress." So pulling Ukon near Yûgao, he advanced to the entrance of the saloon. He saw all was dark in the adjoining chambers. The wind was high, and blew gustily round the mansion. The few servants, consisting of a son of the steward, footman, and page, were all buried in profound slumber. Genji called to them loudly, and they awoke with a start. "Come," said he, "bring a light. Valet, twang your bow-string, and drive away the fiend. How can you sleep so soundly in such a place? But has Koremitz come?"

"Sir, he came in the evening, but you had given no command, and so he went away, saying he would return in the morning," answered one.

The one who gave this reply was an old knight, and he twanged his bow-strings vigorously, "Hiyôjin! hiyôjin!" (Be careful of the fire! be careful of the fire!) as he walked round the rooms.

The mind of Genji instinctively reverted at this moment to the comfort of the palace. "At this hour of midnight," he thought, "the careful knights are patrolling round its walls. How different it is here!"

He returned to the room he had left; it was still dark. He found Yûgao lying half dead and unconscious as before, and Ukon rendered helpless by fright.

"What is the matter? What does it mean? What foolish fear is this?" exclaimed Genji, greatly alarmed. "Perhaps in lonely places like this the fox, for instance, might try to exercise his sorcery to alarm us, but I am here, there is no cause for fear," and he pulled Ukon's sleeve as he spoke, to arouse her.

"I was so alarmed," she replied; "but my lady must be more so; pray attend to her."

"Well," said Genji, and bending over his beloved, shook her gently, but she neither spoke nor moved. She had apparently fainted, and he became seriously alarmed.

At this juncture the lights were brought. Genji threw a mantle over his mistress, and then called to the man to bring the light to him. The servant remained standing at a distance (according to etiquette), and would not approach.

"Come near," exclaimed Genji, testily. "Do act according to circumstances," and taking the lamp from him threw its light full on the face of the lady, and gazed upon it anxiously, when at this very moment he beheld the apparition of the same woman he had seen before in his terrible dream, float before his eyes and vanish. "Ah!" he cried, "this is like the phantoms in old tales. What is the matter with the girl?" His own fears were all forgotten in his anxiety on her account. He leaned over and called upon her, but in vain. She answered not, and her glance was fixed. What was to be done? There was no one whom he could consult. The exorcisms of a priest, he thought, might do some good, but there was no priest. He tried to compose himself with all the resolution he could summon, but his anguish was too strong for his nerves. He threw himself beside her, and embracing her passionately, cried, "Come back! come back to me, my darling! Do not let us suffer such dreadful events." But she was gone; her soul had passed gently away.

The story of the mysterious power of the demon, who had threatened a certain courtier possessed of considerable strength of mind, suddenly occurred to Genji, who thought self-possession was the only remedy in present circumstances, and recovering his composure a little, said to Ukon, "She cannot be dead! She shall not die yet!" He then called the servant, and told him. "Here is one who has been strangely frightened by a vision. Go to Koremitz and tell him to come at once; and if his brother, the priest, is there, ask him to come also. Tell them cautiously; don't alarm their mother."

The midnight passed, and the wind blew louder, rushing amongst the branches of the old pines, and making them moan more and more sadly. The cries of strange weird birds were heard, probably the shrieks of the ill-omened screech-owl, and the place seemed more and more remote from all human sympathy. Genji could only helplessly repeat, "How could I have chosen such a retreat." While Ukon, quite dismayed, cried pitifully at his side. To him it seemed even that this girl might become ill, might die! The light of the lamp flickered and burnt dim. Each side of the walls seemed to his alarmed sight to present numberless openings one after another (where the demon might rush in), and the sound of mysterious footsteps seemed approaching along the deserted passages behind them. "Ah! were Koremitz but here," was the only thought of Genji; but it would seem that Koremitz was from home, and the time Genji had to wait for him seemed an age. At last the crowing cocks announced the coming day, and gave him new courage.

He said to himself, "I must now admit this to be a punishment for all my inconsiderateness. However secretly we strive to conceal our faults, eventually they are discovered. First of all, what might not my father think! and then the general public? And what a subject for scandal the story of my escapades will become."

Koremitz now arrived, and all at once the courage with which Genji had fought against calamity gave way, and he burst into tears, and then slowly spoke. "Here a sad and singular event has happened; I cannot explain to you why. For such sudden afflictions prayers, I believe, are the only resource. For this reason I wished your brother to accompany you here."

"He returned to his monastery only yesterday," replied Koremitz. "But tell me what has happened; any unusual event to the girl?"

"She is dead," returned Genji in a broken voice; "dead without any apparent cause."

Koremitz, like the Prince, was but young. If he had had greater experience he would have been more serviceable to Genji; indeed, they both were equally perplexed to decide what were the best steps to be taken under the trying circumstances of the case.

At last Koremitz said, "If the steward should learn this strange misfortune it might be awkward; as to the man himself he might be relied on, but his family, who probably would not be so discreet, might hear of the matter. It would, therefore, be better to quit this place at once."

"But where can we find a spot where there are fewer observers than here?" replied Genji.

"That is true. Suppose the old lodgings of the deceased. No, there are too many people there. I think a mountain convent would be better, because there they are accustomed to receive the dead within their walls, so that matters can be more easily concealed."

And after a little reflection, he continued, "There is a nun whom I know living in a mountain convent in Higashi-Yama. Let us take the corpse there. She was my father's nurse; she is living there in strict seclusion. That is the best plan I can think of."

This proposal was decided on, and the carriage was summoned.

Presuming that Genji would not like to carry the dead body in his arms, Koremitz covered it with a mantle, and lifted it into the carriage. Over the features of the dead maiden a charming calmness was still spread, unlike what usually happens, there being nothing repulsive. Her wavy hair fell outside the mantle, and her small mouth, still parted, wore a faint smile. The sight distressed both the eyes and heart of Genji. He fain would have followed the body; but this Koremitz would not permit.

"Do take my horse and ride back to Nijiô at once," he said, and ordered the horse for him. Then taking Ukon away in the same carriage with the dead, he, girding up his dress, followed it on foot. It was by no means a pleasant task for Koremitz, but he put up with it cheerfully.

Genji, sunk in apathy, now rode back to Nijiô; he was greatly fatigued, and looked pale. The people of the mansion noticed his sad and haggard appearance.

Genji said nothing, but hurried straight away to his own private apartment.

"Why did I not go with her?" he still vainly exclaimed. "What would she think of me were she to return to life?" And these thoughts affected him so deeply that he became ill, his head ached, his pulse beat high, and his body burned with fever. The sun rose high, but he did not leave his couch. His domestics were all perplexed. Rice gruel was served up to him, but he would not touch it. The news of his indisposition soon found its way out of the mansion, and in no time a messenger arrived from the Imperial Palace to make inquiries. His brother-in-law also came, but Genji only allowed Tô-no-Chiûjiô to enter his room, saying to him, "My aged nurse has been ill since last May, and has been tonsured, and received consecration; it was, perhaps, from this sacrifice that at one time she became better, but lately she has had a relapse, and is again very bad. I was advised to visit her, moreover, she was always most kind to me, and if she had died without seeing me it would have pained her, so I went to see her. At this time a servant of her house, who had been ill, died suddenly. Being rendered 'unclean' by this event, I am passing the time privately. Besides, since the morning, I have become ill, evidently the effects of cold. By the bye, you must excuse me receiving you in this way."

"Well, sir," replied Tô-no-Chiûjiô, "I will represent these circumstances to his Majesty. Your absence last night has given much inquietude to the Emperor. He caused inquiries to be made for you everywhere, and his humor was not very good." And thereupon Tô-no-Chiûjiô took his leave, thinking as he went, "What sort of 'uncleanness' can this really be. I cannot put perfect faith in what he tells me."

Little did Tô-no-Chiûjiô imagine that the dead one was no other than his own long-lost Tokonatz (Pinks).

In the evening came Koremitz from the mountain, and was secretly introduced, though all general visitors were kept excluded on the pretext of the "uncleanness."

"What has become of her?" cried Genji, passionately, when he saw him. "Is she really gone?"

"Her end has come," replied Koremitz, in a tone of sadness; "and we must not keep the dead too long. To-morrow we will place her in the grave: to-morrow 'is a good day.' I know a faithful old priest. I have consulted with him how to arrange all."

"And what has become of Ukon?" asked Genji. "How does she bear it?"

"That is, indeed, a question. She was really deeply affected, and she foolishly said, 'I will die with my mistress.' She was actually going to throw herself headlong from the cliff; but I warned, I advised, I consoled her, and she became more pacified."

"The state of her feelings may be easily conceived. I am myself not less deeply wounded than she. I do not even know what might become of myself."

"Why do you grieve so uselessly? Every uncertainty is the result of a certainty. There is nothing in this world really to be lamented. If you do not wish the public to know anything of this matter, I, Koremitz, will manage it."

"I, also, am aware that everything is fated. Still, I am deeply sorry to have brought this misfortune on this poor girl by my own inconsiderate rashness. The only thing I have now to ask you, is to keep these events in the dark. Do not mention them to any one— nay, not even to your mother."

"Even from the priests to whom it must necessarily be known, I will conceal the reality," replied Koremitz.

"Do manage all this most skilfully!"

"Why, of course I shall manage it as secretly as possible," cried Koremitz; and he was about to take his departure, but Genji stopped him.

"I must see her once more," said Genji, sorrowfully. "I will go with you to behold her, before she is lost to my sight forever." And he insisted on accompanying him.

Koremitz, however, did not at all approve of this project; but his resistance gave way to the earnest desire of Genji, and he said, "If you think so much about it, I cannot help it."

"Let us hasten, then, and return before the night be far advanced."

"You shall have my horse to ride."

Genji rose, and dressed himself in the ordinary plain style he usually adopted for his private expeditions, and started away with one confidential servant, besides Koremitz.

They crossed the river Kamo, the torches carried before them burning dimly. They passed the gloomy cemetery of Toribeno, and at last reached the convent.

It was a rude wooden building, and adjoining was a small Buddha Hall, through whose walls votive tapers mysteriously twinkled. Within, nothing but the faint sound of a female's voice repeating prayers was to be heard. Outside, and around, the evening services in the surrounding temples were all finished, and all Nature was in silent repose. In the direction of Kiyomidz alone some scattered lights studding the dark scene betrayed human habitations.

They entered. Genji's heart was beating fast with emotion. He saw Ukon reclining beside a screen, with her back to the lamp. He did not speak to her, but proceeded straight to the body, and gently drew aside the mantle which covered its face. It still wore a look of tranquil calmness; no change had yet attacked the features. He took the cold hand in his own, crying out as he did so:—

"Do let me hear thy voice once more! Why have you left me thus bereaved?" But the silence of death was unbroken!

He then, half sobbing, began to talk with Ukon, and invited her to come to his mansion, and help to console him. But Koremitz now admonished him to consider that time was passing quickly.

On this Genji threw a long sad farewell glance at the face of the dead, and rose to depart. He was so feeble and powerless that he could not mount his horse without the help of Koremitz. The countenance of the dead girl floated ever before his sight, with the look she wore when living, and it seemed as if he were being led on by some mysterious influence.

The banks of the river Kamo were reached, when Genji found himself too weak to support himself on horseback, and so dismounted.

"I am afraid," he exclaimed, "I shall not be able to reach home."

Koremitz was a little alarmed. "If I had only been firm," he thought, "and had prevented this journey, I should not have exposed him to such a trial." He descended to the river, and bathing his hands,[58] offered up a prayer to Kwannon of Kiyomidz, and again assisted Genji to mount, who struggled to recover his energy, and managed somehow to return to Nijiô, praying in silence as he rode along.

The people of the mansion entertained grave apprehensions about him; and not unnaturally, seeing he had been unusually restless for some days, and had become suddenly ill since the day before, and they could never understand what urgency had called him out on that evening.

Genji now lay down on his couch, fatigued and exhausted, and continued in the same state for some days, when he became quite weak.

The Emperor was greatly concerned, as was also Sadaijin. Numerous prayers were offered, and exorcisms performed everywhere in his behalf, all with the most careful zeal. The public was afraid he was too beautiful to live long.

The only solace he had at this time was Ukon; he had sent for her, and made her stay in his mansion.

And whenever he felt better he had her near him, and conversed with her about her dead mistress.

In the meantime, it might have been the result of his own energetic efforts to realize the ardent hopes of the Emperor and his father-in-law, that his condition became better, after a heavy trial of some three weeks; and towards the end of September he became convalescent. He now felt as though he had been restored to the world to which he had formerly belonged. He was, however, still thin and weak, and, for consolation, still resorted to talk with Ukon.

"How strange," he said to her, as they were conversing together one fine autumn evening. "Why did she not reveal to me all her past life? If she had but known how deeply I loved her, she might have been a little more frank with me."

"Ah! no," replied Ukon; "she would not intentionally have concealed anything from you; but it was, I imagine, more because she had no choice. You at first conducted yourself in such a mysterious manner; and she, on her part, regarded her acquaintance with you as something like a dream. That was the cause of her reticence."

"What a useless reticence it was," exclaimed Genji. "I was not so frank as, perhaps, I ought to have been; but you may be sure that made no difference in my affection towards her. Only, you must remember, there is my father, the Emperor, besides many others, whose vigilant admonitions I am bound to respect. That was the reason why I had to be careful. Nevertheless, my love to your mistress was singularly deep; too deep, perhaps, to last long. Do tell me now all you know about her; I do not see any reason why you should conceal it. I have carefully ordered the weekly requiem for the dead; but tell me in whose behalf it is, and what was her origin?"

"I have no intention of concealing anything from you. Why should I? I only thought it would be blamable if one should reveal after death what another had thought best to reserve," replied Ukon. "Her parents died when she was a mere girl. Her father was called Sammi-Chiûjiô, and loved her very dearly. He was always aspiring to better his position, and wore out his life in the struggle. After his death, she was left helpless and poor. She was however, by chance, introduced to Tô-no-Chiûjiô, when he was still Shiôshiô, and not Chiûjiô. During three years they kept on very good terms, and he was very kind to her. But some wind or other attacks every fair flower; and, in the autumn of last year, she received a fearful menace from the house of Udaijin, to whose daughter, as you know, Tô-no-Chiûjiô is married. Poor girl, she was terrified at this. She knew not what to do, and hid herself, with her nurse, in an obscure part of the capital. It was not a very agreeable place, and she was about removing to a certain mountain hamlet, but, as its 'celestial direction' was closed this year, she was still hesitating, and while matters were in this state, you appeared on the scene. To do her justice, she had no thought of wandering from one to another; but circumstances often make things appear as if we did so. She was, by nature, extremely reserved, so that she did not like to speak out her feelings to others, but rather suffered in silence by herself. This, perhaps, you also have noticed."

"Then it was so, after all. She was the Tokonatz of Tô-no-Chiûjiô," thought Genji; and now it also transpired that all that Koremitz had stated about Tô-no-Chiûjiô's visiting her at the Yûgao house was a pure invention, suggested by a slight acquaintance with the girl's previous history.

"The Chiûjiô told me once," said Genji, "that she had a little one. Was there any such?"

"Yes, she had one in the spring of the year before last—a girl, a nice child," replied Ukon.

"Where is she now?" asked Genji, "perhaps you will bring her to me some day. I should like to have her with me as a memento of her mother. I should not mind mentioning it to her father, but if I did so, I must reveal the whole sad story of her mother's fate, and this would not be advisable at present; however, I do not see any harm if I were to bring her up as my daughter. You might manage it somehow without my name being mentioned to any one concerned."

"That would be a great happiness for the child," exclaimed Ukon, delighted, "I do not much appreciate her being brought up where she is."

"Well, I will do so, only let us wait for some better chance. For the present be discreet."

"Yes, of course. I cannot yet take any steps towards that object; we must not unfurl our sails before the storm is completely over."

The foliage of the ground, touched with autumnal tints, was beginning to fade, and the sounds of insects (*mushi*) were growing faint, and both Genji and Ukon were absorbed by the sad charm of the scene. As they meditated, they heard doves cooing among the bamboo woods.

To Genji it brought back the cries of that strange bird, which cry he had heard on that fearful night in Rokjiô, and the subject recurred to his mind once more, and he said to Ukon, "How old was she?"

"Nineteen."

"And how came you to know her?"

"I was the daughter of her first nurse, and a great favorite of her father's, who brought me up with her, and from that time I never left her. When I come to think of those days I wonder how I can exist without her. The poet says truly, 'The deeper the love, the more bitter the parting.' Ah! how gentle and retiring she was. How much I loved her!"

"That retiring and gentle temperament," said Genji, "gives far greater beauty to women than all beside, for to have no natural pliability makes women utterly worthless."

The sky by this time became covered, and the wind blew chilly. Genji gazed intently on it and hummed:—

"When we regard the clouds above,Our souls are filled with fond desire,To me the smoke of my dead love,Seems rising from the funeral pyre."

The distant sound of the bleacher's hammer reached their ears, and reminded him of the sound he had heard in the Yûgao's house. He bade "Good-night" to Ukon, and retired to rest, humming as he went:—

"In the long nights of August and September."

On the forty-ninth day (after the death of the Yûgao) he went to the Hokke Hall in the Hiye mountain, and there had a service for the dead performed, with full ceremony and rich offerings. The monk-brother of Koremitz took every pains in its performance.

The composition of requiem prayers was made by Genji himself, and revised by a professor of literature, one of his intimate friends. He expressed in it the melancholy sentiment about the death of one whom he had dearly loved, and whom he had yielded to Buddha. But who she was was not stated. Among the offerings there was a dress. He took it up in his hands and sorrowfully murmured,

"With tears to-day, the dress she woreI fold together, when shall IBright Elysium's far-off shoreThis robe of hers again untie?"

And the thought that the soul of the deceased might be still wandering and unsettled to that very day, but that now the time had come when her final destiny would be decided,[59] made him pray for her more fervently.

So closed the sad event of Yûgao.

Now Genji was always thinking that he should wish to see his beloved in a dream.

The evening after his visit to the Hokke Hall, he beheld her in his slumbers, as he wished, but at the same moment the terrible face of the woman that he had seen on that fearful evening in Rokjiô again appeared before him; hence he concluded that the same mysterious being who tenanted that dreary mansion had taken advantage of his fears and had destroyed his beloved Yûgao.

A few words more about the house in which she had lived. After her flight no communication had been sent to them even by Ukon, and they had no idea of where she had gone to. The mistress of the house was a daughter of the nurse of Yûgao. She with her two sisters lived there. Ukon was a stranger to them, and they imagined that her being so was the reason of her sending no intelligence to them. True they had entertained some suspicions about the gay Prince, and pressed Koremitz to confide the truth to them, but the latter, as he had done before, kept himself skilfully aloof.

They then thought she might have been seduced and carried off by some gallant son of a local Governor, who feared his intrigue might be discovered by Tô-no-Chiûjiô.

During these days Kokimi, of Ki-no-Kami's house, still used to come occasionally to Genji. But for some time past the latter had not sent any letter to Cicada. When she heard of his illness she not unnaturally felt for him, and also she had experienced a sort of disappointment in not seeing his writing for some time, especially as the time of her departure for the country was approaching. She therefore sent him a letter of inquiry with the following:—

"If long time passes slow away,Without a word from absent friend,Our fears no longer brook delay,But must some kindly greeting send."

To this letter Genji returned a kind answer and also the following:—

"This world to me did once appearLike Cicada's shell, when cast away,Till words addressed by one so dear,Have taught my hopes a brighter day."

This was written with a trembling hand, but still bearing nice traits, and when it reached Cicada, and she saw that he had not yet forgotten past events, and the scarf he had carried away, she was partly amused and partly pleased.

It was about this time that the daughter of Iyo-no-Kami was engaged to a certain Kurando Shiôshiô, and he was her frequent visitor. Genji heard of this, and without any intention of rivalry, sent her the following by Kokimi:—

"Like the green reed that grows on highBy river's brink, our love has been,And still my wandering thoughts will flyBack to that quickly passing scene."

She was a little flattered by it, and gave Kokimi a reply, as follows:—

"The slender reed that feels the windThat faintly stirs its humble leaf,Feels that too late it breathes its mind,And only wakes, a useless grief."

Now the departure of Iyo-no-Kami was fixed for the beginning of October.

Genji sent several parting presents to his wife, and in addition to these some others, consisting of beautiful combs, fans, *nusa*,[60] and the scarf he had carried away, along with the following, privately through Kokimi:—

"I kept this pretty souvenirIn hopes of meeting you again,I send it back with many a tear,Since now, alas! such hope is vain."

There were many other minute details, which I shall pass over as uninteresting to the reader.

Genji's official messenger returned, but her reply about the scarf was sent through Kokimi:—

"When I behold the summer wingsCicada like, I cast aside;Back to my heart fond memory springs,And on my eyes, a rising tide."

The day of the departure happened to be the commencement of the winter season. An October shower fell lightly, and the sky looked gloomy.

Genji stood gazing upon it and hummed:—

"Sad and weary Autumn hours,Summer joys now past away,Both departing, dark the hours,Whither speeding, who can say?"

All these intrigues were safely kept in strict privacy, and to have boldly written all particulars concerning them is to me a matter of pain. So at first I intended to omit them, but had I done so my history would have become like a fiction, and the censure I should expect would be that I had done so intentionally, because my hero was the son of an Emperor; but, on the other hand, if I am accused of too much loquacity, I cannot help it.

FOOTNOTES:

[52]Name of an ecclesiastical office.

[53]Sasinuki is a sort of loose trousers, and properly worn by men only, hence some commentators conclude, the attendant here mentioned to mean a boy, others contend, this garment was worn by females also when they rode.

[54]A mythological repulsive deity who took part in the building of a bridge at the command of a powerful magician.

[55]A popular superstition in China and Japan believes foxes to have mysterious powers over men.

[56]Upasaka, a sect of the followers of Buddhism who are laymen though they observe the rules of clerical life.

[57]Meitreya, a Buddhisatva destined to reappear as a Buddha after the lapse of an incalculable series of years.

[58]It is the Oriental custom that when one offers up a prayer, he first washes his hands, to free them from all impurity.

[59]According to the Buddhist's doctrine of the Hosso sect, all the souls of the dead pass, during seven weeks after death, into an intermediate state, and then their fate is decided. According to the Tendai sect, the best and the worst go immediately where they deserve, but those of a medium nature go through this process.

[60]An offering made of paper, to the God of roads, which travellers were accustomed to make, before setting out on a journey.

CHAPTER V

YOUNG VIOLET

I t was the time when Genji became subject to periodical attacks of ague, that many exorcisms and spells were performed to effect a cure, but all in vain. At length he was told by a friend that in a certain temple on the northern mountain (Mount Kurama) there dwelt a famous ascetic, and that when the epidemic had prevailed during the previous summer, many people had recovered through his exorcisms. "If," added the friend, "the disease is neglected it becomes serious; try therefore, this method of procuring relief at once, and before it is too late."

Genji, therefore, sent for the hermit, but he declined to come, saying that he was too old and decrepit to leave his retreat. "What shall I do?" exclaimed Genji, "shall I visit him privately?" Eventually, taking four or five attendants, he started off early one morning for the place, which was at no great distance on the mountain.

It was the last day of March, and though the height of the season for flowers in the capital was over, yet, on the mountain, the cherry-trees were still in blossom. They advanced on their way further and further. The haze clung to the surface like a soft sash does round the waist, and to Genji, who had scarcely ever been out of the capital, the scenery was indescribably novel. The ascetic lived in a deep cave in the rocks, near the lofty summit. Genji did not, however, declare who he was, and the style of his retinue was of a very private character. Yet his nobility of manners was easily recognizable.

"Welcome your visit!" cried the hermit, saluting him. "Perhaps you are the one who sent for me the other day? I have long since quitted the affairs of this world, and have almost forgotten the secret of my exorcisms. I wonder why you have come here for me." So saying, he pleasingly embraced him. He was evidently a man of great holiness. He wrote out a talismanic prescription, which he gave to Genji to drink in water, while he himself proceeded to perform some mysterious rite. During the performance of this ceremony the sun rose high in the heavens. Genji, meantime, walked out of the cave and looked around him with his attendants. The spot where they stood was very lofty, and numerous monasteries were visible, scattered here and there in the distance beneath. There was immediately beyond the winding path in which they were walking a picturesque and pretty building enclosed by hedges. Its well arranged balconies and the gardens around it apparently betokened the good taste of its inhabitants. "Whose house may that be?" inquired Genji of his attendants. They told him it was a house in which a certain priest had been living for the last two years. "Ah! I know him," said Genji. "Strange, indeed, would it be if he were to discover that I am here in this privacy." They noticed a nun and a few more females with her walking in the garden, who were carrying fresh water for their offerings, and were gathering flowers. "Ah! there are ladies walking there," cried the attendants in tones of surprise. "Surely, the Reverend Father would not indulge in flirtations! Who can they be?" And some of them even descended a little distance, and peered over the enclosure, where a pretty little girl was also seen amongst them.

Genji now engaged in prayer until the sun sank in the heavens. His attendants, who were anxious about his disease, told him that it would be good for him to have a change from time to time. Hereupon, he advanced to the back of the temple, and his gaze fell on the far-off Capital in the distance, which was enveloped in haze as the dusk was setting in, over the tops of the trees around. "What a lovely landscape!" exclaimed Genji. "The people to whom such scenery is familiar, are perhaps happy and contented." "Nay," said the attendants, "but were you to see the beautiful mountain ranges and the sea-coast in our various provinces, the pictures would indeed be found lovely." Then some of them described to him Fuji Yama, while others told him of other mountains, diverting his attention by their animated description of the beautiful bays and coasts of the Western Provinces; thus as they depicted them to him, they cheered and gladdened his mind. One of them went on to say: "Among such sights and at no great distance, there is the sea-coast of Akashi, in the Province of Harima, which is, I think, especially beautiful. I cannot, indeed, point out in detail its most remarkable features, but, in general, the blue expanse of the sea is singularly charming. Here, too, the home of the former Governor of the Province constitutes an object of great attraction. He has assumed the tonsure, and resides there with his beautiful daughter. He is the descendant of a high personage, and was not without hope of elevation at Court, but, being of an eccentric character, he was strongly averse to society. He had formerly been a Chiûjiô of the Imperial Guard, but having resigned that office, had become Governor of Harima. He was not, however, popular in that office. In this state of affairs he reflected within himself, no doubt, that his presence in the Capital could not but be disagreeable. When, therefore, his term of office expired, he determined still to remain in the province. He did not, however, go to the mountainous regions of the interior, but chose the sea-coast. There are in this district several places which are well situated for quiet retirement, and it would have seemed inconsistent in him had he preferred a part of the sea-coast so near the gay world; nevertheless, a retreat in the too remote interior would have been too solitary, and might have met with objections on the part of his wife and child. For this reason, it appears, that he finally selected the place which I have already alluded to for the sake of his family. When I went down there last time, I became acquainted with the history and circumstances of the family, and I found that though he may not have been well received in the Capital, yet, that here, having been formerly governor, he enjoys considerable popularity and respect. His residence, moreover, is well appointed and of sufficient magnitude, and he performs with punctuality and devoutness his religious duties—nay, almost with more earnestness than many regular priests." Here Genji interrupted. "What is his daughter like?" "Without doubt," answered his companion, "the beauty of her person is unrivalled, and she is endowed with corresponding mental ability. Successive governors often offer their addresses to her with great sincerity, but no one has ever yet been accepted. The dominant idea of her father seems to be this: 'What, have I sunk to such a position! Well, I trust, at least, that my only daughter may be successful and prosperous in her life!' He often told her, I heard, that if she survived him, and if his fond hopes for her should not be realized, it would be better for her to cast herself into the sea."

Genji was much interested in this conversation, and the rest of the company laughingly said, "Ah! she is a woman who is likely to become the Queen of the Blue Main. In very truth her father must be an extraordinary being!"

The attendant who had given this account of the ex-governor and his daughter, was the son of the present Governor of the Province. He was until lately a Kurand, and this year had received the title of Jugoi. His name was Yoshikiyo, and he, too, was a man of gay habits, which gave occasion to one of his companions to observe: "Ah! perhaps you also have been trying to disappoint the hopes of the aged father." Another said, "Well, our friend has given us a long account, but we must take it with some reserve. She must be, after all, a country maiden, and all that I can give credit to is this much: that her mother may be a woman of some sense, who takes great care of the girl. I am only afraid that if any future governor should be seized with an ardent desire to possess her, she would not long remain unattached."

"What possible object could it serve if she were carried to the bottom of the sea? The natives of the deep would derive no pleasure from her charms," remarked Genji, while he himself secretly desired to behold her.

"Ay," thought his companions, "with his susceptible temperament, what wonder if this story touches him."

The day was far advanced, and the Prince prepared to leave the mountain. The Hermit, however, told him that it would be better to spend the evening in the Temple, and to be further prayed for. His attendants also supported this suggestion. So Genji made up his mind to stay there, saying, "Then I shall not return home till to-morrow."

The days at this season were of long duration, and he felt it rather tiresome to pass a whole evening in sedate society, so, under the cover of the shades of the evening, he went out of the Temple, and proceeded to the pretty building enclosed by hedges. All the attendants had been despatched home except Koremitz, who accompanied him. They peeped at this building through the hedges. In the western antechamber of the house was placed an image of Buddha, and here an evening service was performed. A nun, raising a curtain before Buddha, offered a garland of flowers on the altar, and placing a Kiô (or Sutra, i.e., Buddhist Bible) on her "arm-stool," proceeded to read it. She seemed to be rather more than forty years old. Her face was rather round, and her appearance was noble. Her hair was thrown back from her forehead and was cut short behind, which suited her very well. She was, however, pale and weak, her voice, also, being tremulous. Two maiden attendants went in and out of the room waiting upon her, and a little girl ran into the room with them. She was about ten years old or more, and wore a white silk dress, which fitted her well and which was lined with yellow. Her hair was waved like a fan, and her eyes were red from crying. "What is the matter? Have you quarrelled with the boy?" exclaimed the nun, looking at her. There was some resemblance between the features of the child and the nun, so Genji thought that she possibly might be her daughter.

"Inuki has lost my sparrow, which I kept so carefully in the cage," replied the child.

"That stupid boy," said one of the attendants. "Has he again been the cause of this? Where can the bird be gone? And all this, too, after we had tamed it with so much care." She then left the room, possibly to look for the lost bird. The people who addressed her called her Shiônagon, and she appeared to have been the little girl's nurse.

"To you," said the nun to the girl, "the sparrow may be dearer than I may be, who am so ill; but have I not told you often that the caging of birds is a sin? Be a good girl; come nearer!"

The girl advanced and stood silent before her, her face being bathed in tears. The contour of the child-like forehead and of the small and graceful head was very pleasing. Genji, as he surveyed the scene from without, thought within himself, "If she is thus fair in her girlhood, what will she be when she is grown up?" One reason why Genji was so much attracted by her was, that she greatly resembled a certain lady in the Palace, to whom he, for a long time, had been fondly attached. The nun stroked the beautiful hair of the child and murmured to herself, "How splendid it looks! Would that she would always strive to keep it thus. Her extreme youth makes me anxious, however. Her mother departed this life when she only a very young girl, but she was quite sensible at the age of this one. Supposing that I were to leave her behind, I wonder what would happen to her!" As she thus murmured, her countenance became saddened by her forebodings.

The sight moved Genji's sympathy as he gazed. It seemed that the tender heart of the child was also touched, for she silently watched the expression of the nun's features, and then with downcast eyes bent her face towards the ground, the lustrous hair falling over her back in waves.

The nun hummed, in a tone sufficiently audible to Genji,

"The dews that wet the tender grass,At the sun's birth, too quickly pass,Nor e'er can hope to see it riseIn full perfection to the skies."

Shiônagon, who now joined them, and heard the above distich, consoled the nun with the following:—

"The dews will not so quickly pass,Nor shall depart before they seeThe full perfection of the grass,They loved so well in infancy."

At this juncture a priest entered and said, "Do you know that this very day Prince Genji visited the hermit in order to be exorcised by him. I must forthwith go and see him."

Genji observing this movement quickly returned to the monastery, thinking as he went what a lovely girl he had seen. "I can guess from this," thought he, "why those gay fellows (referring to his attendants) so often make their expeditions in search of good fortune. What a charming little girl have I seen to-day! Who can she be? Would that I could see her morning and evening in the palace, where I can no longer see the fair loved one whom she resembles!"

He now returned to the monastery, and retired to his quarters. Soon after a disciple of the priest came and delivered a message from him through Koremitz, saying, "My master has just heard of the Prince's visit to the mountain, and would have waited on him at once, but thought it better to postpone calling. Nevertheless he would be much pleased to offer a humble welcome, and feels disappointed that he has not yet had an opportunity of doing so."

Genji said in reply, "I have been afflicted with constant attacks of ague for the last few weeks, and, therefore, by the advice of my friends, I came to this mountain to be exorcised. If, however, the spells of the holy man are of no avail to me, his reputation might suffer in consequence. For that reason I wish to keep my visit as private as possible, nevertheless I will come now to your master." Thereupon the priest himself soon made his appearance, and, after briefly relating the circumstances which had occasioned his retirement to this locality, he offered to escort Genji to his house, saying, "My dwelling is but a rustic cottage, but still I should like you to see, at least, the pretty mountain streamlet which waters my garden."

Genji accepted the offer, thinking as he went, "I wonder what the priest has said at home about myself to those to whom I have not yet been introduced. But it will be pleasant to see them once more."

The night was moonless. The fountain was lit up by torches, and many lamps also were lighted in the garden. Genji was taken to an airy room in the southern front of the building, where incense which was burning threw its sweet odors around. The priest related to him many interesting anecdotes, and also spoke eloquently of man's future destiny. Genji as he heard him, felt some qualms of conscience, for he remembered that his own conduct was far from being irreproachable. The thought troubled him that he would never be free from the sting of these recollections through his life, and that there was a world to come, too! "Oh, could I but live in a retreat like this priest!" As he thus thought of a retreat, he was involuntarily taken by a fancy, that how happy would he be if accompanied to such a retreat by such a girl as he had seen in the evening, and with this fancy her lovely face rose up before him.

Suddenly he said to the priest, "I had once a dream which made me anxious to know who was living in this house, and here to-day that dream has again come back to my memory!" The priest laughed, and said, "A strange dream! even were you to obtain your wish it might not gratify you. The late Lord Azechi Dainagon died long ago, and perhaps you know nothing about him. Well! his widow is my sister, and since her husband's death her health has not been satisfactory, so lately she has been living here in retirement."

"Ah, yes," said Genji, venturing upon a guess, "and I heard that she bore a daughter to Dainagon."

"Yes, she had a daughter, but she died about ten years ago. After her father's death the sole care of her fell upon her widowed mother alone. I know not how it came to pass, but she became secretly intimate with Prince Hiôbkiô. But the Prince's wife was very jealous and severe, so she had much to suffer and put up with. I saw personally the truth that 'care kills more than labor.'"

"Ah, then," thought Genji, "the little one is her daughter, and no wonder that she resembles the one in the palace (because Prince Hiôbkiô was the brother of the Princess Wistaria). How would it be if I had free control over her, and had her brought up and educated according to my own notions?" So thinking, he proceeded to say how sad it was that she died! "Did she leave any offspring?"

"She gave birth to a child at her death, which was also a girl, and about this girl the grandmother is always feeling very anxious."

"Then," said Genji, "let it not appear strange to you if I say this, but I should be very happy to become the guardian of this girl. Will you speak to her grandmother about it? It is true that there is one to whom my lot is linked, but I care but little for her, and indeed usually lead a solitary life."

"Your offer is very kind," replied the priest, "but she is extremely young. However every woman grows up under the protecting care of some one, and so I cannot say much about her, only it shall be mentioned to my sister."

The priest said this with a grave and even a stern expression on his countenance, which caused Genji to drop the subject.

He then asked the Prince to excuse him, for it was the hour for vespers, and as he quitted the room to attend the service, said he would return as soon as it was finished.

Genji was alone. A slight shower fell over the surrounding country, and the mountain breezes blew cool. The waters of the torrent were swollen, and the roar of them might be heard from afar. Broken and indistinct, one might hear the melancholy sound of the sleepy intonation of prayers. Even those people who have no sorrow of their own often feel melancholy from the circumstances in which they are placed. So Genji, whose mind was occupied in thought, could not slumber here. The priest said he was going to vespers, but in reality it was later than the proper time for them. Genji perceived that the inmates had not yet retired to rest in the inner apartments of the house. They were very quiet, yet the sound of the telling of beads, which accidentally struck the lectern, was heard from time to time. The room was not far from his own. He pulled the screen slightly aside, and standing near the door, he struck his fan on his hand, to summon someone.

"What can be the matter," said an attendant, and as she came near to the Prince's room she added, "Perhaps my ear was deceived," and she began to retire.

"Buddha will guide you; fear not the darkness, I am here," said Genji.

"Sir!" replied the servant, timidly.

"Pray do not think me presumptuous," said Genji; "but may I beg you to transmit this poetical effusion to your mistress for me?

Since first that tender grass I viewed,My heart no soft repose e'er feels,But gathering mist my sleeve bedews,And pity to my bosom steals."

"Surely you should know, sir, that there is no one here to whom such things can be presented!"

"Believe me, I have my own reasons for this," said Genji. "Let me beseech you to take it."

So the attendant went back, and presented it to the nun.

"I do not see the real intent of the effusion," thought the nun. "Perhaps he thinks that she is already a woman. But"—she continued, wonderingly—"how could he have known about the young grass?" And she then remained silent for a while. At last, thinking it would be unbecoming to take no notice of it, she gave orally the following reply to the attendant to be given to Genji:—

"You say your sleeve is wet with dew,'Tis but one night alone for you,But there's a mountain moss grows nigh,Whose leaves from dew are never dry."

When Genji heard this, he said: "I am not accustomed to receive an answer such as this through the mouth of a third person. Although I thank the lady for even that much, I should feel more obliged to her if she would grant me an interview, and allow me to explain to her my sincere wishes."

This at length obliged the nun to have an interview with the Prince. He then told her that he called Buddha to witness that, though his conduct may have seemed bold, it was dictated by pure and conscientious motives.

"All the circumstances of your family history are known to me," continued he. "Look upon me, I pray, as a substitute for your once loved daughter. I, too, when a mere infant, was deprived by death of my best friend—my mother—and the years and months which then rolled by were fraught with trouble to me. In that same position your little one is now. Allow us, then, to become friends. We could sympathize with each other. 'Twas to reveal these wishes to you that I came here, and risked the chance of offending you in doing so."

"Believe me, I am well disposed at your offer," said the nun; "but you may have been incorrectly informed. It is true that there is a little girl dependent upon myself, but she is but a child. Her society could not afford you any pleasure; and forgive me, therefore, if I decline your request."

"Yet let there be no reserve in the expression of your ideas," interrupted Genji; but, before they could talk further, the return of the priest put an end to the subject, and Genji retired to his quarters, after thanking the nun for his kind reception.

The night passed away, and dawn appeared. The sky was again hazy, and here and there melodious birds were singing among the mountain shrubs and flowers that blossomed around. The deer, too, which were to be seen here, added to the beauty of the picture. Gazing around at these Genji once more proceeded to the temple. The hermit—though too infirm to walk—again contrived to offer up his prayers on Genji's behalf, and he also read from the Darani.[61] The tremulous accents of the old man—poured forth from his nearly toothless mouth—imparted a greater reverence to his prayers.

Genji's attendants now arrived from the capital, and congratulated him on the improvement in his health. A messenger was despatched from the Imperial Palace for the same purpose. The priest now collected wild and rare fruits, not to be met with in the distant town, and, with all respect, presented them to Genji, saying: "The term of my vow has not yet expired; and I am, therefore, sorry to say that I am unable to descend the mountain with you on your departure." He then offered to him the parting cup of *saké*.

"This mountain, with its waters, fill me with admiration," said Genji, "and I regret that the anxiety of my father the Emperor obliges me to quit the charming scene; but before the season is past, I will revisit it: and—

The city's folk from me shall hearHow mountain cherries blossom fair,And ere the Spring has passed away,I'll bid them view the prospect gay."

To this the priest replied—

"Your noble presence seems to meLike the rare flowers of Udon tree,[62]Nor does the mountain cherry white,Attract my gaze while you're in sight."

Genji smiled slightly, and said: "That is a very great compliment; but the Udon tree does not blossom so easily."

The hermit also raised the cup to his lips, and said:—

"Opening my lonely hermit's door,Enclosed around by mountain pine,A blossom never seen beforeMy eyes behold that seems divine."

And he presented to him his *toko* (a small ecclesiastical wand). On seeing this, the priest also made him the following presents:—A rosary of Kongôji (a kind of precious stone), which the sage Prince Shôtok obtained from Corea, enclosed in the original case in which it had been sent from that country; some medicine of rare virtue in a small emerald jar; and several other objects, with a spray of Wistaria, and a branch of cherry blossoms.

Genji, too, on the other hand, made presents, which he had ordered from the capital, to the hermit and his disciples who had taken part in the religious ceremonies, and also to the poor mountaineers. He also sent the following to the nun, by the priest's page:—

"In yester-eve's uncertain light,A flower I saw so young and bright,But like a morning mist. Now painImpels me yet to see again."

A reply from the nun was speedily brought to him, which ran thus:—

"You say you feel, perhaps 'tis true,A pang to leave these mountain bowers,For sweet the blossoms, sweet the view,To strangers' eyes of mountain flowers."

While this was being presented to him in his carriage, a few more people came, as if accidentally, to wait upon him on his journey. Among them was Tô-no-Chiûjiô, and his brother Ben, who said: "We are always pleased to follow you; it was unkind of you to leave us behind."

Just as the party were on the point of starting, some of them observed that it was a pity to leave so lovely a spot without resting awhile among the flowers. This was immediately agreed to, and they took their seats on a moss-grown rock, a short distance from which a little streamlet descended in a murmuring cascade.

They there began to drink *saké*, and Tô-no-Chiûjiô taking his flute, evoked from it a rich and melodious strain; while Ben, tapping his fan in concert, sang "The Temple of Toyora," while the Prince, as he leaned against a rock, presented a picturesque appearance, though he was pale and thin.

Among the attendants was one who blew on a long flute, called Hichiriki, and another on a Shiô flute. The priest brought a *koto*, and begged Genji to perform upon it, saying: "If we are to have music at all, let us have a harmonious concert." Genji said that he was no master of music; but, nevertheless, he played, with fair ability, a pleasing air. Then they all rose up, and departed.

After they had quitted the mountain, Genji first of all went to the Palace, where he immediately had an interview with the Emperor, who considered his son to be still weak in health; and who asked him several questions with regard to the efficacy of the prayers of the reverend hermit. Genji gave him all particulars of his visit to the mountain.

"Ah!" said the Emperor, "he may some day be entitled to become a dean (Azali). His virtue and holiness have not yet been duly appreciated by the government and the nation."

Sadaijin, the father-in-law of the Prince, here entered, and entreated Genji to accompany him to his mansion, and spend a few days. Genji did not feel very anxious to accept this invitation, but was persuaded to do so. Sadaijin conveyed him in his own carriage, and gave up to him the seat of honor.

They arrived; but, as usual, his bride did not appear, and only presented herself at last at the earnest request of her father. She was one of those model princesses whom one may see in a picture—very formal and very sedate—and it was very difficult to draw her into conversation. She was very uninteresting to Genji. He thought that it would only lead to a very unpleasant state of affairs, as years grew on, if they were to be as cool and reserved to each other as they had been hitherto. Turning to her, he said, with some reproachfulness in his accents, "Surely you should sometimes show me a little of the ordinary affection of people in our position!"

She made no reply; but, glancing coolly upon him, murmured with modest, yet dignified, tone—

"When   you   cease   to   care   for   me,
What can I then do for thee?"

"Your words are few; but they have a sting in them. You say I cease to care for you; but you do me wrong in saying so. May the time come when you will no longer pain me thus," said Genji; and he made every effort to conciliate her. But she was not easily appeased. He was unsuccessful in his effort, and presently they retired to their apartment, where he soon relapsed into sleepy indifference. His thoughts began to wander back into other regions, and hopes of the future growth and charms of the young mountain-violet again occupied his mind. "Oh! how difficult it is to secure a prize," thought he. "How can I do so? Her father, Prince Hiôbkiô, is a man of rank, and affable, but he is not of prepossessing appearance. Why does his daughter resemble so much, in her personal attractions, the lovely one in the chamber of Wistaria. Is it that the mother of her father and of Wistaria is the same person? How charming is the resemblance between them! How can I make her mine?"

Some days afterwards he sent a letter to the mountain home, and also a communication—perhaps with some hint in it—to the priest. In his letter to the nun he said that her indifference made it desirable to refrain from urging his wishes; but, nevertheless, that he should be deeply gratified if she would think more favorably of the idea which was now so deeply rooted in his mind. Inside the letter he enclosed a small folded slip of paper, on which was written:—

"The mountain flower I left behindI strive but vainly to forget,Those lovely traits still rise to mindAnd fill my heart with sad regret."

This ludicrous effusion caused the nun to be partly amused and partly vexed. She wrote an answer as follows:—

"When you came into our neighborhood your visit was very pleasing to us, and your special message does us honor. I am, however, at a loss how to express myself with regard to the little one, as yet she cannot even manage the naniwadz."[63]

Enclosed in the note were the following lines, in which she hinted as to her doubts of the steadfastness of Genji's character:

"Your heart admires the lowly flowerThat dwells within our mountain bower.Not long, alas! that flower may lastTorn by the mountain's angry blast."

The tenor of the priest's answer was much the same, and it caused Genji some vexation.

About this time the Lady Wistaria, in consequence of an attack of illness, had retired from the palace to her private residence, and Genji, while sympathizing with the anxiety of the Emperor about her, longed greatly for an opportunity of seeing her, ill though she was. Hence at this time he went nowhere, but kept himself in his mansion at Nijiô, and became thoughtful and preoccupied. At length he endeavored to cajole Ô Miôbu, Wistaria's attendant, into arranging an opportunity for him to see her. On Wistaria's part there were strong doubts as to the propriety of complying with his request, but at last the earnestness of the Prince overcame her scruples, and Ô Miôbu managed eventually to bring about a meeting between them.[64]

Genji gave vent to his feelings to the Princess, as follows:—

"Though now we meet, and not againWe e'er may meet, I seemAs though to die, I were full fainLost in this blissful dream."

Then the Princess replied to him, full of sadness:—

"We might dream on but fear the name,The envious world to us may give,Forgetful of the darkened fame,That lives when we no longer live."

For some time after this meeting had taken place, Genji found himself too timid to appear at his father's palace, and remained in his mansion. The Princess, too, experienced a strong feeling of remorse. She had, moreover, a cause of anxiety special in its nature and peculiar to herself as a woman, for which she alone felt some uneasiness of conscience.

Three months of the summer had passed away, and her secret began to betray itself externally. The Emperor was naturally anxious about the health of his favorite, and kind inquiries were sent from time to time to her. But the kinder he was to her the more conscience-stricken she felt.

Genji at this time was often visited by strange dreams. When he consulted a diviner about them, he was told that something remarkable and extraordinary might happen to him, and that it behooved him to be cautious and prudent.

"Here is a pretty source of embarrassment," thought Genji.

He cautioned the diviner to be discreet about it, especially because he said the dreams were not his own but another person's. When at last he heard authentically about the condition of the Princess, he was extremely anxious to communicate with her, but she now peremptorily objected to any kind of correspondence between them, and Ô Miôbu too refused any longer to assist him.

In July Wistaria returned to the palace. There she was received by the Emperor with great rejoicing, and he thought that her condition did but add to her attractiveness.

It was now autumn, the season when agreeable receptions were often held by the Emperor in Court, and it was awkward when Genji and the Princess happened to face each other on these occasions, as neither of them could be free from their tender recollections.

During these autumn evenings the thoughts of Genji were often directed to the granddaughter of the nun, especially because she resembled the Princess so much. His desire to possess her was considerably increased, and the recollection of the first evening when he heard the nun intoning to herself the verses about the tender grass, recurred to his mind. "What," thought he, "if I pluck this tender grass, would it then be, would it then grow up, as fair as now."

"When will be mine this lovely flowerOf tender grace and purple hue?Like the Wistaria of the bower,Its charms are lovely to my view."

The Emperor's visit to the Palace Suzak-in was now announced to take place in October, and dancers and musicians were selected from among the young nobles who were accomplished in these arts, and Royal Princes and officers of State were fully engaged in preparation for the *fête*. After the Royal festivities, a separate account of which will be given hereafter, he sent again a letter to the mountain. The answer, however, came only from the priest, who said that his sister had died on the twentieth day of the last month; and added that though death is inevitable to all of us, still he painfully felt her loss.

Genji pondered first on the precariousness of human life, and then thought how that little one who had depended on her must be afflicted, and gradually the memory of his own childhood, during which he too had lost his mother, came back to his mind.

When the time of full mourning was over, Shiônagon, together with the young girl, returned to their house in the capital. There one evening Genji paid them a visit. The house was rather a gloomy one, and was tenanted by fewer inmates than usual.

"How timid the little girl must feel!" thought Genji, as he was shown in. Shiônagon now told him with tearful eyes every circumstance which had taken place since she had seen him. She also said that the girl might be handed over to her father, who told her that she must do so, but his present wife was said to be very austere. The girl is not young enough to be without ideas and wishes of her own, but yet not old enough to form them sensibly; so were she to be taken to her father's house and be placed with several other children, much misery would be the result. Her grandmother suffered much on this account. "Your kindness is great," continued she, "and we ought not, perhaps, to think too anxiously about the future. Still she is young, too young, and we cannot think of it without pity."

"Why do you recur to that so often?" said Genji, "it is her very youthfulness which moves my sympathy. I am anxious to talk to her,

Say, can the wave that rolls to land,Return to ocean's heaving breast,Nor greet the weed upon the strandWith one wild kiss, all softly pressed.

How sweet it would be!"

"That is very beautifully put, sir," said Shiônagon, "but,

Half trembling at the coming tideThat rolls about the sea-beat sand,Say, can the tender weed untried,Be trusted to its boisterous hand?"

Meanwhile the girl, who was with her companions in her apartment, and who was told that a gentleman in Court dress had arrived, and that perhaps it was the Prince, her father, came running in, saying, "Shiônagon, where is the gentleman in Court dress; has the Prince, my father, arrived?"

"Not the Prince, your father," uttered Genji, "but I am here, and I too am your friend. Come here!"

The girl, glancing with shy timidity at Genji, for whom she already had some liking, and thinking that perhaps there was impropriety in what she had spoken, went over to her nurse, and said, "Oh! I am very sleepy, and wish to lie down!"

"See how childish she still is," remarked Shiônagon.

"Why are you so timid, little one, come here and sleep on my knees," said Genji.

"Go, my child, as you are asked," observed Shiônagon, and she pushed her towards Genji.

Half-unconsciously she took her place by his side. He pushed aside a small shawl which covered her hair, and played with her long tresses, and then he took her small hand in his. "Ah, my hand!" cried she, and drawing it back, she ran into a neighboring room. Genji followed her, and tried to coax her out of her shyness, telling her that he was one of her best friends, and that she was not to be so timid.

By this time darkness had succeeded to the beautiful evening, and hail began to fall.

"Close the casement, it is too fearful, I will watch over you this evening," said Genji, as he led the girl away, to the great surprise of Shiônagon and others who wondered at his ease in doing this.

By and by she became sleepy, and Genji, as skilfully as any nurse could, removed all her outer clothing, and placed her on the couch to sleep, telling her as he sat beside her, "some day you must come with me to some beautiful palace, and there you shall have as many pictures and playthings as you like." Many other similar remarks he added to arrest her attention and to please her.

Her fears gradually subsided, and as she kept looking on the handsome face of Genji, and taking notice of his kindness, she did not fall asleep for some time.

When the night was advanced, and the hailstorm had passed away, Genji at last took his departure. The temperature now suddenly changed, and the hail was lying white upon the grass. "Can it be," thought he, "that I am leaving this place as a lover?" At that moment he remembered that the house of a maiden with whom he had had an acquaintance was on his road home. When he came near to it he ordered one of his attendants to knock at the door. No one, however, came forth. Thereupon Genji turned to another, who had a remarkably good voice, and ordered him to sing the following lines:—

"Though wandering in the morning gray,This gate is one I cannot pass,A tender memory bids me stayTo see once more a pretty lass."

This was repeated twice, when presently a man came to the door and sang, in reply, as follows:—

"If you cannot pass the gate,Welcome all to stop and wait.Nought prevents you. Do not fear,For the gate stands always here."

And then went in, slamming the door in their faces, and appearing no more. Genji, therefore disappointed, proceeded on his way home.

On the morrow he took up his pen to write a letter to Violet, but finding that he had nothing in particular to say, he laid it aside, and instead of a letter several beautiful pictures were sent for her.

From this time Koremitz was sent there very often, partly to do them service, and partly to watch over their movements. At last the time when the girl's father was to take her home approached within a night, and Shiônagon was busily occupied in sewing a dress for the girl, and was thus consequently unable to take much notice of Koremitz when he arrived. Noting these preparatory arrangements, Koremitz at once hastened to inform Genji about them. He happened to be this evening at the mansion of Sadaijin, but Lady Aoi was not, as was often the case, with him, and he was amusing himself there with thumping a *wagon* as he sang a "Hitachi" song. Koremitz presented himself before him, and gave him the latest information of what was going on.

Genji, when he had listened to Koremitz, thought, "This will never do; I must not lose her in this way. But the difficulty is indeed perplexing. If, on the one hand, she goes to her father, it will not become me to ask him for her. If, on the other hand, I carry her off, people may say that I stole her. However, upon consideration, this latter plan, if I can manage to shut people's mouths beforehand, will be much better than that I should demand her from her father."

So, turning to Koremitz, he said, "I must go there. See that the carriage is ready at whatever hour I may appoint. Let two or three attendants be in readiness." Koremitz, having received these orders, retired.

Long before dawn broke, Genji prepared to leave the mansion. Lady Aoi, as usual, was a little out of temper, but Genji told her that he had some particular arrangements to make at his mansion at Nijiô, but that he would soon return to her. He soon started, Koremitz alone following him on horseback.

On their arrival Koremitz proceeded to a small private entrance and announced himself. Shiônagon recognized his voice and came out, and upon this he informed her that the Prince had come. She, presuming that he did so only because he happened to pass by them, said, "What! at this late hour?" As she spoke, Genji came up and said:—

"I hear that the little one is to go to the Prince, her father, and I wish to say a few words to her before she goes."

"She is asleep; really, I am afraid that she cannot talk with you at this hour. Besides, what is the use?" replied Shiônagon, with a smile.

Genji, however, pressed his way into the house, saying:—

"Perhaps the girl is not awake yet, but I will awake her," and, as the people could not prevent his doing so, he proceeded to the room where she was unconsciously sleeping on a couch. He shook her gently. She started up, thinking it was her father who had come.

Genji pushed the hair back from her face, as he said to her, "I am come from your father;" but this she knew to be false, and was alarmed. "Don't be frightened," said Genji; "there is nothing in me to alarm you." And in spite of Shiônagon's request not to disturb her, he lifted her from the couch, abruptly saying that he could not allow her to go elsewhere, and that he had made up his mind that he himself would be her guardian. He also said she should go with him, and that some of them should go with her.

Shiônagon was thunderstruck. "We are expecting her father to-morrow, and what are we to say to him?" She added, "Surely, you can find some better opportunity to manage matters than this."

"All right, you can come afterward; we will go first," retorted Genji, as he ordered his carriage to drive up.

Shiônagon was perplexed, and Violet also cried, thinking how strange all this was. At last Shiônagon saw it was no use to resist, and so having hurriedly changed her own dress for a better one, and taking with her the pretty dress of Violet which she had been making in the evening, got into the carriage, where Genji had already placed the little one.

It was no great distance to Nijiô, and they arrived there before dawn. The carriage was driven up to the western wing of the mansion. To Shiônagon the whole affair seemed like a dream. "What am I to do?" she said to Genji, who teasingly answered, "What you choose. You may go if you like; so long as this darling is here I am content." Genji lifted the girl out and carried her into the house. That part of the mansion in which they now were, had not been inhabited, and the furniture was scanty and inappropriate; so, calling Koremitz, the Prince ordered him to see that proper furniture was brought. The beds were therefore taken from the eastern wing, where he himself lived.

Day broke, and Shiônagon surveyed with admiration all the magnificence with which she was surrounded. Both the exterior of the building and its internal arrangements left nothing to be desired. Going to the casement, she saw the gravelled walks flashing brightly in the sun. "Ah," thought she, "where am I amidst all this splendor? This is too grand for me!"

Bath water for their ablutions, and rice soup were now brought into the apartment, and Genji afterward made his appearance.

"What! no attendants? No one to play with the girl? I will send some," and he then ordered some young persons from the eastern wing of the mansion. Four accordingly came.

Violet was still fast asleep in her night-dress, and now Genji gently shook and woke her. "Do not be frightened any more," he said quietly to her; "a good girl would not be so, but would know that it is best to be obedient." She became more and more pleasing to him, and he tried to please her by presenting to her a variety of pretty pictures and playthings, and by consulting her wishes in whatever she desired. She was still wearing the dress of mourning, of sombre color and of soft material, and it was only now at last that she began to smile a little, and this filled Genji with delight. He now had to return to the eastern wing, and Violet, for the first time, went to the casement and looked out on the scenery around. The trees covered with foliage, a small lake, and the plantations round about expanded before her as in a picture. Here and there young people were going in and out. "Ah! what a pretty place," she exclaimed, charmed as she gazed around. Then, turning again into the apartment, she saw beautiful pictures painted on the screens and walls, which could not but please her.

Genji did not go to the Palace for two or three days, but spent his time in trying to train Violet. "She must soon take lessons in writing," he thought, and he wrote several writing copies for her. Among these was one in plain characters on violet-colored paper, with the title, "Musashi-no" (The field of Musashi is known for its violets). She took it up, and in handwriting plain and clear though small, she found the following:

Though still a bud the violet be,A still unopened blossom here,Its tenderness has charms for me,Recalling one no longer near.

"Come, *you* must write one now," said Genji.

"I cannot write well enough," said Violet, looking up at him, with an extremely charming look.

"Never mind, whether good or bad," said he, "but still write something, to refuse is unkind. When there is any difficulty I will help you through with it."

Thereupon she turned aside shyly and wrote something, handling the pen gracefully with her tiny fingers. "I have done it badly," she cried out, and tried to conceal what she had written, but Genji insisted on seeing it and found the following:—

I wonder what's the floweret's name, From which that bud its charm may claim!

This was, of course, written in a childish hand, but the writing was large and plain, giving promise of future excellence.

"How like her grandmother's it is," thought Genji. "Were she to take lessons from a good professor she might become a master of the art."

He ordered for her a beautiful doll's house, and played with her different innocent and amusing games.

In the meantime, the Prince, her father, had duly arrived at the old home of Violet and asked for her. The servants were embarrassed, but as they had been requested by Genji not to tell, and as Shiônagon had also enjoined them to keep silence, they simply told him that the nurse had taken her and absconded. The Prince was greatly amazed, but he remembered that the girl's grandmother never consented to send his daughter to his house, and knowing Shiônagon to be a shrewd and intelligent woman, he concluded that she had found out the reasons which influenced her, and that so out of respect to her, and out of dislike to tell him the reason of it, she had carried the girl off in order that she might be kept away from him. He therefore merely told the servants to inform him at once if they heard anything about them, and he returned home.

Our story again brings us back to Nijiô. The girl gradually became reconciled to her new home, as she was most kindly treated by Genji. True, during those evenings when Genji was absent she thought of her dead grandmother, but the image of her father never presented itself to her, as she had seldom seen him. And now, naturally enough, Genji, whom she had learned to look upon as a second father, was the only one for whom she cared. She was the first to greet him when he came home, and she came forward to be fondled and caressed by him without shame or diffidence. Girls at her age are usually shy and under restraint, but with her it was quite different. And again, if a girl has somewhat of jealousy in her disposition, and looks upon every little trifle in a serious light, a man will have to be cautious in his dealings with her, and she herself, too, will often have to undergo vexation. Thus many disagreeable and unexpected incidents might often result. In the case of Violet, however, things were very different, and she was ever amiable and invariably pleasant.

FOOTNOTES:

[61]An Indian theological writing.

[62]In the Buddhist Bible it is stated that there is in Paradise a divine tree, called Udon, which rarely blossoms. When, however, it does

blossom, Buddha is said to appear in the world, therefore we make use of this expression when referring to any rare event.

[63]The name of a song which in those days formed the first lesson in writing.

[64]The authoress represents her in a subsequent chapter as suffering punishment in the next world for this sin. The real cause of Genji's exile is also supposed to have resulted from the same sin.

CHAPTER VI

SAFFRON FLOWER

The beauteous Yûgao of Genji was lost, but memory of her never vanished from his mind. Her attractive nature, thoughtfulness, and patient manner had seemed to him surpassingly charming. At last he began to think of seeking for some other maiden who might resemble her in these qualities. True, his thoughts had often reverted to Cicada, and to her young friend; but it was now of little use thinking of them, for one had gone to the country, and the other was married.

Now, Genji had another nurse, next in degree to Daini. The daughter of this nurse, Tayû-no-Miôbu, was in Court service. She was still young, and full of mirth and life. Genji was wont to make her useful when in the palace. Her father, who had been remotely connected with the Royal blood, was an official in the War Department. Her mother, however, had been married again to the Governor of the province of Chikzen, and had gone there with her husband; so Tayû made her father's house her home, and went from there backwards and forwards to the palace. She was an intimate acquaintance of a young Princess, the daughter of the late Lord-Lieutenant of Hitachi, and she had been the child of his old age, and was at this time his survivor. The life that she passed was somewhat lonely, and her circumstances miserable. Tayû mentioned this young lady to Genji, who exclaimed:—

"How sad! Tell me all about her."

"I cannot say that I know so much about her," replied Tayû. "She leads a very retired life, and is seldom seen in society. Perhaps, some favorable evening, you might see her from a hiding-place. The *koto* is her favorite instrument, and the favorite amusement of her solitude."

"Ah!" said Genji, "I see, one of the three friends (as the Chinese poets call them)—Music, Poetry, and Wine; but, of the other two, one is not always a good friend." And he added, "Well, you may manage some time to let me hear her *koto*. The Prince, her father, had great taste and reputation in such arts; so, I believe, she is no ordinary performer."

"But, perhaps, after all, not so good as you imagine," replied Tayû, disingenuously.

"Oh! that remains to be discovered," cried Genji, nibbling at the bait. "One of these evenings I will come, and you had better be there also."

Now, the home of Tayû's father was at some distance from the Princess's mansion; but Tayû used to spend her time very often with the Princess, when she had leave of absence from the Court, chiefly because she did not like being at home with her stepmother. For this reason Tayû had plenty of chances for gratifying the wish of Genji to see the Princess; so a certain evening was appointed.

It was a sweet balmy day in spring, and the grounds of the palace were full of silence and repose. Tayû left the palace, and proceeded to the mansion of the Princess, attracted more by the beauty of the evening than by the appointment made. Genji also appeared on the scene, with the newly risen moon, and was soon prattling with Tayû.

"You have not come at a very favorable time," said she. "This is not the sort of evening when the *koto* sounds sweetest."

"But take me somewhere, so that I may hear her voice. I cannot go away without hearing that."

Tayû then led him into a private room, where she made him sit down, and left him, saying, as she went away, "I am sorry to make you wait, but you must have a little patience." She proceeded to another part of the palace occupied by the Princess, whom she found sitting pensively near an open casement, inhaling the rich perfume of the plum blossoms.

"A good opportunity," thought Tayû; and, advancing to the Princess, said: "What a lovely evening! How sweet at such an hour is the music of the *koto*! My official going to and fro to the palace prevents me from having the pleasure of hearing it often; so do now, if you please, play me a tune."

"You appreciate music," said the Princess; "but I am afraid that mine is not good enough to charm the ear of courtiers; but, if you wish it, I will play one tune." And she ordered the *koto* to be brought, and began to strike it. Her skill was certainly not super-excellent; but she had been well instructed, and the effect was by no means displeasing to the ear.

Tayû, however, it must be remembered, was rather a sharp girl. She did not like Genji to hear too much, so as to criticise; and, therefore, said to the Princess, casting a glance upwards, "How changed and dull the sky has become. A friend of mine is waiting; and is, perhaps, impatient. I must have more of this pleasure some other time; at present I must go and see him." Thus she caused the Princess to cease playing, and went to Genji, who exclaimed, when she returned, "Her music seems pretty good; but I had better not have heard it at all. How can we judge by so little? If you are willing to oblige me at all, let me hear and see more closely than this." Tayû made a difficulty. "She is so retiring," she said, "and always keeps herself in the strictest privacy. Were you to intrude upon her, it would not be acting rightly."

"Truly so," replied Genji; "her position insures her from intrusion. Let us, then, seek for some better opportunity." And then he prepared to take leave, as if he had some other affairs on his hands. Tayû observed, with a knowing smile, "The Emperor, your father, always thinks of you as quite guileless, and actually says so. When I hear these remarks I often laugh in my sleeve. Were his Majesty to see you in these disguises, what would he then think?"

Genji answered, with a slight laugh: "Nonsense! If these trifling amusements were thought so improper, how cheerless the life of woman would be!"

Tayû made no remark in reply; so Genji then left the house, and took a stroll round the garden, intending to reach that part of the mansion where the Princess had her apartments. As he sauntered along, he came to a thick hedge, in which there was a dark bower, and here wished to stop awhile. He stepped cautiously into it, when he suddenly perceived a tall man concealed there. "Who can this be?" thought Genji, as he withdrew to a corner where the moonlight did not reach. This was Tô-no-Chiûjiô, and the reason of his being there was this:

He had left the Palace that evening in company with Genji, who did not go to his house in Nijiô, nor to his bride, but separated from him on the road. Tô-no-Chiûjiô was very anxious to find out where Genji was going. He therefore followed him unperceived. When he saw Genji enter the mansion of the Princess, he wished to see how the business would end; so he waited in the garden, in order that he might witness Genji's departure, listening, at the same time, to the *koto* of the Princess. Genji did not know who the man was, nor did he wish to be recognized. He therefore began to retreat slowly on tip-toe, when Tô-no-Chiûjiô came up to him from behind, and addressed him: "You slighted me, but I have come to watch over you:—

Though like two wandering moons on highWe left our vast imperial home,We parted on our road, and IKnew not where you were bent to roam."

Genji at once recognized his companion; and, being somewhat amused at his pertinacity, exclaimed: "What an unexpected surprise!

We all admire the moon, 'tis true,Whose home unknown to mortal eyels in the mountains hid, but whoTo find that far-off home, would try?"

Hereupon Tô-no-Chiûjiô gave him a taunt: "What would you do," said he, "if I were to follow you very often? Were you to maintain true propriety in your position, you ought always to have trustworthy attendants; and I am sure, by so doing, you will meet with better fortune. I cannot say that it is very decorous of you to go wandering about in such a fashion. It is too frivolous!"

"How very tiresome!" mentally exclaimed Genji; "but he little knows about his Nadeshiko (little darling). I have him there!"

Neither of them ventured to go to any other rendezvous that night; but, with many mutual home-thrusts, they got into a carriage together, and proceeded home, amusing themselves all the way with a duet on their flutes. Entering the mansion, they went to a small apartment, where they changed their dresses, and commenced playing the flutes in such a manner as if they had come from the Palace. The Sadaijin, hearing this music, could not forbear joining them, and blew skilfully a Corean flute in concert with theirs. Lady Aoi, also, in her room, catching the impulse, ordered some practised players on the *koto* to perform.

Meantime, both Genji and Tô-no-Chiûjiô, in their secret minds, were thinking of the notes of the *koto* heard before on that evening, and of the bare and pitiable condition of the residence of the Princess whom they had left—a great contrast to the luxury of their present quarters. Tô-no-Chiûjiô's idea about her took something of this shape: "If girls who, from a modest propriety, keep themselves aloof for years from our society, were at last to be subdued by our attentions, our affection for them would become irresistible, even braving whatever remarks popular scandal might pass upon us. She may be like one of these. The Prince Genji seems to have made her the object of some attentions. He is not one to waste his time without reason. He knows what he is doing."

As these thoughts arose in his mind, a slight feeling of jealousy disturbed him, and made him ready to dare a little rivalry in that quarter; for, it would appear, that after this day amatory letters were often sent both by him and Genji to the Princess, who, however, returned no answer to either.

This silence on her part made Tô-no-Chiûjiô, more especially, think thus: "A strange rejection; and from one, too, who possesses such a secluded life. True, her birth is high; but that cannot be the only reason which makes her bury herself in retirement. There must be some stronger reason, I presume."

As we have before mentioned, Genji and Tô-no-Chiûjiô were so intimate that all ceremony was dispensed with between them, and they could ask each other any question without reserve. From this circumstance Tô-no-Chiûjiô one day boldly inquired of Genji: "I dare say you have received some replies from the Princess. Have you not? I for my part have thrown out some hints in that quarter by way of experiment, but I gave up in disappointment."

"Ah, then, he too has been trying there," thought Genji, smiling slightly, and he replied very vaguely, "I am not particularly concerned whether I get an answer or not, therefore I cannot tell you whether I have received any."

"I understand that," thought Tô-no-Chiûjiô; "perhaps he has got one; I suspect so."

To state the truth, Genji was not very deeply smitten by the Princess, and he was but little concerned at her sending no reply to his letter; but when he heard the confession of his brother-in-law's attempts in the same quarter, the spirit of rivalry stirred him once more. "A girl," thought he, "will yield to him who pays her the most attentions. I must not allow him to excel me in that." And Genji determined to achieve what he intended to do, and with this object still enlisted the aid of Tayû. He told her that the Princess's treating his letter with such indifference was an act of great cruelty. "Perhaps she does this," said he, "because she suspects I am changeable. I am not, however, such a one as that. It is often only the fault of ladies themselves that causes men to appear so; besides a lady, like the Princess, who has neither parent nor brother to interfere with her, is a most desirable acquaintance, as we can maintain our friendship far better than we could otherwise do."

"Yes! what you say is all very well," replied Tayû, "but the Princess is not exactly so placed that any one can make himself quite at ease with her. As I told you before she is very bashful and reserved; but yet is perhaps more desirable for this very reason," and she detailed many more particulars about her. This enabled Genji to fully picture the general bearing of the Princess's character; and he thought, "Perhaps her mind is not one of brilliant activity, but she may be modest, and of a quiet nature, worthy of attention." And so he kept the recollection of her alive in his mind. Before, however, he met her, many events had taken place. He had been attacked by the ague, which led to his journey to the mountain and his discovery of Violet, and his secret affection for a certain one in the palace.

His mind being thus otherwise occupied, the spring and summer passed away without anything further transpiring about the Princess. As the autumn advanced his thoughts recurred to past times, and even the sound of the fuller's hammer, which he had listened to in the home of Yûgao, came back to his mental ear; and these reveries again brought him to the recollection of the Princess Hitachi, and now once more he began to urge Tayû to contrive a meeting.

It would seem that there was no difficulty for Tayû to bring the matter about, but at the same time no one knew better than herself that the natural gifts and culture of the Princess were far from coming up to Genji's standard. She thought, however, that it would matter very little if he did not care for her, but if, on the other hand, he did so, he was quite free to come and see her without any interference. For this reason she at last made up her mind to bring them together, and she gave several hints to the Princess.

Now it so happened towards the end of August that Tayû was on one occasion engaged in conversing with the Princess. The evening was as yet moonless, the stars alone twinkled in the heavens, and the gentle winds blew plaintively over the tall trees around the mansion. The conversation gradually led to times gone by, and the Princess was rendered sad by the contrast of her present circumstances with those of her father's time. "This is a good opportunity," thought Tayû, and she sent, it seems, a message to Genji, who soon hastened to the mansion with his usual alacrity. At the moment when he arrived on the scene the long-looked-for moon had just made her appearance over the tops of a distant mountain, and as he looked along the wildly growing hedges around the residence, he heard the sound of the *koto*, which was being played by the Princess at Tayû's request. It sounded a little too old-fashioned, but that was of no consequence to the eager ears of the Prince. He soon made his way to the entrance, and requested a domestic to announce him to Tayû.

When the latter heard of this she affected great surprise, and said to the Princess, "The Prince has come. How annoying! He has often been displeased because I have not yet introduced him to you. I have often told him that you do not particularly like it, and therefore I cannot think what makes him come here. I had better see him and send him away, but what shall I say. We cannot treat him like an ordinary person. I am really puzzled what to do. Will you not let me ask you if you will see him for a few minutes, then all matters will end satisfactorily?"

"But I am not used to receive people," said the Princess, blushing. "How simple minded!" rejoined Tayû, coaxingly, "I am sorry for that, for the bashfulness of young ladies who are under the care of their parents may sometimes be even desirable, but how then is that parallel with your case? Besides, I do not see any good in a friendless maiden refusing the offer of a good acquaintance."

"Well, if you really insist upon it," said the Princess, "perhaps I will; but don't expose me too much to the gaze of a stranger."

Having thus cunningly persuaded the Princess, Tayû set the reception-room in order, into which Genji was soon shown. The

Princess was all the while experiencing much nervousness, and as she did not know exactly how to manage, she left everything to Tayû, and was led by her to the room to receive her visitor. The room was arranged in such a way that the Princess had her back to the light so that her face and emotions could be obscured.

The perfume which she used was rich, still preserving the trait of high birth, but her demeanor was timid, and her deportment awkward.

Genji at once noticed this. "Just as I imagined. She is so simple," thought he, and then he commenced to talk with her, and to explain how passionately he had desired to see her. She, however, listened to him almost in silence, and gave no plain answer. Genji was disconcerted, and at last said,

"From you I sought so oft reply,But you to give one would not deign,If you discard me, speak, and IWill cease to trouble you again."

The governess of the Princess, Kojijiû by name, who was present, was a sagacious woman, and noticing the embarrassment of the lady, she advanced to her side, and made the following reply in such a well-timed manner that her real object, which was to conceal the deficiencies of her mistress, did not betray itself—

"Not by the ringing of a bell,Your words we wish to stay;But simply, she has nought to tell,And nothing much to say."

"Your eloquence has so struck me that my mouth is almost closed," said Genji, smiling—

"Not speaking is a wiser part,And words are sometimes vain,But to completely close the heartIn silence, gives me pain."

He then tried to speak of this thing and that indifferently, but all hopes of agreeable responsiveness on the lady's part being vain, he coolly took his leave, and left the mansion, much disappointed.

This evening he slept in his mansion at Nijiô. The next morning Tô-no-Chiûjiô appeared before he had risen.

"How late, how late!" he cried, in a peculiar tone. "Were you fatigued last night, eh?"

Genji rose and presently came out, saying, "I have overslept myself, that is all; nothing to disturb me. But have you come from the palace? Was it your official watch-night?"[65]

"Yes," replied Tô-no-Chiûjiô, "and I must inform you that the dancers and musicians for the *fête* in Suzak-in are to be nominated to-day. I came from the palace to report this to my father, so I must now go home, but I will soon return to you."

"I will go with you," said Genji, "but let us breakfast before we start."

Breakfast was accordingly brought, of which they partook. Two carriages, Genji's and Tô-no-Chiûjiô's, were driven to the door, but Tô-no-Chiûjiô invited the Prince to take a seat with him. Genji complied, and they drove off. Going along Tô-no-Chiûjiô observed with an envious tone in his voice, "You look very sleepy;" to which Genji returned an indifferent reply. From the house of Sadaijin they proceeded to the Imperial Palace to attend the selection of the dancers and musicians. Thence Genji drove with his father-in-law to the mansion of the latter.

Here in the excitement of the coming *fête* were assembled several young nobles, in addition to Genji himself. Some practised dancing, others music, the sound of which echoed everywhere around. A large *hichiriki* and a *shakuhachi* (two kinds of flute) were blown with the utmost vigor. Even large drums were rolled upon a balcony and beaten with a will.

During the following days, therefore, Genji was so busily engaged that no thought came across his mind of revisiting the Princess Hitachi. Tayû certainly came now and then, and strove to induce him to pay the Princess another visit, but he made an excuse on the pretext of being so much occupied.

It was not until the *fête* was over that one evening he resolved to pay a visit there. He did not, however, announce his intention openly, but went there in strict secrecy, making his way to the house unobserved, as there was no one about.

On his arrival he went up to the latticed window and peeped through. The curtains were old and half worn out, yet were still left to hang in the once pretty and decorated chamber. There were a few domestic maidens there partaking of supper. The table and service seemed to be old Chinese, but everything else betrayed a scantiness of furniture.

In the further room where the mistress was probably dining, an old waitress was passing in and out, wearing a peculiar white dress rather faded in appearance, and an awkward-looking comb in her hair, after the old-fashioned style of those formerly in the service of the aristocratic class, of whom a few might still be retained in a family.

"Ah," thought Genji, smiling, "we might see this kind of thing in the college of ceremonies." One of the maids happened to say, "This poor cold place! when one's life is too long, such fate comes to us."

Another answered her, "How was it we did not like the mansion when the late Prince was living?"

Thus they talked about one thing or another connected with their mistress's want of means.

Genji did not like that they should know that he had seen and heard all this, so he slyly withdrew some distance, and then advancing with a firm step, approached the door and knocked.

"Some one is come," cried a servant, who then brought a light, opened the door, and showed him into a room where he was soon joined by the Princess, neither Tayû nor Kojijiû being there on this occasion. The latter was acquainted with the Saiin (the sacred virgin at the Temple of Kamo),[66] and often spent some time with her. On this occasion she happened to be visiting her, a circumstance which was not very convenient for the Princess. The dilapidated state of the mansion was just as novel to Genji as that which he had seen in the lodge of Yûgao, but the great drawback consisted in the Princess's want of responsiveness. He spoke much, she but little. Outside, in the meantime, the weather had become boisterous and snow fell thickly, while within in the room where they sat the lamp burned dimly, no one waiting there even to trim the light.

Some hours were spent between them, and then Genji rose, and throwing up the shutter in the same way as he did in the lodge of Yûgao, looked upon the snow which had fallen in the garden. The ground was covered with a sheet of pure whiteness; no footstep had left its trace, betraying the fact that few persons came to the mansion. He was about to take his departure, but some vague impulse arrested him. Turning to the Princess, he asked her to come near him, and to look out on the scene, and she somewhat unreadily complied.

The evening was far advanced, but the reflection of the snow threw a faint light over all. Now, for the first time, he discovered the imperfections of the personal attractions of the Princess. First, her stature was very tall, the upper part of her figure being out of proportion to the lower, then one thing which startled him most was her nose. It reminded him of the elephant of Fugen. It was high and long; while its peak, a little drooping, was tinged with pink. To the refined eyes of Genji this was a sad defect. Moreover, she was thin, too thin; and her shoulders drooped too much, as if the dress was too heavy for them.

"Why am I so anxious to examine and criticise?" thought Genji, but his curiosity impelled him to continue his examination. Her hair and the shape of her head were good, in no way inferior to those of others he liked so well. Her complexion was fair, and her forehead well developed. The train of her dress, which hung down gracefully, seemed about a foot too long. If I described everything which she wore I should become loquacious, but in old stories the dress of the personages is very often more minutely described than anything else; so I must, I suppose, do the same. Her vest and skirt dress were double, and were of light green silk, a little worn, over which was a robe of dark color. Over all this she wore a mantle of sable of good quality, only a little too antique in fashion. To all these things, therefore, he felt no strong objection; but the two things he could not pass unnoticed were her nose, and her style of movement. She moved in a stiff and constrained manner, like a master of the ceremonies in some Court procession, spreading out his arms and looking important. This afforded him amusement, but still he felt for her. "If I say too much, pardon me," said Genji, "but you seem apparently friendless. I should advise you to take interest in one with whom you have made acquaintance. He will sympathize with you. You are much too reserved. Why are you so?

The icicle hangs at the gable end,But melts when the sun is high,Why does your heart not to me unbend,And warm to my melting sigh."

A smile passed over the lips of the Princess, but they seemed too stiff to reply in a similar strain. She said nothing.

The time had now come for Genji to depart. His carriage was drawn up to the middle gate, which, like everything else that belonged to the mansion, was in a state of dilapidation. "The spot overgrown with wild vegetation, spoken of by Sama-no-Kami might be such as this," he thought. "If one can find a real beauty of elevated character and obtain her, how delightful would it not be! The spot answers the description, but the girl does not quite equal the idea; however, I really pity her, and will look after her. She is a fortunate girl, for if I were not such a one as I am, I should have little sympathy for the unfortunate and unfavored. But this is not what I shall do."

He saw an orange tree in the garden covered with snow. He bade his servant shake it free. A pine tree which stood close by suddenly jerked its branches as if in emulation of its neighbor, and threw off its load of snow like a wave. The gate through which he had to drive out was not yet opened. The gatekeeper was summoned to open it. Thereupon an aged man came forth from his lodge. A miserable-looking girl with a pinched countenance stood by, his daughter or his granddaughter, whose dress looked poorer from the whiteness of the surrounding snow. She had something containing lighted charcoal which she held to her breast for warmth.

When she observed that her aged parent could scarcely push back the gate, she came forward and helped him. And the scene was quite droll. Genji's servant also approached them, and the gates were thrown open.

Again Genji hummed:—

"The one who on the time-bent head of age,Beholds the gathered snow,Nor less his tears of grief may shed,For griefs that youth can only know."

and added, "Youth with its body uncovered."[67] Then the pitiable image of one with a tinged flower[68] on her face presented itself once more to his thoughts and made him smile.

"If Tô-no-Chiûjiô observed this, what would he not have to say?" thought he, as he drove back slowly to his mansion.

After this time communications were frequently sent from Genji to the Princess. This he did because he pitied the helpless condition and circumstances he had witnessed more than for any other reason. He also sent her rolls of silk, which might replace the old-fashioned sable-skins, some damask, calico and the like. Indeed, presents were made even to her aged servants and to the gatekeeper.

In ordinary circumstances with women, particular attention such as this might make a blush, but the Princess did not take it in such a serious light, nor did Genji do this from any other motive than kindness.

The year approached its end! He was in his apartment in the Imperial Palace, when one morning Tayû came in. She was very useful to him in small services, such as hairdressing, so she had easy access to him, and thus she came to him this morning.

"I have something strange to tell you, but it is somewhat trying for me to do so," she said, half smiling.

"What can it be? There can be nothing to conceal from me!"

"But I have some reason for my hesitation to reveal it," replied Tayû.

"You make a difficulty, as usual," rejoined Genji.

"This is from the Princess," she said, taking a letter from her pocket and presenting it.

"Is this a thing of all others that you ought to conceal," cried Genji, taking the letter and opening it. It was written on thick and coarse paper of Michinok manufacture. The verse it contained ran as follows:—

"Like this, my sleeves are worn away, By weeping at your long delay."

These words puzzled Genji. Inclining his head in a contemplative way, he glanced from the paper to Tayû, and from Tayû to the paper. Then she drew forth a substantial case of antique pattern, saying, "I cannot produce such a thing without shame, but the Princess expressly sent this for your New Year. I could not return it to her nor keep it myself; I hope you will just look at it."

"Oh, certainly," replied Genji. "It is very kind of her," at the same time thinking, "What a pitiful verse! This may really be her own composition. No doubt Kojijiû has been absent, besides she seems to have had no master to improve her penmanship. This must have been written with great effort. We ought to be grateful for it, as they say." Here a smile rose on Genji's cheeks, and a blush upon Tayû's. The case was opened, and a Naoshi (a kind of gown), of scarlet, shabby and old-fashioned, of the same color on both sides, was found inside. The sight was almost too much for Genji from its very absurdity. He stretched out the paper on which the verse had been written, and began to write on one side, as if he was merely playing with the pen. Tayû, glancing slyly, found that he had written:—

This color pleases not mine eye,Too fiery bright its gaudy hue,And when the saffron flower was nigh,The same pink tinge was plain to view.

He then erased what he had written, but Tayû quickly understood what he really meant by "saffron flower," referring to the pinkness of its flower, so she remarked:—

"Although the dress too bright in hue,And scarlet tints may please you not,At least to her, who sends, be true,Soon will Naoshi be forgot."

While they were thus prattling on the matter, people were entering the room to see him, so Genji hastily put the things aside, and Tayû retired.

A few days after, Genji one morning looked into the Daihan-sho (large parlor), where he found Tayû, and threw a letter to her, saying, "Tayû, here is the answer. It has cost me some pains," and then passed through, humming as he went, with a peculiar smile,

"Like that scarlet-tinged plum."

None but Tayû understood the real allusion. One of the women observed, "The weather is too frosty, perhaps he has seen some one reddened by the frost." Another said, "What an absurdity! There is no one among us of that hue, but perhaps Sakon or Unemé may be like this," and thus they chattered on till the matter dropped.

The letter was soon sent by Tayû to the Princess, who assembled all her attendants round her, and they all read it together, when the following was found in it:—

Of my rare visits you complain,But can the meaning be,Pray come not often, nor again,For I am tired of thee.

On the last day of the year he made the following presents to the Princess, sending them in the same case as the Naoshi had been sent to him: stuff for a complete dress, which had originally been presented to himself; also rolls of silk, one of the color of the purple grape, another of the Kerria japonica color, and others. All these were handed to the Princess by Tayû. It should be observed that these presents were made by Genji to the Princess chiefly on account of her reduced circumstances. Her attendants, however, who wished to flatter their mistress, exclaimed, "Our scarlet dress was very good, too. Scarlet is a color which never fades. The lines we sent were also excellent. Those of the Prince are, no doubt, a little amusing, but nothing more."

The Princess, flattered by the remarks, wrote down her verse in her album, as if worthy of preservation.

The New Year began with the morrow; and it was announced that the Otoko-dôka (gentlemen's singing dances) would soon take place in which Genji would take part. Hence he was busy in going backwards and forwards, to practise, but the lonely residence of the saffron flower began to draw his thoughts in that direction. So after the ceremony of the State Festival, on the seventh day, he betook himself there in the evening, after he had left the Emperor's presence, having made a pretence of retiring to his own private apartments. On this occasion the appearance of the lady happened to be a little more attractive, and Genji was pleased, thinking there might be a time when she would improve still more. When the sun shone forth he rose to leave. He opened the casement on the western side of the mansion, and, looking at the corridor, perceived that its roof was broken. Through it the sunshine peeped, and shone upon the slight cover of snow scattered in the crevices. The scene, as we have before said, betrayed everywhere dilapidation and decay.

The mirror-stand, combs, and dressing-case were brought in by an attendant. They were all of an extremely antique pattern. He drew an "arm-stool" near him, and resting himself upon it began combing his hair. He was amused at the sight of these articles, which were doubtless a legacy from her parents. The dress of the Princess was in every way nicer. It had been made out of the silk of Genji's present. He recognized it by the tasteful pattern. Turning to her he said, "This year you might become a little more genial, the only thing I wait for above all is a change in your demeanor." To which she, with some awkwardness, said,

"In the spring, when numerous birds sing."

Such poetic responses were a great delight to Genji, who thought they were the silent touches of time, and that she had made some improvement. He then left and returned to his mansion in Nijiô, where he saw the young Violet innocently amusing herself. She wore with grace a long close-fitting cherry-colored dress of plain silk. She had not yet blackened her teeth,[69] but he now made her do so, which gave a pleasant contrast to her eyebrows. He played at their usual games at toys with her, trying in every way to please her. She drew pictures and painted them, so did he also. He drew the likeness of a lady with long hair, and painted her nose with pink.

Even in caricature it was odd to see. He turned his head to a mirror in which he saw his own image reflected in great serenity. He then took the brush and painted his own nose pink. Violet, on seeing this, screamed.

"When I become ornamented in this way what shall I be like?" inquired Genji.

"That would be a great pity. Do wipe it off, it might stain," she replied.

Genji partly wiped it off, saying, "Need I wipe it off any more? Suppose I go with this to the Palace?"

On this Violet approached and carefully wiped it for him. "Don't put any more color," cried Genji, "and play upon me as Heijiû."[70]

The mild sun of spring descended in the west, and darkness slowly gathered over the forest tops, obscuring all but the lovely white plum blossoms which were still visible amidst the gloom. At the front of the porch, also, a red plum blossom, which usually opens very early, was deeply tinged with glowing hues. Genji murmured:—

"The 'red-tinged flower' is far from fair,Nor do my eyes delight to see,But yon red plum which blossoms there,Is full of loveliness to me."

What will become of all these personages!

FOOTNOTES:

[65]Young nobles spent a night in the palace in turns, to attend to any unexpected official business.

[66]When a new emperor succeeded, two virgins, chosen from the royal princesses, were sent—one to the Shintô temple at Ise, the other to the same temple at Kamo—to become vestals, and superintend the services.

[67]From a Chinese poem about poor people "night advancing, snow and hail fly white around. Youth with its body uncovered, and the aged with chilly pain, grief and cold come together, and make them both sob."

[68]A play upon the word "hana," which means a nose, as well as a flower.

[69]An old custom in Japan for girls when married, or even betrothed, is to blacken their teeth. This custom, however, is rapidly disappearing.

[70]In an old tale it is stated that this man had a sweetheart. He often pretended to be weeping, and made his eyes moist by using the water which he kept in his bottle for mixing ink, in order to deceive her. She discovered this ruse; so one day she put ink into it secretly. He damped his eyes as usual, when, giving him a hand mirror, she hummed, "You may show me your tears, but don't show your blackened face to strangers."

CHAPTER VII

MAPLE FÊTE

T he Royal visit to the Suzak-in was arranged to take place towards the middle of October, and was anticipated to be a grand affair. Ladies were not expected to take part in it, and they all regretted their not being able to be present.

The Emperor, therefore, wished to let his favorite, the Princess Wistaria, above others, have an opportunity of witnessing a rehearsal that would represent the coming *fête*, and ordered a preliminary concert to be performed at the Court, in which Genji danced the "Blue Main Waves," with Tô-no-Chiûjiô for his partner. They stood and danced together, forming a most pleasing contrast—one, so to speak, like a bright flower; the other, an everlasting verdure beside it. The rays of the setting sun shone over their heads, and the tones of the music rose higher and higher in measure to their steps. The movements both of hand and foot were eminently graceful; as well, also, was the song of Genji, which was sung at the end of his dance, so that some of the people remarked that the sound of the holy bird, Kariôbinga,[71] might be even like this. And so the rehearsal ended.

When the day of the *fête* came, all the Royal Princes, including the Heir-apparent, and all personages of State, were present at the scene. On the lake, "the music boat," filled with selected musicians, floated about, as usual on such occasions; and in the grounds, the bands, which were divided into two divisions on the right and left, under the direction of two Ministers and two Yemon-no-Kami, played. With this music different dances, including Chinese and

Corean, were performed, one after another, by various dancers. As the performance went on, the high winds rustled against the tall fir-trees, as though Divine strains of music had broken forth on high in harmony with them. The tune of the bands became quick and thrilling, as different colored leaves whirled about overhead.

Then, at length, the hero of the "Blue Main Waves" made his appearance, to the delight of the suddenly startled spectators, from the midst of a knoll in the grounds, covered with maple leaves. The twigs of maple which crowned his head, became thinned as he danced, and a Sadaishiô, plucking a bunch of chrysanthemums from in front of the Royal stand, replaced the lessened maple leaves. The sun was by this time descending, and the sky had become less glaring, while the face of Nature seemed as if it were smiling on the scene. Genji danced with unusual skill and energy. All the pages and attendants, who were severally stationed here under the side of the rock, there under the shade of the foliage, were quite impressed with the effects of the performance.

After Genji, a little prince, the child of the Niogo of Jiôkiô-den, danced the "Autumn Gales," with a success next to that of Genji. Then, the principal interest of the day being over, as these dances were finished, the *fête* ended. This very evening Genji was invested with the title of Shôsammi, and Tô-no-Chiûjiô with that of Shôshii. Many other persons also received promotion in rank according to their merits.

It was after this *fête* that the young Violet was taken into the mansion of Genji at Nijiô, and she lived with him. The more care he took of her the more amiable she became, while nothing pleased him more than teaching her to read and write.

The full extent of her mourning for her grandmother was three months, as it is for the maternal side; and on the last day of

December her dress was changed. As she, however, had been always brought up under the care of her grandmother, her indebtedness to the latter was not to be held lightly; consequently any bright colors were not advisable for her, so she wore plain scarlet, mauve, and light yellow, without trimmings or ornament on them.

The dawn ushered in the New Year's day. Genji was about to leave his mansion to attend the New Year's *levée*. Just before starting, he came into Violet's room to see her.

"How are you? Are you becoming less childish now?" said he, with a smile to the girl who was playing with her Hina (toys).

"I am trying to mend this. Inuki damaged it when he was playing what he called 'driving out devils,'"[72] replied the girl.

"What carelessness! I will soon get it mended for you. Don't cry this day, please," said Genji, and he went off, the maidens who attended on Violet accompanying him to the door. This example was also followed by Violet herself.

She went back again to her toys, and presented a toy prince, whom she called Genji, at the Court of her toy house. Shiônagon was beside her. She said:—

"You might really be a little more womanly, as the Prince told you. How very childish! a girl older than ten always playing with toys!"

Violet said nothing; but she seemed, for the first time, to have become aware that she was expected to be a woman in the course of time.

From the Court, Genji went to the mansion of Sadaijin. Lady Aoi was as cool to him as ever. His persuasive eloquence availed him but little. She was older than Genji by four years, and was as cold and stately in her mien as ever. Her father, however, received him joyfully whenever he called, although he was not always satisfied with the capriciousness of his son-in-law.

The next morning Genji rose early, and was arranging his toilet, with a view of making his New Year's visits, when Sadaijin entered the room, and officiously assisted him in putting on his dress, except, perhaps, his boots. He, moreover, had brought him a belt mounted with rare jewels, and requested him to wear it.

Genji observed: "Such a belt is more suited for some special occasion—such as a Royal banquet, or the like." But Sadaijin insisted on his putting it on, telling him that for that sort of occasion he possessed a much more valuable one.

These New Year's visits were only paid to the Emperor, to the Heir-apparent, and to the Princess Wistaria at her private residence in Sanjiô, where she had retired, but she did not receive him personally. At this time, the Princess was not in her usual state of health, for she was approaching her confinement. Many people, who thought that they might have heard of the event in December, now began to say, "At least we shall receive the intelligence this month," and the Emperor himself became impatient; but the month passed away, and yet it did not happen. In the middle of February, however, she was safely delivered of a Prince. During the following April the child was presented to the Emperor.[73] He was rather big for his age, and had already begun to notice those around him.

In these days much of Genji's time was passed at Nijiô with Violet, and Lady Aoi was still greatly neglected. The circumstances which induced him to stay at home more than ever were these: He would order his carriage to be brought in readiness to take him; but, before it was ready, he would proceed to the western wing, where Violet lived. Perhaps, with eyes drowsy after dozing, and playing on a flute as he went, he would find her moping on one side of the room, like a fair flower moistened with dews. He would then approach her side, and say, "How are you? Are you not well?" She, without being startled, would slowly open her eyes, and murmur: "Sad like the weed in a creek," and then put her hand on her mouth deprecatingly. On this he would remark, "How knowing you are! Where did you learn such things?" He would then call for a *koto*, and saying "The worst of the *soh-koto* is that its middle chord should break so easily," would arrange it for a Hiôjiô tune, and when he had struck a few chords on it, would offer it to her, asking her to play, and would presently accompany her with his flute. They would then play some difficult air, perhaps Hosoroguseri, a very ugly name, but a very lively tune, and she would keep very good time, and display her skill. The lamp would be presently brought in, and they would look over some pictures together. In due time, the carriage would be announced. Perhaps it might be added, "It is coming on to rain." Upon hearing this, she would, perhaps, put her pictures aside, and become downcast. He would then smooth her wavy hair, and say, "Are you sorry when I am not here?" To this question she would indicate her feelings by slightly nodding an affirmative, and she would lean on his knee and begin to doze.

He would then say, "I shall not go out to-night." The servant having brought in supper, would tell her that Genji was not going out that evening. Then she would manifest the greatest delight, and would partake of the supper. And thus it came to pass that he often disappointed one who was expecting him.

The way that Genji neglected his bride gradually became known to the public—nay, to the Emperor himself, who sometimes admonished him, telling him that his father-in-law always took great interest in him and great care from his earliest childhood, and saying that he hoped that he would surely not forget all these benefits, and that it was strange to be unkind to his daughter. But when these remarks were made to Genji, he answered nothing.

Let us now change our subject. The Emperor, though he had already passed the meridian of life, was still fond of the society of the fair sex. And his Court was full of ladies who were well versed in the ways of the world. Some of these would occasionally amuse themselves by paying attentions to Genji. We will here relate the following amusing incident:—

There was at the Court a Naishi-no-Ske, who was already no longer young, and commonly called Gen-Naishi-no-Ske. Both her family and character were good. She was, however, in spite of her age, still coquettish, which was her only fault. Genji often felt amused at her being so young in temperament, and he enjoyed occasionally talking nonsense with her. She used to attend on the Emperor while his hair was being dressed. One day, after he had retired into his dressing-room, she remained in the other room, and was smoothing her own hair. Genji happened to pass by. He stole unperceived into the room, and slyly tugged the skirt of her robe. She started, and instinctively half concealed her face with an old-fashioned fan, and looked back at Genji with an arch glance in her sunken eyes. "What an unsuitable fan for you!" exclaimed Genji, and took it from her hand. It was made of reddish paper, apparently long in use, and upon it an ancient forest had been thickly painted. In a corner was written, in antique style, the following words:—

"On grasses old, 'neath forest trees,No steed will browse or swain delay,However real that grass may be,'Tis neither good for food nor play."

Genji was highly amused. "There are many things one might write on fans," thought he; "what made her think of writing such odd lines as these?"

"Ah!" said Genji, "I see, 'its summer shade is still thick though!'"[74]

While he was joking he felt something like nervousness in thinking what people might say if anyone happened to see him flirting with such an elderly lady. She, on her side, had no such fear. She replied—

"If beneath that forest tree,The steed should come or swain should be,Where that ancient forest grows,Is grass for food, and sweet repose."

"What?" retorted Genji,

"If my steed should venture near,Perhaps he'd find a rival there,Some one's steed full well, I ween,Rejoices in these pastures green."

And quitted the room.

The Emperor, who had been peeping unobserved into it, after he had finished his toilet, laughed heartily to himself at the scene.

Tô-no-Chiûjiô was somehow informed of Genji's fun with this lady, and became anxious to discover how far he meant to carry on the joke. He therefore sought her acquaintance. Genji knew nothing of this. It happened on a cool summer evening that Genji was sauntering round the Ummeiden in the palace yard. He heard the sound of a *biwa* (mandolin) proceeding from a veranda. It was played by this lady. She performed well upon it, for she was often accustomed to play it before the Emperor along with male musicians. It sounded very charming. She was also singing to it the "Melon grower."

"Ah!" thought Genji, "the singing woman in Gakshoo, whom the poet spoke of, may have been like this one," and he stood still and listened. Slowly he approached near the veranda, humming slowly, as he went, "Adzmaya," which she soon noticed, and took up the song, "Do open and come in! but

I do not believe you're in the rain,Nor that you really wish to come in."

Genji at once responded,

"Whose love you may be I know not,But I'll not stand outside your cot,"

and was going away, when he suddenly thought, "This is too abrupt!" and coming back, he entered the apartment.

How great was the joy of Tô-no-Chiûjiô, who had followed Genji unperceived by him, when he saw this. He contrived a plan to frighten him, so he reconnoitred in order to find some favorable opportunity.

The evening breeze blew chill, and Genji it appears was becoming very indifferent. Choosing this moment Tô-no-Chiûjiô slyly stepped forth to the spot where Genji was resting.

Genji soon noticed his footsteps, but he never imagined that it was his brother-in-law. He thought it was Suri-no-Kami, a great friend of the lady. He did not wish to be seen by this man. He reproached her for knowing that he was expected, but that she did not give him any hint. Carrying his Naoshi on his arm, he hid himself behind a folding screen. Tô-no-Chiûjiô, suppressing a laugh, advanced to the side of the screen, and began to fold it from one end to the other, making a crashing noise as he did so. The lady was in a dilemma, and stood aloof. Genji would fain have run out, and concealed himself elsewhere, but he could not get on his Naoshi, and his head-dress was all awry. The Chiûjiô spoke not a word lest he should betray himself, but making a pretended angry expostulation, he drew his sword. All at once the lady threw herself at his feet, crying, "My lord! my lord!" Tô-no-Chiûjiô could scarcely constrain himself from laughing. She was a woman of about fifty seven, but her excitement was more like that of a girl of twenty.

Genji gradually perceived that the man's rage was only simulated, and soon became aware who it was that was there; so he suddenly rushed out, and catching hold of Tô-no-Chiûjiô's sword-arm, pinched it severely. Tô-no-Chiûjiô no longer maintained his disguise, but burst into loud laughter.

"How are you my friend, were you in earnest?" exclaimed Genji, jestingly—"but first let me put on my Naoshi." But Tô-no-Chiûjiô caught it, and tried to prevent him putting it on.

"Then I will have yours," cried Genji, seizing the end of Tô-no-Chiûjiô's sash, and beginning to unfasten it, while the latter resisted. Then they both began to struggle, and their Naoshi soon began to tear.

"Ah," cried Tô-no-Chiûjiô,

"Like   the   Naoshi   to   the   eye,
Your secrets all discovered lie."

"Well," replied Genji,

"This   secret   if   so   well   you   know,
Why am I now disturbed by you?"

And they both quitted the room without much noticing the state of their garments.

Tô-no-Chiûjiô proceeded to his official chamber, and Genji to his own apartment. The sash and other things which they had left behind them were soon afterwards sent to Genji by the lady.

The sash was that of Tô-no-Chiûjiô. Its color was somewhat deeper than his own, and while he was looking at this, he suddenly noticed that one end of a sleeve of his own Naoshi was wanting. "Tô-no-Chiûjiô, I suppose, has carried it off, but I have him also, for here is his sash!" A page boy from Tô-no-Chiûjiô's office hereupon entered, carrying a packet in which the missing sleeve was wrapped, and a message advising Genji to get it mended before all things. "Fancy if I had not got this sash?" thought Genji, as he made the boy take it back to his master in return.

In the morning they were in attendance at Court. They were both serious and solemn in demeanor, as it happened to be a day when there was more official business than on other days; Tô-no-Chiûjiô (who being chief of the Kurand, which office has to receive and despatch official documents) was especially much occupied. Nevertheless they were amused themselves at seeing each other's solemn gravity.

In an interval, when free from duty, Tô-no-Chiûjiô came up to Genji and said, with envious eyes, "Have you not been a little scared in your private expedition?" when Genji replied, "No, why so? there was nothing serious in it; but I do sympathize with one who took so much useless trouble."

They then cautioned each other to be discreet about the matter, which became afterwards a subject for laughter between them.

Now even some Royal Princes would give way to Genji, on account of his father's favor towards him, but Tô-no-Chiûjiô, on the contrary, was always prepared to dispute with him on any subject, and did not yield to him in any way. He was the only brother of the Lady Aoi by the same Royal mother, with an influential State personage for their father, and in his eyes there did not seem to be much difference between himself and Genji.

The incidents of the rivalry between them, therefore, were often very amusing, though we cannot relate them all.

In the month of July the Princess Wistaria was proclaimed Empress. This was done because the Emperor had a notion of abdication in favor of the Heir-apparent and of making the son of the Princess Wistaria the Heir-apparent to the new Emperor, but there was no appropriate guardian or supporter, and all relations on the mother's side were of the Royal blood, and thereby disqualified from taking any active part in political affairs.

For this reason the Emperor wished to make the position of the mother firmer.

The mother of the Heir-apparent, whom this arrangement left still a simple Niogo, was naturally hurt and uneasy at another being proclaimed Empress. Indeed she was the mother of the Heir-apparent, and had been so for more than twenty years. And the public remarked that it was a severe trial for her to be thus superseded by another.

FOOTNOTES:

[71]Kalavinka, the beautifully singing holy birds in Paradise, to whose singing the voice of Buddha is compared.

[72]On New Year's Eve, in Japan, some people fry peas, and throw them about the rooms, saying, "Avaunt, Devil, avaunt! Come in happiness!" This is called driving out devils.

[73]An infant born to the Emperor is presented to him only when it has attained the age of some months.

[74]From an old poem,

"The shade of Ôaraki forest is thick:The summer has come there, the summer has come!"

This is a mere metaphorical pun referring to her still being lively in spite of age.

CHAPTER VIII

FLOWER-FEAST

T owards the end of February the cherry flowers at the front of the Southern Palace were coming into blossom, and a feast was given to celebrate the occasion. The weather was most lovely, and the merry birds were singing their melody to the charms of the scene. All the Royal Princes, nobles and *literati* were assembled, and among them the Emperor made his appearance, accompanied by the Princess Wistaria (now Empress) on the one side, and the Niogo of Kokiden, the mother of the Heir-apparent on the other; the latter having constrained herself to take part with her rival in the *fête*, in spite of her uneasiness at the recent promotion of that rival.

When all the seats were taken the composing[75] of poems, as was the custom, commenced, and they began picking up the rhymes. The turn came in due course to Genji, who picked up the word spring. Next to Genji, Tô-no-Chiûjiô took his.

Many more followed them, including several aged professors, who had often been present on similar occasions, with faces wrinkled by time, and figures bowed by the weight of years. The movements and announcements[76] both of Genji and his brother-in-law were elegant and graceful, as might be expected; but among those who followed there were not a few who showed awkwardness, this being more the case with scholars of ordinary accomplishments, since this was an epoch when the Emperor, the Heir-apparent and others of high distinction were more or less accomplished in these arts.

Meanwhile, they all partook of the feast; the selected musicians joyfully played their parts, and as the sun was setting, "The Spring-lark Sings" (name of a dance) was danced. This reminded those present of Genji's dance at the maple *fête*, and the Heir-apparent pressed him to dance, at the same moment putting on his head a wreath of flowers. Upon this Genji stood up, and waving his sleeves, danced a little. Tô-no-Chiûjiô was next requested by the Emperor to do the same thing, and he danced the "Willow Flower Gardens" most elaborately, and was honored by the Emperor with a present of a roll of silk. After them, many young nobles danced indiscriminately, one after another, but we cannot give an opinion about them as the darkness was already gathering round. Lamps were at length brought, when the reading of the poems took place, and late in the evening all present dispersed.

The palace grounds now became quite tranquil, and over them the moon shone with her soft light.

Genji, his temper mellowed by *saké*, was tempted to take a stroll to see what he could see. He first sauntered round Fuji-Tsubo (the chamber of Wistaria) and came up by the side of the corridor of Kokiden. He noticed a small private door standing open. It seems that the Niogo was in her upper chamber at the Emperor's quarters, having gone there after she retired from the feast. The inner sliding door was also left open, and no human voice was heard from within.

"Such are occasions on which one often compromises one's self," thought he, and yet slowly approached the entrance. Just at that moment he heard a tender voice coming toward him, humming, "Nothing so sweet as the *oboro*[77] moon-night." Genji waited her approach, and caught her by the sleeve. It made her start. "Who are you?" she exclaimed. "Don't be alarmed," he replied, and gently led her back to the corridor. He then added, "Let us look out on the moonlight together." She was, of course, nervous, and would fain have cried out. "Hush," said he; "know that I am one with whom no one will interfere; be gentle, and let us talk a little while." These words convinced her that it was Prince Genji, and calmed her fears.

It appears that he had taken more *saké* than usual, and this made him rather reckless. The girl, on the other hand, was still very young, but she was witty and pleasantly disposed, and spent some time in conversing with him.

He did not yet know who she was, and asked, "Can't you let me know your name? Suppose I wish to write to you hereafter?" But she gave no decided answer; so Genji, after exchanging his fan with hers, left her and quietly returned to his apartments.

Genji's thoughts were now directed to his new acquaintance. He was convinced that she was one of the younger sisters of the Niogo. He knew that one of them was married to a Prince, one of his own relations, and another to his brother-in-law, Tô-no-Chiûjiô. He was perfectly sure that his new acquaintance was not either of these, and he presumed her to be the fifth or sixth of them, but was not sure which of these two.

"How can I ascertain this?" he thought. "If I compromise myself, and her father becomes troublesome, that won't do; but yet I must know."

The fan which he had just acquired was of the color of cherry. On it was a picture representing the pale moon coming out of a purple cloud, throwing a dim light upon the water.

To Genji this was precious. He wrote on one side the following, and kept it carefully, with a longing for the chance of making it useful:—

"The moon I love has left the sky,And where 'tis hid I cannot tell;I search in vain, in vain I tryTo find the spot where it may dwell."

Now, it so happened that on a certain day at the end of March, an archery meeting was to be held at Udaijin's, in which numerous noble youths were to be present, and which was to be succeeded by the Wistaria flower-feast. The height of the flower season was past, but there were two cherry-trees, besides the Wistaria in the gardens, which blossomed later. A new building in the ground, which had been decorated for the occasion of the Mogi[78] of the two Princesses, was being beautifully arranged for this occasion.

Genji also had been told one day at Court by Udaijin that he might join the meeting. When the day came Genji did not arrive early. Udaijin sent by one of his sons the following haughty message to Genji, who was at the time with the Emperor:—

"If the flowers of my home were of every-day hue, Why should they so long a time have tarried for you?"

Genji at once showed this to the Emperor, asking whether he had better go. "Ah!" said the latter, smiling, "This is from a great personage. You had better go, I should think; besides there are the Princesses there."

Thereupon he prepared to go, and made his appearance late in the afternoon.

The party was very pleasant, although the archery-match was almost finished, and several hours were spent in different amusements. As twilight fell around, Genji affected to be influenced by the *saké* he had taken, left the party, and went to that part of the Palace where the Princesses lived. The Wistaria flowers in the gardens could also be seen from this spot, and several ladies were looking out on them.

"I have been too much pressed. Let me take a little quiet shelter here," said Genji, as he joined them. The room was nicely scented with burning perfume. There he saw his two half-sisters and some others with whom he was not acquainted. He was certain that the one he wished to ascertain about was among them, but from the darkness of the advancing evening he was unable to distinguish her. He adopted a device for doing so. He hummed, as he looked vacantly around, the "Ishi-kawa,"[79] but instead of the original line, "My belt being taken," artfully, and in an arch tone, substituted the word "fan" for "belt."

Some were surprised at this change, while others even said, "What a strange Ishi-kawa!" One only said nothing, but looked down, and thus betrayed herself as the one whom he was seeking, and Genji was soon at her side.

FOOTNOTES:

[75]Composing poems in Chinese was a principal part of the feast. The form of it is this, a Court scholar selects in obedience to Imperial command, the subject, and then writes different words on pieces of paper and places them on a table in the gardens, folded up. Two of these are first picked out for the Emperor, and then each one after another, according to precedence, goes to the table, takes one, and these words form their rhymes.

[76]It was also the custom, when each had taken his paper, to read it aloud, and also to announce his particular title or station.

[77]"Oboro" is an adjective meaning calm, and little glaring, and is specially attributed to the moon in spring. The line is from an old ode.

[78]The ceremony of girls putting on a dress marking the commencement of womanhood, corresponding to the Gembuk in the case of boys. These princesses were the daughters of the Niogo of Kokiden. It was the custom that royal children should be brought up at the home of the mother.

[79]Name of a well-known ballad.

CHAPTER IX

HOLLYHOCK

T he Emperor has at last abdicated his throne, as he has long intended, in favor of the Heir-apparent, and the only child of the Princess Wistaria is made Heir-apparent to the new Emperor.

The ex-Emperor now lived in a private palace with this Princess in a less royal style; and the Niogo of Kokiden, to whom was given the honorary title of ex-Empress, resided in the Imperial Palace with the Emperor, her son, and took up a conspicuous position. The ex-Emperor still felt some anxiety about the Heir-apparent, and appointed Genji as his guardian, as he had not yet a suitable person for that office.

This change in the reigning Emperor, and the gradual advancement of Genji's position, gave the latter greater responsibility, and he had to restrain his wandering.

Now, according to usage, the Saigû[80] and Saiin[81] were selected; for the latter the second sister of the Emperor was chosen, and for the former the only daughter of the Lady of Rokjiô, whose husband had been a Royal Prince.

The day of the departure of the Saigû for Ise was not yet fixed; and the mind of her mother, who had some reasons for dissatisfaction with Genji, was still wavering in her indecision, whether or not she should go to Ise with her daughter.

The case of the Saiin, however, was different, and the day of her installation was soon fixed. She was the favorite child of her mother as well as of her father, and the ceremonies for the day of consecration were arranged with especial splendor. The number of persons who take a share in the procession on this occasion is defined by regulations; yet the selection of this number was most carefully made from the most fashionable of the nobles of the time, and their dresses and saddles were all chosen of beautiful appearance. Genji was also directed by special order to take part in the ceremony.

As the occasion was expected to be magnificent, every class of the people showed great eagerness to witness the scene, and a great number of stands were erected all along the road. The day thus looked forward to at last arrived.

Lady Aoi seldom showed herself on such occasions; besides, she was now in a delicate state of health, near her confinement, and had, therefore, no inclination to go out. Her attendants, however, suggested to her that she ought to go. "It is a great pity," they said, "not to see it; people come from a long distance to see it." Her mother also said, "You seem better to-day. I think you had better go. Take these girls with you."

Being pressed in this way, she hastily made up her mind, and went with a train of carriages. All the road was thronged by multitudes of people, many dressed in a style which is called Tsubo-Shôzok. Many of great age prostrated themselves in an attitude of adoration, and many others, notwithstanding their natural plainness, looked almost blooming, from the joy expressed in their countenances—nay, even nuns and aged women, from their retreats, were to be seen amongst them. Numerous carriages were also squeezed closely together, so that the broad thoroughfare of the Ichijiô road was made almost spaceless. When, however, the carriages of the Lady Aoi's party appeared, her attendants ordered several others to make way, and forced a passage to the spot where the best view could be obtained, and where the common people were not allowed. Among these happened to be two *ajiro*[82] carriages, and their inmates were plainly incognito and persons of rank.

These belonged to the party of the Lady of Rokjiô. When these carriages were forced to give place, their attendants cried out, "These carriages do not belong to people who ought to be so abruptly forced away." But the attendants of the Lady Aoi, who were slightly under the influence of drink, would not listen to their expostulations, and they at last made their way and took up their position, pushing the other two back where nothing could be seen, even breaking their poles.

The lady so maltreated was of course extremely indignant, and she would fain have gone home without seeing the spectacle, but there was no passage for retiring. Meanwhile the approach of the procession was announced, and only this calmed her a little.

Genji was as usual conspicuous in the procession. There were several carriages along the roads on whose occupants his glance was cast; that of Lady Aoi, however, was the most striking, and as he passed by the attendants saluted him courteously, which act Genji acknowledged. What were the feelings of the Lady of Rokjiô, who had been driven back, at this moment!

In due course the procession passed, and the exciting scene of the day was over. The quarrels about the carriage naturally came to the ears of Genji. He thought that Lady Aoi was too modest to be the instigator of such a dispute; but her house was one of great and powerful families famous for overweening pride, a tendency shared by its domestics; and they, for other motives, also of rivalry, were glad to have an opportunity of mortifying the Lady of Rokjiô.

He felt for the wounded lady, and hastened to see her; but she, under some pretext, refused to see him.

The day of the hollyhock *fête* of the same temple came. It was especially grand, as it was the first one after the installation of the new Saiin, but neither Lady Aoi or the Lady of Rokjiô was present, while Genji privately took Violet with him in a close carriage to see the festival, and saw the horse-races.

We have already mentioned that the mind of the Lady of Rokjiô was still wavering and unsettled whether or not she should go to Ise with her daughter; and this state of mind became more and more augmented and serious after the day of the dispute about the carriages, which made her feel a bitter disdain and jealousy towards the Lady Aoi. Strange to say, that from about the same time, Lady Aoi became ill, and began to suffer from spiritual influences. All sorts of exorcisms were duly performed, and some spirits came forth and gave their names. But among them was a spirit, apparently a "living one,"[83] which obstinately refused to be transmitted to the third party. It caused her great suffering, and seemed not to be of a casual nature, but a permanent hostile influence. Some imagined this to be the effect of fearful jealousy of some one who was intimately known to Genji and who had most influence over him; but the spirit gave no information to this effect. Hence some even surmised that the wandering spirit of some aged nurse, or the like, long since dead, still haunted the mansion, and might have seized the opportunity of the lady's delicate health, and taken possession of her. Meanwhile at the mansion of Rokjiô, the lady, when she was informed of the sufferings of Lady Aoi, felt somewhat for her, and began to experience a sort of compassion.

This became stronger when she was told that the sufferings of the Lady Aoi were owing to some living spirit. She thought that she never wished any evil to her; but, when she reflected, there were several times when she began to think that a wounded spirit, such as her own, might have some influence of the kind. She had sometimes dreams, after weary thinking, between slumber and waking, in which she seemed to fly to some beautiful girl, apparently Lady Aoi, and to engage in bitter contention and struggle with her. She became even terrified at these dreams; but yet they took place very often. "Even in ordinary matters," she thought, "it is too common a practice, to say nothing of the good done by people, but to exaggerate the bad; and so, in such cases, if it should be rumored that mine was that living spirit which tormented Lady Aoi, how trying it would be to me! It is no rare occurrence that one's disembodied spirit, after death, should wander about; but even that is not a very agreeable idea. How much more, then, must it be disagreeable to have the repute that one's living spirit was inflicting pain upon another!"

These thoughts still preyed upon her mind, and made her listless and depressed.

In due course, the confinement of Lady Aoi approached. At the same time, the jealous spirit still vexed her, and now more vigorous exorcising was employed. She became much affected by it, and cried out, "Please release me a little; I have something to tell the Prince."

Hereupon he was ushered into the room. The curtain was dropped, and the mother of the lady left the room, as she thought her daughter might prefer to speak to him in private. The sound of the spells performed in the next chamber ceased, and Hoke-kiô was read in its place. The lady was lying on her couch, dressed in a pure white garment, with her long tresses unfastened. He approached her, and taking her hand, said: "What sad affliction you cause us!" She then lifted her heavy eyelids, and gazed on Genji for some minutes.

He tried to soothe her, and said, "Pray don't trouble yourself too much about matters. Everything will come right. Your illness, I think, will soon pass away. Even supposing you quit this present world, there is another where we shall meet, and where I shall see you once more cheerful, and there will be a time when your mother and father will also join you."

"Ah! no. I only come here to solicit you to give me a little rest. I feel extremely disturbed. I never thought of coming here in such a way; but it seems the spirit of one whose thoughts are much disconcerted wanders away unknown even to itself.

Oh, bind my wandering spirit, pray,Dear one, nor let it longer stray."

The enunciation of these words was not that of Lady Aoi herself; and when Genji came to reflect, it clearly belonged to the Lady of Rokjiô. Always before, when anyone had talked with him about a living spirit coming to vex Lady Aoi, he felt inclined to suppress such ideas; but now he began to think that such things might really happen, and he felt disturbed. "You speak thus," said Genji, as if he was addressing the spirit, "but you do not tell me who you are. Do, therefore, tell me clearly." At these words, strange to say, the face of the Lady Aoi seemed momentarily to assume the likeness of that of Rokjiô. On this, Genji was still more perplexed and anxious, and put a stop to the colloquy. Presently she became very calm, and people thought that she was a little relieved. Soon after this, the lady was safely delivered of a child.

Now, to perform due thanksgiving for this happy deliverance, the head of the monastery on Mount Hiye and some other distinguished priests were sent for. They came in all haste, wiping off the perspiration from their faces as they journeyed; and, from the Emperor and Royal princes down to the ordinary nobles, all took an interest in the ceremony of Ub-yashinai (first feeding), and the more so as the child was a boy.

To return to the Lady of Rokjiô. When she heard of the safe delivery of Lady Aoi, a slightly jealous feeling once more seemed to vex her; and when she began to move about, she could not understand how it was, but she perceived that her dress was scented with a strange odor.[84] She thought this most surprising, and took baths and changed her dress, in order to get rid of it; but the odor soon returned, and she was disgusted with herself.

Some days passed, and the day of autumn appointments arrived. By this time, Lady Aoi's health seemed progressing favorably, and Genji left her in order to attend the Court.

When he said good-by to her, there was a strange and unusual look in her eyes. Sadaijin also went to Court, as well as his sons, who had some expectation of promotion, and there were few people left in the mansion.

It was in the evening of that day that Lady Aoi was suddenly attacked by a spasm, and before the news of this could be carried to the Court, she died.

These sad tidings soon reached the Court, and created great distress and confusion: even the arrangements for appointments and promotion were disturbed. As it happened late in the evening there was no time to send for the head of the monastery, or any other distinguished priest. Messengers of inquiry came one after another to the mansion, so numerous that it was almost impossible to return them all answers. We need not add how greatly affected were all her relations.

As the death took place from a malign spiritual influence, she was left untouched during two or three days, in the hope that she might revive; but no change took place, and now all hope was abandoned. In due course the corpse was taken to the cemetery of Toribeno. Numerous mourners and priests of different churches crowded to the spot, while representatives of the ex-Emperor, Princess Wistaria, and the Heir-apparent also were present. The ceremony of burial was performed with all solemnity and pathos.

Thus the modest and virtuous Lady Aoi passed away forever.

Genji forthwith confined himself to his apartment in the grand mansion of Sadaijin, for mourning and consolation. Tô-no-Chiûjiô, who was now elevated to the title of Sammi, constantly bore him company, and conversed with him both on serious and amusing subjects. Their struggle in the apartment of Gen-naishi, and also their rencontre in the garden of the "Saffron Flower," were among the topics of their consoling conversation.

It was on one of these occasions that a soft shower of rain was falling. The evening was rendered cheerless, and Tô-no-Chiûjiô came to see him, walking slowly in his mourning robes of a dull color. Genji was leaning out of a window, his cheek resting on his hand; and, looking out upon the half-fading shrubberies, was humming—

"Has she become rain or cloud?'Tis now unknown."

Tô-no-Chiûjiô gently approached him. They had, as usual, some pathetic conversation, and then the latter hummed, as if to himself—

"Beyond the cloud in yonder sky,From which descends the passing rain,Her gentle soul may dwell,Though we may cease to trace its form in vain."

This was soon responded to by Genji:—

"That cloudy shrine we view on high,Where my lost love may dwell unseen,Looks gloomy now to this sad eyeThat looks with tears on what has been."

There was among the faded plants of the garden a solitary Rindô-nadeshko.[85] When Tô-no-Chiûjiô had gone, Genji picked this flower, and sent it to his mother-in-law by the nurse of the infant child, with the following:—

"In bowers where all beside are deadSurvives alone this lovely flower,Departed autumn's cherished gem,Symbol of joy's departed hour."[86]

Genji still felt lonely. He wrote a letter to the Princess Momo-zono (peach-gardens). He had known her long. He admired her, too. She had been a spectator, with her father, on the day of the consecration of the Saiin, and was one of those to whom the appearance of Genji was most welcome. In his letter he stated that she might have a little sympathy with him in his sorrow, and he also sent with it the following:—

"Many an autumn have I pastIn gloomy thought, but none I weenHas been so mournful as the last,Which rife with grief and change hath been."

There was, indeed, nothing serious between Genji and this princess; yet, as far as correspondence was concerned, they now and then exchanged letters, so she did not object to receiving this communication. She felt for him much, and an answer was returned, in which she expressed her sympathy at his bereavement.

Now, in the mansion of Sadaijin every performance of requiem was celebrated. The forty-ninth day had passed, and the mementoes of the dead, both trifling and valuable, were distributed in a due and agreeable manner; and Genji at length left the grand mansion with the intention of first going to the ex-Emperor, and then of returning to his mansion at Nijiô. After his departure, Sadaijin went into the apartment occupied till lately by him. The room was the same as before, and everything was unchanged; but his only daughter, the pride of his old days, was no more, and his son-in-law had gone too.

He looked around him for some moments. He saw some papers lying about. They were those on which Genji had been practising penmanship for amusement—some in Chinese, others in Japanese; some in free style, others in stiff. Among these papers he saw one on which the words "Old pillows and old quilts" were written, and close to these the following:—

"How much the soul departed, stillMay love to linger round this couch,My own heart tells me, even IReluctant am to leave it now."

And on another of these papers, accompanying the words, "The white frost lies upon the tiles," the following:—

"How many more of nights shall IOn this lone bed without thee lie;The flower has left its well-known bed,And o'er its place the dews are shed."

As Sadaijin was turning over these papers a withered flower, which seems to have marked some particular occasion, dropped from amongst them.

Return we now to Genji. He went to the ex-Emperor, to whom he still seemed thin and careworn. He had some affectionate conversation with him, remained till evening, and then proceeded to his mansion at Nijiô. He went to the western wing to visit the young Violet. All were habited in new winter apparel, and looked fresh and blooming.

"How long it seems since I saw you!" he exclaimed. Violet turned her glance a little aside. She was apparently shy, which only increased her beauty.

He approached, and after having a little conversation, said, "I have many things to say to you, but now I must have a little rest," and returned to his own quarters.

The next morning, first of all he sent a letter to Sadaijin's, making inquiry after his infant child.

At this time he confined himself more than usual to his own house, and for companionship he was constantly with Violet, who was now approaching womanhood. He would sometimes talk with her differently from the manner in which he would speak to a mere girl; but on her part she seemed not to notice the difference, and for their daily amusement either Go or Hentski[87] was resorted to, and sometimes they would play on till late in the evening.

Some weeks thus passed away, and there was one morning when Violet did not appear so early as usual. The inmates of the house, who did not know what was the reason, were anxious about her, thinking she was indisposed. About noon Genji came. He entered the little room, saying, "Are you not quite well? Perhaps you would like to play at Go again, like last night, for a change;" but she was more than ever shy.

"Why are you so shy?" he exclaimed; "be a little more cheerful—people may think it strange," said he, and stayed with her a long time trying to soothe her; but to no effect—she still continued silent and shy.

This was the evening of Wild Boar's day, and some *mochi* (pounded rice cake) was presented to him, according to custom, on a tray of plain white wood.

He called Koremitz before him and said, "To-day is not a very opportune day; I would rather have them to-morrow evening. Do send in some to-morrow.[88] It need not be of so many colors." So saying, he smiled a little, and sharp Koremitz soon understood what he meant. And this he accordingly did on the morrow, on a beautiful flower-waiter.

Up to this time nothing about Violet had been publicly known, and Genji thought it was time to inform her father about his daughter; but he considered he had better have the ceremony of Mogi first performed, and ordered preparations to be made with that object.

Let us here notice that the young daughter of Udaijin, after she saw Genji, was longing to see him again. This inclination was perceived by her relations. It seems that her father was not quite averse to this liking, and he told his eldest daughter, the reigning Emperor's mother, that Genji was recently bereaved of his good consort, and that he should not feel discontented if his daughter were to take the place of Lady Aoi; but this the royal mother did not approve. "It would be far better for her to be introduced at Court," she said, and began contriving to bring this about.

FOOTNOTES:

[80]The sacred virgin of the temple of Ise.

[81]The same of Kamo, which is situated in the neighborhood of Kiôto, the then capital.

[82]"Ajiro" means woven bamboo, and here it signifies a carriage made of woven bamboo.

[83]Before proceeding with the story, it is necessary for the reader to peruse the following note: In Japan there existed, and still more or less exists, a certain superstition which is entertained, that the spirits of the dead have the power of inflicting injury on mankind; for instance, a woman when slighted or deserted, dies, her spirit often works evil on the man who forsook her, or on her rival. This is the spirit of the dead. There is also another belief that the spirits of the living have sometimes the same power, but in this case it only takes place when one is fiercely jealous. When this spirit works upon the rival, the owner of the spirit is not aware of it; but she herself becomes more gloomy, as if she had, as it were, lost her own spirit. These spirits can be exorcised, and the act is performed by a certain sect of priests; but the living one is considered far more difficult to exorcise than the other, because it is imagined that the dead spirit can be easily "laid," or driven back to the tomb, while the living one, being still in its present state, cannot be settled so easily. The method of exorcism is as follows: Certain spells are used on the sufferer, and certain religious addresses are read from the Buddhist bibles, and then the sufferer is made to speak out all his subjects of complaint; but it is supposed not to be the man himself who speaks and tells these causes of complaint, but the spirit of which he is possessed. This process is sometimes performed on a third party; in that case the priest temporarily transmits the spirit from the sufferer to the substitute and makes it speak with his

mouth. When he has told all the causes of his complaint and wrongs, the priest sometimes argues with him, sometimes chides, sometimes soothes, and sometimes threatens, and at last says to the spirit, "If you do not go out quietly, I will confine you by my sacred power." By such means the spirit is exorcised; the process resembles mesmerism in some points, but of course has no sensible foundation. In other cases the spirits of those who have either recently, or even years before, met with cruel wrongs or death, may in their wanderings seize upon some person in the vicinity, though totally unconnected with the crime done upon them, and may cause them suffering, or even spirits, who from any cause, are unable to obtain rest, may do the same thing.

[84]In the ceremony of exorcism a sacred perfume is burnt, and it was this scent which the Lady of Rokjiô perceived in her garment because her spirit was supposed to go to and fro between herself and Lady Aoi, and to bring with it the smell of this perfume.

[85]A kind of pink; some translate it Gentian.

[86]Here the flower is compared to the child, and autumn to the mother.

[87]"Hentski," a children's game. It consists in choosing beforehand a "hen" or half-character, opening a book and seeing which of the players can most quickly pick out the words beginning with this "hen."

[88]It seemed to have been the ancient custom, that on the third night of a wedding, the same kind of rice cake, but only of one color, was served up.

CHAPTER X

DIVINE TREE

The departure of the Saigû, the daughter of the Lady of Rokjiô, for her destination in the Temple of Ise, which was postponed from time to time, owing to different circumstances, was at length arranged to take place in September. This definite arrangement delighted the Saigû, to whom the uncertainty of the event had been somewhat tiresome. Her mother also made up her mind to accompany her to the temple. Although there was no precedent for the mother of the Saigû accompanying her daughter, this lady made up her mind to do so, because she would not allow her young daughter to go alone.

In a suburban field the "field palace" was built.[89] It was of wood, and surrounded by a fence of newly cut branches of trees. In front stood a huge *torii*[90] of logs, and within the compound were the quarters of the Kandzkasa.[91] Here the Saigû took up her residence, where her mother also accompanied her. When the sixteenth of September, which was fixed for the departure, arrived, the ceremony of her last consecration was duly performed on the banks of the River Katzra, whence the sacred virgin went to the Imperial Palace to have the farewell audience with the Emperor. She was accompanied by her mother. The father of the latter had been a great personage of State, and she had been married to a Royal Prince at sixteen, when there had been every possibility of her coming to the Court in a position far superior to what she now enjoyed. She was, however, bereaved of him at the age of twenty; and now at thirty she comes to take leave at her departure for a far-off province with her only daughter. The Saigû was about fourteen years of age, was extremely delicate and fair to look upon, and when presented to the Emperor he was struck by the charms of her youthful appearance.

Numerous carriages were ranged at the front of eight State departments to see her off in state, besides many others along the road, full of spectators.

Late in the afternoon her party left the palace, and turned away from Nijiô round to the highway of Tôin, and passed by the mansion of Genji, who witnessed their passing, and sent the following to the lady-mother with a twig of Sakaki (divine tree):—

"Bravely you quit this scene, 'tis true;But though you dauntless fly so far,Your sleeve may yet be wet with dew,Before you cross Suzukah."[92]

The answer to this was sent to him from beyond the barrier of Ausaka (meeting-path) in the following form:—

"Whether my sleeve be wet or not,In the waters of the Suzukah,Who will care? Too soon forgotWill Ise be that lies so far."

And thus the Lady of Rokjiô and her daughter disappear for some time from our scenes in the capital.

It was about this time that the ex-Emperor was indisposed for some time, and in October his state became precarious. The anxiety of the public was general, and the Emperor went to visit him. Notwithstanding his weakness, the former gave him every injunction, first about the Heir-apparent, then about Genji, and said:—

"Regard him as your adviser, both in large and small matters, without reserve, and not otherwise than if I were still alive. He is not incapable of sharing in the administration of public affairs, notwithstanding his youth. He has a physiognomy which argues great qualities, and for this reason, I made him remain in an ordinary position, without creating him a Royal Prince, with the object that he should be able to take part in public affairs. Do not misconstrue these ideas."

There were some more injunctions given of like nature relating to public matters, and the Emperor sorrowfully and repeatedly assured him that he would not neglect them. Such, however, are not subjects which we women are supposed to understand, and even thus much that I have mentioned is given not without some apprehension.

A few days after the visit of the Emperor the Heir-apparent was brought before his dying father. There had been some idea that he should be brought on the day when the Emperor paid his visit, but it was postponed to avoid any possible confusion. The boy Prince was apparently more pleased at seeing his father than concerned at his illness. To him the ex-Emperor told many things, but he was too young to heed them. Genji was also present, and the ex-Emperor explained to him in what way he should serve the Government, and how he should look after this young Prince. When their interview concluded it was already merging towards the evening, and the young Prince returned to the palace.

The Royal mother of the reigning Emperor (formerly Koki-den-Niogo) would also have visited the ex-Emperor but for her repugnance to encounter the Princess Wistaria, who never left his side.

In the course of a few days the strength of the Emperor began to decline, and at last he quietly and peacefully passed away.

And now the Court went into general mourning, and Genji, being one of the principal mourners, put on a dress of Wistaria cloth;[93] so frequently did misfortune fall on him in the course of a few years, and his cares became really great.

The funeral and the weekly requiems were performed with all due pomp and ceremony, and when the forty-ninth day had passed, all the private household of his late Majesty dispersed in the midst of the dreary weather of the latter part of December to their own homes; the Princess Wistaria retiring to her own residence in Sanjiô, accompanied by her brother, Prince Hiôbkiô.

True, it is that his late Majesty had been for some time off the throne, but his authority had by no means diminished on that account. But his death now altered the state of things, and the ascendancy of the family of Udaijin became assured. The people in general entertained great fear that infelicitous changes would take place in public affairs, and among these Genji and the Princess Wistaria were the most disturbed by such anxieties.

The new year came in, but nothing joyful or exciting accompanied its presence—the world was still.

Genji kept himself to his mansion. In those days, when his father was still in power, his courtyard was filled with the carriages of visitors, especially when the days of the appointments were approaching; but now this was changed, and his household secretaries had but little to occupy them.

In January the Princess Momo-zono (peach-gardens) was chosen for the Saiin, of the Temple of Kamo, her predecessor having retired from office, on account of the mourning for her father, the late ex-Emperor.

There were not many precedents for Princesses of the second generation being appointed to this position; but this Princess was so chosen, owing, it seems, to the circumstance that there was no immediate issue of the Imperial blood suitable for this office.

In February the youngest daughter of the Udaijin became the Naishi-no-Kami,[94] in the place of the former one, who had left office and become a nun after the death of the ex-Emperor.

She took up her residence in the Kokiden, which was till lately occupied by her sister, the Empress-mother, who at this period spent most of her time at her father's, and who when she came to the Court made the Ume-Tsubo (the plum-chamber) her apartment.

Meanwhile the Empress-mother, who was by nature sagacious and revengeful, and who during the late Emperor's life had been fain to disguise her spiteful feelings, now conceived designs of vengeance against those who had been adverse to her; and this spirit was directed especially against Genji and his father-in-law, Sadaijin— against the latter because he had married his only daughter to Genji against the wishes of the Emperor when Heir-apparent, and because during the life of the late Emperor his influence eclipsed that of her father, Udaijin, who had long been his political adversary.

The Emperor, it is true, never forgot the dying injunctions of his father, and never failed in sympathy with Genji; but he was still young, with a weak mind, and therefore he was under the influence of his mother and grandfather, Udaijin, and was often constrained by them in his actions to go contrary to his own wishes.

Such being the state of things, Sadaijin seldom appeared at Court, and his loss of influence became manifest. Genji, too, had become less adventurous and more steady in his life; and in his mansion Violet became the favorite object of attraction, in whose behalf the ceremony of Mogi had been duly performed some time before, and who had been presented to her father. The latter had for a long time regarded her as lost, and even now he never forgave the way in which his daughter had been taken away by Genji.

The summer had passed without any particular events, and autumn arrived. Genji, wishing to have a little change, went to the monastery of Unlinin,[95] and spent some days in the chamber of a rissh (discipline-master), who was a brother of his mother. Maple-trees were changing their tints, and the beautiful scenery around this spot made him almost forget his home. His daily amusement was to gather together several monks, and make them discuss before him.

He himself perused the so-called "sixty volumes,"[96] and would get the monks to explain any point which was not clear to his understanding.

When he came to reflect on the various circumstances taking place in the capital, he would have preferred remaining in his present retirement; but he could not forget one whom he had left behind there, and this caused him to return. After he had requested a splendid expiatory service to be performed, he left the monastery. The monks and the neighbors came to see him depart. His carriage was still black, and his sleeves were still of Wistaria, and in this gloomy state he made his return to his mansion in Nijiô.

He brought back some twigs of maple, whose hues, when compared with those in his own garden, he perceived were far more beautiful. He, therefore, sent one of these to the residence of Princess Wistaria, who had it put in a vase, and hung at the side of her veranda.

Next day he went to the Imperial Palace, to see his brother the Emperor, who was passing a quiet and unoccupied leisure, and soon entered into a pleasant conversation on matters both past and present. This Emperor, it must be remembered, was a person of quiet ways and moderate ambition. He was kind in heart, and affectionate to his relatives. His eyes were shut to the more objectionable actions of Genji. He talked with him on different topics of literature, and asked his opinions on different questions. He also talked on several poetical subjects, and on the news of the day—of the departure of the Saigû.

The conversation then led to the little Prince, the Heir-apparent. The Emperor said, "Our father has enjoined me to adopt him as my son, and to be kind to him in every way; but he was always a favorite of mine, and this injunction was unnecessary, for I could not be any more particularly kind to him. I am very glad that he is very clever for his age in penmanship and the like."

Genji replied, "Yes, I also notice that he is of no ordinary promise; but yet we must admit that his ability may be only partial."

After this conversation Genji left. On his way he came across a nephew of the Empress-mother, who seems to have been a person of rather arrogant and rough character. As he crossed Genji's path he stopped for a minute, and loudly reciting,

"The white rainbow crossed the sun, And the Prince was frightened,"[97]

passed on. Genji at once understood what it was intended for, but prudently proceeded on his way homeward without taking any notice of it.

Let us now proceed to the Princess Wistaria. Since she had been bereaved of the late Emperor she retired to her private residence. She fully participated in all those inglorious mortifications to which Genji and his father-in-law were subjected. She was convinced she would never suffer such cruel treatment as that which Seki-Foojin[98] did at the hands of her rival, but she was also convinced that some sort of misfortune was inevitable. These thoughts at last led her to determine to give up the world. The fortune of her child, however, had been long a subject of anxiety to her; and though she had determined to do so, the thought of him had affected her mind still more keenly. She had hitherto rarely visited the Court, where he was residing; for her visits might be unpleasing to the feelings of her rival, the other ex-Empress, and prejudicial to his interests.

However, she now went there unceremoniously, in order to see him before she carried out her intention to retire. In the course of her chatting with him, she said, "Suppose, that while I do not see you for some time, my features become changed, what would you think?"

The little Prince, who watched her face, replied, "Like Shikib?[99]—no—that can't be." The Princess smiled a little, and said, "No, that is not so; Shikib's is changed by age, but suppose mine were different from hers, and my hair became shorter than hers, and I wore a black dress like a chaplain-in-waiting, and I could not see you often, any longer." And she became a little sad, which made the Prince also a little downcast.

Serene was his face, and finely pencilled were his eyebrows. He was growing up fast, and his teeth were a little decayed and blackened,[100] which gave a peculiar beauty to his smile, and the prettiness of his appearance only served to increase her regret; and with a profound pensiveness she returned to her residence.

In the middle of December she performed Mihakkô (a grand special service on the anniversary of death), which she was carefully preparing for some days. The rolls of the Kiô (Buddhist Bible) used for this occasion were made most magnificently—the spindle of jade, the covering of rich satin, and its case of woven bamboo ornamented likewise, as well as the flower-table.

The first day's ceremony was for her father, the second for her mother, and the third for the late Emperor. Several nobles were present, and participated, Genji being one of them. Different presents were made by them all. At the end of the third day's performance her vows of retirement were, to the surprise of all, announced by the priest. At the conclusion of the whole ceremony, the chief of the Hiye monastery, whom she had sent for, arrived, and from whom she received the "commandments." She then had her hair cut off by her uncle, Bishop of Yokogawa.

These proceedings cast a gloom over the minds of all present, but especially on those of Hiôb-Kiô, her brother, and Genji; and soon after every one departed for his home.

Another New Year came in, and the aspect of the Court was brighter. A royal banquet and singing dances were soon expected to take place, but the Princess Wistaria no longer took any heed of them, and most of her time was devoted to prayer in a new private chapel, which she had had built expressly for herself in her grounds.

Genji came to pay his New Year's visit on the seventh day, but he saw no signs of the season. All nobles who used to pay visits of felicitation, now shunned her house and gathered at the mansion of Udaijin, near her own. The only things which caught Genji's attention in her mansion was a white horse,[101] which was being submitted to her inspection as on former occasions. When he entered, he noticed that all the hangings of the room and the dresses of the inmates were of the dark hues of conventual life. The only things that there seemed to herald spring, were the melting of the thin ice on the surface of the lake, and the budding of the willows on its banks. The scene suggested many reflections to his mind; and, after the usual greetings of the season, and a short conversation, he quitted the mansion.

It should be here noticed that none of her household officers received any promotion or appointment to any sinecure office, or honorary title, even where the merit of the individual deserved it, or the Court etiquette required it. Nay, even the proper income for her household expenses was, under different pretexts, neglected. As for the Princess, she must have been prepared for such inevitable consequences of her giving up the world; but it ought not to be taken as implying that the sacrifice should be so great. Hence these facts caused much disappointment to her household, and the mind of the Princess herself was sometimes moved by feelings of mortification. Nevertheless, troubled about herself no longer, she only studied the welfare and prosperity of her child, and persevered in the most devout prayers for this. She also remembered a secret sin, still unknown to the world, which tormented the recesses of her soul, and she was constantly praying to Buddha to lighten her burden.

About the same time, tired of the world, both public and private, Sadaijin sent in his resignation. The Emperor had not forgotten how much he was respected by the late ex-Emperor, how the latter had enjoined him always to regard him as a support of the country, and he several times refused to accept his resignation; but Sadaijin persevered in his request, and confined himself to his own mansion. This gave complete ascendancy to the family of Udaijin. All the sons of Sadaijin, who formerly had enjoyed considerable distinction at Court, were now fast sinking into insignificance, and had very little influence. Tô-no-Chiûjiô, the eldest of them, was one of those affected by the change of circumstances. True, he was married to the fourth daughter of Udaijin; but he passed little time with her, she still residing with her father, and he was not among the favorite sons-in-law. His name was also omitted in the appointment list on promotion day, which seems to have been intended by his father-in-law as a warning.

Under such circumstances he was constantly with Genji, and they studied and played together. They both well remembered how they used to compete with each other in such matters as studying and playing, and they still kept their rivalry alive. They would sometimes send for some scholars, and would compose poems together, or play the "Covering Rhymes."[102] They seldom appeared at Court, while in the outer world different scandals about them were increasing day by day.

One day in summer Tô-no-Chiûjiô came to pay his usual visit to Genji. He had brought by his page several interesting books, and Genji also ordered several rare books from his library. Many scholars were sent for, in such a manner as not to appear too particular; and many nobles and University students were also present. They were divided into two parties, the right and the left, and began betting on the game of "Covering Rhymes." Genji headed the right, and Tô-no-Chiûjiô the left. To his credit the former often hit on the most difficult rhymes, with which the scholars were puzzled. At last the left was beaten by the right, consequently Tô-no-Chiûjiô gave an entertainment to the party, as arranged in their bet.

They also amused themselves by writing prose and verse. Some roses were blossoming in front of the veranda, which possessed a quiet charm different from those of the full season of spring.

The sight of these afforded them a delightful enjoyment while they were partaking of refreshment. A son of Tô-no-Chiûjiô, about eight or nine years old, was present. He was the second boy by his wife, Udaijin's daughter, and a tolerable player on the Sôh-flute. Both his countenance and disposition were amiable. The party was in full enjoyment when the boy rose and sang "Takasago" (high sand).[103] When he proceeded to the last clause of his song,

"Oh, could I see that lovely flower,That blossomed this morn!"

Tô-no-Chiûjiô offered his cup to Genji, saying,

"How glad am I to see your gentleness,Sweet as the newly blooming flower!"

Genji, smiling, took the cup as he replied,

"Yet that untimely flower, I fear,The rain will beat, the wind will tear,Ere it be fully blown."

And added,

"Oh, I myself am but a sere leaf."

Genji was pressed by Tô-no-Chiûjiô to take several more cups, and his humor reached its height. Many poems, both in Chinese and Japanese, were composed by those present, most of whom paid high compliment to Genji. He felt proud, and unconsciously exclaimed, "The son of King Yuen, the brother of King Mu;" and would have added, "the King Ching's ----"[104] but there he paused.

To describe the scene which followed at a time such as this, when every mind is not in due equilibrium, is against the warning of Tsurayuki, the poet, so I will here pass over the rest.

Naishi-no-Kami, the young daughter of Udaijin, now retired to her home from the Court, having been attacked by ague; and the object of her retirement was to enjoy rest and repose, as well as to have spells performed for her illness.

This change did her great good, and she speedily recovered from the attack.

We had mentioned before that she always had a tender yearning for Genji, and she was the only one of her family who entertained any sympathy or good feeling towards him. She had seen, for some time, the lack of consideration and the indifference with which he was treated by her friends, and used to send messages of kind inquiry. Genji, on his part also, had never forgotten her, and the sympathy which she showed towards him excited in his heart the most lively appreciation.

These mutual feelings led at length to making appointments for meeting during her retirement. Genji ran the risk of visiting her secretly in her own apartments. This was really hazardous, more especially so because her sister, the Empress-mother, was at this time staying in the same mansion. We cannot regard either the lady or Genji as entirely free from the charge of imprudence, which, on his part, was principally the result of his old habits of wandering.

It was on a summer's evening that Genji contrived to see her in her own apartment, and while they were conversing, a thunderstorm suddenly broke forth, and all the inmates got up and ran to and fro in their excitement. Genji had lost the opportunity of escape, and, besides, the dawn had already broken.

When the storm became lighter and the thunder ceased, Udaijin went first to the room of his royal daughter, and then to that of Naishi-no-Kami. The noise of the falling rain made his footsteps inaudible, and all unexpectedly he appeared at the door and said: "What a storm it has been! Were you not frightened?"

This voice startled both Genji and the lady. The former hid himself on one side of the room, and the latter stepped forth to meet her father. Her face was deeply flushed, which he soon noticed. He said, "You seem still excited; is your illness not yet quite passed?" While he was so saying he caught sight of the sash of a man's cloak, twisted round her skirt.

"How strange!" thought he. The next moment he noticed some papers lying about, on which something had been scribbled. "This is more strange!" he thought again; and exclaimed, "Whose writings are these?" At this request she looked aside, and all at once noticed the sash round her skirt, and became quite confused. Udaijin was a man of quiet nature; so, without distressing her further, bent down to pick up the papers, when by so doing he perceived a man behind the screen, who was apparently in great confusion and was endeavoring to hide his face. However, Udaijin soon discovered who he was, and without any further remarks quitted the room, taking the papers with him.

The troubled state of Genji and the lady may be easily imagined, and in great anxiety he left the scene.

Now it was the character of Udaijin that he could never keep anything to himself, even his thoughts. He therefore went to the eldest daughter—that is, the Empress-mother, and told her that he had found papers which clearly were in the handwriting of Genji, and that though venturesomeness is the characteristic of men, such conduct as that which Genji had indulged in was against all propriety. "People said," continued Udaijin, "that he was always carrying on a correspondence with the present Saiin. Were this true, it would not only be against public decorum, but his own interest; although I did not entertain any suspicion before."

When the sagacious Empress-mother heard this, her anger was something fearful. "See the Emperor," she said; "though he is Emperor, how little he is respected! When he was Heir-apparent, the ex-Sadaijin, not having presented his daughter to him, gave her to Genji, then a mere boy, on the eve of his Gembuk; and now this Genji boldly dares to carry on such intrigues with a lady who is intended to be the Royal consort! How daring, also, is his correspondence with the sacred Saiin! On the whole, his conduct, in every respect, does not appear to be as loyal as might be expected, and this only seems to arise from his looking forward to the ascent of the young Prince to the throne."

Udaijin somehow felt the undesirability of this anger, and he began to change his tone, and tried to soothe her, saying: "You have some reason for being so affected; yet don't disclose such matters to the public, and pray don't tell it to the Emperor. It is, of course, an impropriety on the part of the Prince, but we must admit that our girl, also, would not escape censure. We had better first warn her privately among ourselves; and if the matter does not even then come all right, I will myself be responsible for that."

The Empress-mother, however, could not calm her angry feelings. It struck her as a great disrespect to her dignity, on Genji's part, to venture to intrude into the very mansion where she was staying. And she began to meditate how to turn this incident into a means of carrying out the design which she had been forming for some time.

FOOTNOTES:

[89]A temporary residence expressly built for the Saigû to undergo purification.

[90]A peculiar gate erected in front of the sacred places.

[91]Shinto priests.

[92]Name of a river of the province of Ise, which the travellers had to cross.

[93]A dress made of the bark of the Wistaria was worn by those who were in deep mourning for near relatives.

[94]This was an office held by a Court lady, whose duty it was to act as a medium of communication in the transmitting of messages between the Emperor and State officials.

[95]It is said that the tomb of the authoress of this work is to be found at this spot.

[96]In the Tendai sect of Buddhists there are sixty volumes of the theological writings which are considered most authoritative for their doctrine.

[97]A passage of a Chinese history. The story is, that a Prince of a certain Chinese kingdom contrived to have assassinated an Emperor, his enemy. When he sent off the assassin this event took place. The allusion here seems to imply the allegation that Genji intended high treason.

[98]She was the favorite of the first Emperor of the Hung dynasty in China, and the rival of the Empress. When the Emperor died, the Empress, a clever and disdainful woman, revenged herself by cutting off her feet, and her arms, and making away with her son.

[99]This seems to have been the name of an aged attendant.

[100]Among Japanese children it often happens that the milk teeth become black and decayed, which often gives a charm to their expression.

[101]It was the custom to show a white horse on the seventh day of the new year to the Empress, the superstition being that this was a protestation against evil spirits.

[102]A game consisting in opening Chinese poetry books and covering the rhymes, making others guess them.

[103]Name of a ballad.

[104]In Chinese history it is recorded that in giving an injunction to his son, Duke Choau, a great statesman of the eleventh century b.c., used these words: "I am the son of King Yuen, the brother of King Mu, and the uncle of King Ching; but I am so ready in receiving men in any way distinguished, that I am often interrupted three times at my dinner, or in my bath." It would seem that Genji, in the pride of his feeling, unconsciously made the above quotation in reference to himself.

CHAPTER XI

VILLA OF FALLING FLOWERS

The troubles of Genji increased day by day, and the world became irksome to him. One incident, however, deserves a brief notice before we enter into the main consequences of these troubles.

There was a lady who had been a Niogo at the Court of the late ex-Emperor, and who was called Reikeiden-Niogo, from the name of her chamber. She had borne no child to him, and after his death she, together with a younger sister, was living in straitened circumstances. Genji had long known both of them, and they were often aided by the liberality with which he cheerfully assisted them, both from feelings of friendship, and out of respect to his late father.

He, at this time, kept himself quiet at his own home, but he now paid these ladies a visit one evening, when the weather, after a long-continued rain, had cleared up. He conversed with them on topics of past times until late in the evening. The waning moon threw her faint light over the tall trees standing in the garden, which spread their dark shadows over the ground. From among them an orange-tree in full blossom poured forth its sweet perfume, and a Hototo-gisu[105] flew over it singing most enchantingly.

"'Ah! how he recollects his own friend!'" said Genji, and continued:—

"To this home of 'falling flower,'The odors bring thee back again,And now thou sing'st, in evening hour,Thy faithful loving strain."

To this the elder lady replied:—

"At the home where one lives, all sadly alone,And the shadow of friendship but seldom is cast,These blossoms reach the bright days that are goneAnd bring to our sadness the joys of the past."

And, after a long and friendly conversation, Genji returned to his home. One may say that the character of Genji was changeable, it is true, yet we must do him justice for his kind-heartedness to his old acquaintances such as these two sisters, and this would appear to be the reason why he seldom estranged the hearts of those whom he liked.

FOOTNOTES:

[105]The name of a small bird which appears about the time when the orange trees are in blossom. It sings, and is most active in the evening. In poetry, therefore, the orange blossom and this bird are associated, and they are both, the blossom and the bird, emblems of old memories.

CHAPTER XII

EXILE AT SUMA

Genji at last made up his mind to undergo a voluntary exile, before the opinion of the Imperial Court should be publicly announced against him. He heard that the beautiful sea-coast along Suma was a most suitable place for retirement, and that, though formerly populous, there were now only a few fishermen's dwellings scattered here and there. To Suma he finally determined to go into voluntary exile.

When he had thus made up his mind he became somewhat regretful to leave the capital, although it had hitherto appeared ungenial. The first thing which disturbed his mind was the young Violet, whom he could not take with him. The young lady, also, in the "Villa of Falling Flowers" (notwithstanding that he was not a frequent visitor) was another object of his regret.

In spite of these feelings he prepared to set off at the end of March, and at length it came within a few days of the time fixed for his departure, when he went privately, under the cover of the evening, to the mansion of the ex-Sadaijin, in an ajiro carriage, generally used by women. He proceeded into the inner apartments, where he was greeted by the nurse of his little child. The boy was growing fast, was able to stand by this time and to toddle about, and run into Genji's arms when he saw him. The latter took him on his knee, saying, "Ah! my good little fellow, I have not seen you for some time, but you do not forget me, do you?" The ex-Sadaijin now entered. He said, "Often have I thought of coming to have a talk with you, but you see my health has been very bad of late, and I seldom appear at Court, having resigned my office. It would be impolitic to give cause to be talked about, and for it to be said that I stretch my old bones when private matters please me. Of course, I have no particular reason to fear the world; still, if there is anything dreadful, it is the demagogical world. When I see what unpleasant things are happening to you, which were no more probable than that the heavens should fall, I really feel that everything in the world is irksome to me."

"Yes, what you say is indeed true," replied Genji. "However, all things in the world—this or that—are the outcome of what we have done in our previous existence. Hence if we dive to the bottom we shall see that every misfortune is only the result of our own negligence. Examples of men's losing the pleasures of the Court are, indeed, not wanting. Some of these cases may not go so far as a deprivation of titles and honors, as is mine;[106] still, if one thus banished from the pleasures of Court, behaves himself as unconcernedly as those to whom no such misfortune has happened, this would not be becoming. So, at least, it is considered in a foreign country. Repentance is what one ought to expect in such circumstances, and banishment to a far-off locality is a measure generally adopted for offences different from ordinary ones. If I, simply relying on my innocence, pass unnoticed the recent displeasure of the Court, this would only bring upon me greater dishonor. I have, therefore, determined to go into voluntary exile, before receiving such a sentence from the Court."

Then the conversation fell back, as usual, on the times of the late ex-Emperor, which made them sad; while the child also, who innocently played near, made them still more gloomy. The ex-Sadaijin went on to say:—"There is no moment when I ever forget the mother of the boy, but now I almost dare to think that she was fortunate in being short lived, and being free from witnessing the dreamlike sorrow we now suffer. With regard to the boy, the first thing which strikes me as unbearable is that he may pass some time of his lovely childhood away from the gaze of your eyes. There are, as you say, no want of instances of persons suffering a miserable fate, without having committed any real offence; yet still, in such cases, there was some pretext to justify their being so treated. I cannot see any such against you."

While he was thus speaking Tô-no-Chiûjiô joined them, and, partaking of *saké*, they continued their conversation till late in the evening. This night Genji remained in the mansion.

Early the next morning he returned to his own residence, and he spent the whole day with Violet in the western wing. It should here be noticed that she was scarcely ever with her father, even from childhood. He strongly disapproved of his daughter being with Genji, and of the way in which she had been carried off, so he scarcely ever had any communication with her, or did he visit her. These circumstances made her feel Genji's affection more keenly than she otherwise would have; hence her sorrow at the thought of parting with him in a few days may be easily imagined.

Towards the evening Prince Sotz came with Tô-no-Chiûjiô and some others to pay him a visit. Genji, in order to receive them, rose to put on one of his Naoshi, which was plain, without pattern, as proper for one who had no longer a title. Approaching the mirror, to comb his hair, he noticed that his face had grown much thinner.

"Oh, how changed I appear," he exclaimed. "Am I really like this image which I see of myself?" he said, turning to the girl, who cast on him a sad and tearful glance. Genji continued:—

"Though changed I wander far away,My soul shall still remain with you,Perhaps in this mirror's mystic ray,My face may linger still in view."

To this Violet replied:—

"If in this mirror I could see,Always your face, then it would beMy consolation when thou art gone."

As she said this she turned her face to one side of the room, and by doing so obscured the tears gathering in her soft eyes. Genji then left her to receive his friends, who, however, did not remain long, leaving the mansion after a short conversation of a consolatory nature. This evening Genji paid his visit to the sisters of the "Falling Flower" villa.

On the following day the final arrangements necessary for his household affairs were made at his residence. The management of the mansion was intrusted to a few confidential friends; while that of his lands and pasture, and the charge of his documents, were intrusted to the care of Violet, to whom he gave every instruction what she should do. Besides, he enjoined Shiônagon, in whom he placed his confidence, to give her every assistance. He told all the inmates who wished to remain in the mansion, in order to await his return, that they might do so. He also made an appropriate present to the nurse of his boy, and to the ladies of the "Villa of Falling Flowers." When all these things were accomplished, he occupied himself in writing farewell letters to his intimate friends, such as the young daughter of Udaijin and others, to none of whom he had paid a visit.

On the evening prior to his departure he went on horseback to visit the tomb of his father. On his way he called on the Princess Wistaria, and thence proceeded to the mountain where the remains reposed. The tomb was placed among tall growing grass, under thick and gloomy foliage. Genji advanced to the tomb, and, half kneeling down before it, and half sobbing, uttered many words of remembrance and sorrow. Of course no reply came forth. The moon by this time was hidden behind dark clouds, and the winds blew keen and nipping, when suddenly a shadowy phantom of the dead stood before Genji's eyes.

"How would his image look on me,Knew he the secret of the past;As yonder moon in clouded sky,Looks o'er the scene mysteriously."

He returned to his mansion late in the night.

Early in the morning he sent a letter to Ô Miôbu, the nurse of the Heir-apparent, in which he said: "I at last leave the capital, to-day. I know not when I may come and see the Prince again. On him my thoughts and anxieties are concentrated, above all else. Realize these feelings in your own mind, and tell them to him." He also sent the following, fastened to a bough of cherry flowers, already becoming thin:—

"When shall I see these scenes again,And view the flowers of spring in bloom,Like rustic from his mountain home,A mere spectator shall I come?"

These were carefully read by Ô Miôbu to the Prince, and when he was asked what she should write in answer, he said: "Write that I said that since I feel every longing to see him, when I do not see him for a long time, how shall I feel when he goes away altogether?" Thereupon she wrote an answer, in which she indefinitely stated that she had shown the letter to the Prince, whose answer was simple, yet very affectionate, and so on, with the following:—

"'Tis sad that fair blossoms so soon fade away,In the darkness of winter no flower remains,But let spring return with its sunshiny ray,Then once more the flowers we look on again."

Now, with regard to the recent disgrace of Genji, the public in general did not approve of the severity which the Court had shown to him. Moreover, he had been constantly with the Emperor, his father, since the age of seven, and his requests had been always cheerfully listened to by the latter; hence there were very many, especially among public servants of the ordinary class, who were much indebted to him. However, none of them now came to pay their respects to him. It seems that in a world of intrigue none dares do what is right for fear of risking his own interests. Such being the state of things, Genji, during the whole day, was unoccupied, and the time was entirely spent with Violet. Then, at his usual late hour in the evening, he, in a travelling dress of incognito, at length left the capital, where he had passed five-and-twenty years of his life.

His attendants, Koremitz and Yoshikiyo being among them, were seven or eight in number. He took with him but little luggage. All ostentatious robes, all unnecessary articles of luxury were dispensed with. Among things taken, was a box containing the works of Hak-rak-ten (a famous Chinese poet), with other books, and besides these a *kin-koto* for his amusement. They embarked in a boat and sailed down the river. Early the next morning they arrived at the sea-coast of Naniwa. They noticed the Ôye Palace standing lonely amidst the group of pine trees. The sight of this palace gave a thrill of sadness to Genji, who was now leaving, and not returning, home. He saw the waves rolling on the coast and again sweep back. He hummed, as he saw them:—

"The waves roll back, but unlike me,They come again."

From Naniwa they continued their voyage, sailing in the bay. As they proceeded they looked back on the scenes they had left. They saw all the mountains veiled in haze, growing more and more distant, while the rowers gently pulled against the rippling waves. It seemed to them as if they were really going "three thousand miles' distance."[107]

"Our home is lost in the mist of the mountain,Let us gaze on the sky which is ever the same."

The day was long and the wind was fair, so they soon arrived at the coast of Suma.[108] The place was near the spot where the exiled Yukihira had lived, and had watched the beautiful smoke rising from the salt ovens. There was a thatched house in which the party temporarily took up their residence. It was a very different home from what they had been used to, and it might have appeared even novel, had the circumstances of their coming there been different. The authorities of the neighborhood were sent for, and a lodge was built under the direction of Yoshikiyo, in accordance with Genji's wishes. The work was hurried on, and the building was soon completed. In the garden, several trees, cherries and others, were planted, and water was also conducted into it. Here Genji soon took up his abode. The Governor of the province, who had been at Court, secretly paid attention to the Prince, with as much respect as was possible.

For some time Genji did not feel settled in his new residence. When he had become in some degree accustomed to it, the season of continuous rain had arrived (May); his thoughts more than ever reverted to the old capital.

The thoughtful expression of Violet's face, the childish affection of the Heir-apparent, and the innocent playfulness of his little son, became the objects of his reveries and anxiety, nor did he forget his old companions and acquaintances. He, therefore, sent a special messenger to the capital bearing his letters, so that speedy answers might be returned from every quarter. He also sent a messenger to Ise to make inquiry after the lady, who also sent one to him in return.

Now the young daughter of Udaijin had been remaining repentingly in the mansion of her father since the events of the stormy evening. Her father felt much for her, and interceded with the Empress-mother in her behalf, and also with her son, that is, the Emperor, thus getting permission to introduce her once more into Court, an event which took place in the month of July.

To return to Suma. The rainy season had passed, and autumn arrived. The sea was at some distance from the residence of Genji, but the dash of its waves sounded close to their ears as the winds passed by, of which Yukihira sang,

"The autumn wind which passes the barrier of Suma."

The autumn winds are, it seems, in such a place as this, far more plaintive than elsewhere.

It happened one evening that when all the attendants were fast asleep Genji was awake and alone. He raised his head and rested his arms on his pillow and listened to the sound of the waves which reached his ear from a distance. They seemed nearer than ever, as though they were coming to flood his pillows. He drew his *koto* towards him and struck a melancholy air, as he hummed a verse of a poem in a low tone. With this every one awoke and responded with a sigh.

Such was a common occurrence in the evening, and Genji always felt saddened whenever he came to think that all his attendants had accompanied him, having left their families and homes simply for his sake. In the daytime, however, there were changes. He would then enjoy pleasant conversations. He also joined several papers into long rolls on which he might practise penmanship. He spent a good deal of time in drawing and sketching. He remembered how Yoshikiyo, on one occasion in Mount Kurama, had described the beautiful scenery of the place on which he was now gazing. He sketched every beautiful landscape of the neighborhood, and collected them in albums, thinking how nice it would be if he could send for Tsunenori, a renowned contemporary artist, and get him to paint the sketches which he had made.

Out of all the attendants of Genji there were four or five who had been more especially his favorites, and who had constantly attended on him. One evening they were all sitting together in a corridor which commanded a full view of the sea. They perceived the island of Awaji lying in the distance, as if it were floating on the horizon, and also several boats with sailors, singing as they rowed to the shore over the calm surface of the water, like waterfowl in their native element. Over their heads flocks of wild geese rustled on their way homeward with their plaintive cry, which made the thoughts of the spectators revert to their homes. Genji hummed this verse:—

"Those wandering birds above us flying,Do they our far-off friends resemble.With their voice of plaintive cryingMake us full of thoughtful sighing."

Yoshikiyo took up the idea and replied:—

"Though these birds no friends of oursAre, and we to them are nought,Yet their voice in these still hoursBring those old friends to our thought."

Then Koremitz continued:—

"Before to-day I always thoughtThey flew on pleasure's wing alone,But now their fate to me is fraughtWith some resemblance to our own."

Ukon-no-Jiô added:—

"Though we, like them, have left our homeTo wander forth, yet still for meThere's joy to think where'er I roamMy faithful friends are still with me."

Ukon-no-Jiô was the brother of Ki-no-Kami. His father, Iyo-no-Kami, had now been promoted to be Hitachi-no-Kami (Governor of Hitachi), and had gone down to that province, but Ukon-no-Jiô did not join his father, who would have gladly taken him, and faithfully followed Genji.

This evening happened to be the fifteenth of August, on which day a pleasant reunion is generally held at the Imperial Palace. Genji looked at the silvery pale sky, and as he did so the affectionate face of the Emperor, his brother, whose expression strikingly resembled their father's, presented itself to his mind. After a deep and long sigh, he returned to his couch, humming as he went:—

"Here is still a robeHis Majesty gave to me."

It should be here noticed that he had been presented by the Emperor on a certain occasion with a robe, and this robe he had never parted with, even in his exile.

About this time Daini (the senior Secretary of the Lord-Lieutenant of Kiûsiû) returned to the capital with his family, having completed his official term. His daughter had been a virgin dancer, and was known to Genji. They preferred to travel by water, and slowly sailed up along the beautiful coast. When they arrived at Suma, the distant sound of a *kin*[109] was heard, mingled with the sea-coast wind, and they were told that Genji was there in exile. Daini therefore sent his son Chikzen-no-Kami to the Prince with these words: "Coming back from a distant quarter I expected as soon as I should arrive in the capital to have had the pleasure of visiting you and listening to your pleasant voice, and talking of events which have taken place there, but little did I think that you had taken up your residence in this part of the country. How greatly do I sympathize with you! I ought to land and see you at once, but there are too many people in the same boat, therefore I think it better to avoid the slightest grounds which may cause them to talk. However, possibly I shall pay you a visit soon."

This Chikzen-no-Kami had been for some time previously a Kurand (a sort of equerry) to Genji, therefore his visit was especially welcome to him. He said that since he had left the capital it had become difficult to see any of his acquaintances, and that therefore this especial visit was a great pleasure to him. His reply to the message of Daini was to the same effect. Chikzen-no-Kami soon took his leave, and returning to the boat, reported to his father and others all he had seen. His sister also wrote to Genji privately thus: "Pray excuse me if I am too bold.

Know you not the mind is swayedLike the tow-rope of our boat,At the sounds your Kin has made,Which around us sweetly float."

When Genji received this, his pleasure was expressed by his placid smile, and he sent back the following:—

"If this music moves the mindSo greatly as you say,No one would care to leave behindThese lonely waves of Suma's bay."

This recalls to our mind that there was in the olden time an exile who gave a stanza even to the postmaster of a village.[110] Why then should not Genji have sent to her whom he knew this stanza?

In the meantime, as time went on, more sympathizers with Genji were found in the capital, including no less a personage than the Emperor himself. True it is that before Genji left, many even of his relatives and most intimate friends refrained from paying their respects to him, but in the course of time not a few began to correspond with him, and sometimes they communicated their ideas to each other in pathetic poetry. These things reached the ears of the Empress-mother, who was greatly irritated by them. She said: "The only thing a man who has offended the Court should do is to keep himself as quiet as possible. It is most unpardonable that such a man should haughtily cause scandal to the Court from his humble dwelling. Does he intend to imitate the treacherous example of one who made a deer pass for a horse?[111] Those who intrigue with such a man are equally blamable." These spiteful remarks once more put a stop to the correspondence.

Meanwhile, at Suma, the autumn passed away and winter succeeded, with all its dreariness of scene, and with occasional falls of snow. Genji often spent the evening in playing upon the Kin, being accompanied by Koremitz's flute and the singing of Yoshikiyo. It was on one of these evenings that the story of a young Chinese Court lady, who had been sent to the frozen land of barbarians, occurred to Genji's mind. He thought what a great trial it would be if one were obliged to send away one whom he loved, like the lady in the tale, and as he reflected on this, with some melancholy feelings, it appeared to him as vividly as if it were only an event of yesterday, and he hummed:—

"The sound of the piper's distant strainBroke on her dreams in the frozen eve."

He then tried to sleep, but could not do so, and as he lay the distant cry of Chidori reached his ears.[112] He hummed again as he heard them:—

"Although on lonely couch I lieWithout a mate, yet still so near,At dawn the cries of Chidori,With their fond mates, 'tis sweet to hear."

Having washed his hands, he spent some time in reading a Kiô (Sutra), and in this manner the winter-time passed away.

Towards the end of February the young cherry-trees which Genji had planted in his garden blossomed, and this brought to his memory the well-known cherry-tree in the Southern Palace, and the *fête* in which he had taken part. The noble countenance of the late ex-Emperor, and that of the present one, the then Heir-apparent, which had struck him much at that time, returned to his recollection with the scene where he had read out his poem.

"While on the lordly crowd I muse,Which haunts the Royal festive hours,The day has come when I've put onThe crown of fairest cherry flowers."

While thus meditating on the past, strange to say, Tô-no-Chiûjiô, Genji's brother-in-law, came from the capital to see the Prince. He had been now made Saishiô (privy councillor). Having, therefore, more responsibility, he had to be more cautious in dealing with the public. He had, however, a personal sympathy with Genji, and thus came to see him, at the risk of offending the Court.

The first thing which struck his eyes was, not the natural beauty of the scenery, but the style of Genji's residence, which showed the novelty of pure Chinese fashion. The enclosure was surrounded by "a trellis-work of bamboo," with "stone steps," and "pillars of pine-tree."[113]

He entered, and the pleasure of Genji and Tô-no-Chiûjiô was immense, so much so that they shed tears. The style of the Prince's dress next attracted the attention of Tô-no-Chiûjiô. He was habited in a plain, simple country style, the coat being of an unforbidden color, a dull yellow, the trousers of a subdued green.

The furniture was all of a temporary nature, with Go and Sugorok playing boards, as well as one for the game of Dagi. He noticed some articles for the services of religion, showing that Genji was wont to indulge in devotional exercises. The visitor told Genji many things on the subject of affairs in the capital, which he had been longing to impart to him for many months past; telling him also how the grandfather of his boy always delighted in playing with him, and giving him many more interesting details.

Several fishermen came with the fish which they had caught. Genji called them in and made them show their spoils. He also led them to talk of their lives spent on the sea, and each in his own peculiar local dialect gave him a narration of his joys and sorrows. He then dismissed them with the gift of some stuff to make them clothing. All this was quite a novelty to the eyes of Tô-no-Chiûjiô, who also saw the stable in which he obtained a glimpse of some horses. The attendants at the time were feeding them. Dinner was presently served, at which the dishes were necessarily simple, yet tasteful. In the evening they did not retire to rest early, but spent their time in continuing their conversation and in composing verses.

Although Tô-no-Chiûjiô had, in coming, risked the displeasure of the Court, he still thought it better to avoid any possible slander, and therefore he made up his mind to set out for his home early next morning. The *saké* cup was offered, and they partook of it as they hummed,

"In our parting cup, the tears of sadness fall."

Several presents had been brought from the capital for Genji by Tô-no-Chiûjiô, and, in return, the former made him a present of an excellent dark-colored horse, and also a celebrated flute, as a token of remembrance.

As the sun shed forth his brilliant rays Tô-no-Chiûjiô took his leave, and as he did so he said, "When shall I see you again, you cannot be here long?" Genji replied,

"Yon noble crane that soars on high,[114]And hovers in the clear blue sky,Believe my soul as pure and light;As spotless as the spring day bright.

However, a man like me, whose fortune once becomes adverse seldom regains, even in the case of great wisdom, the prosperity he once fully enjoyed, and so I cannot predict when I may find myself again in the capital."

So Tô-no-Chiûjiô, having replied as follows:—

"The crane mounts up on high, 'tis true,But now he soars and cries alone,Still fondly thinking of his friend,With whom in former days he flew,"

set off on his homeward road, leaving Genji cast down for some time.

Now the coast of Akashi is a very short distance from Suma, and there lived the former Governor of the province, now a priest, of whom we have spoken before. Yoshikiyo well remembered his lovely daughter, and, after he came to Suma with Genji, he wrote to her now and then. He did not get any answer from her, but sometimes heard from her father, to whom Genji's exile became soon known, and who wished to see him for a reason not altogether agreeable to himself. It should be remembered that this old man always entertained aspirations on behalf of his daughter, and in his eyes the successive governors of the province who came after him, and whose influence had been unbounded, were considered as nobodies. To him, his young daughter was everything; and he used to send her twice a year to visit the temple of Sumiyoshi, in order that she might obtain good fortune by the blessing of the god.

She was not of an ideal beauty, but yet expressive in countenance and exalted in mind. She could, in this respect, rival any of those of high birth in the capital.

The priest said one day to his wife, "Prince Genji, the imperial son of the Kôyi of Kiritsubo is now at Suma in exile, having offended the Court. How fortunate it would be if we could take the opportunity of presenting our child to him!"

The wife replied, "Ah, how dreadful, when I heard what the townspeople talk, I understood that he has several mistresses. He went even so far as to carry on a secret intimacy, which happened to be obnoxious to the Emperor, and it is said that this offence was the cause of his exile."

"I have some reason for mentioning this to you," he interrupted, impatiently; "it is not a thing which you understand, so make up your mind, I shall bring the matter about, and take an opportunity of making him come to us."

"No matter how distinguished a personage he is," replied the wife, "it is a fact that he has offended the Court and is exiled. I do not understand why you could take a fancy to such a man for our maiden daughter. It is not a joking matter. I hope you will take it into graver consideration."

"That a man of ability and distinction should meet with adverse fortune is a very common occurrence," said he, still more obstinately, "both in our empire and in that of China. How then do you venture to say such things against the Prince? His mother was the daughter of an Azechi Dainagon, who was my uncle. She enjoyed a good reputation, and when she was introduced at Court, became both prosperous and distinguished. Although her life was shortened by the suffering caused by the fierce jealousy of her rivals, she left behind the royal child, who is no other person than Prince Genji. A woman should always be aspiring, as this lady was. What objection then is there in the idea of introducing our only child to a man like him? Although I am now only a country gentleman, I do not think he would withdraw his favor from me."

Such were the opinions of this old man, and hence his discouragement of the advances of Yoshikiyo.

The first of March came, and Genji was persuaded by some to perform Horai (prayer for purification) for the coming occasion of the Third.[115] He therefore sent for a calendar-priest, with whom he went out, accompanied by attendants, to the sea-shore. Here a tent was erected ceremoniously, and the priest began his prayers, which were accompanied by the launching of a small boat, containing figures representing human images. On seeing this Genji said,

"Never thought I, in my younger day,To be thrown on the wild sea-shore,And like these figures to float away,And perhaps see my home no more."

As he contemplated the scene around him, he perceived that the wild surface of the sea was still and calm, like a mirror without its frame. He offered prayers in profound silence, and then exclaimed,

"Oh, all ye eight millions of gods,[116] hear my cry,Oh, give me your sympathy, aid me, I pray,For when I look over my life, ne'er did ICommit any wrong, or my fellows betray."

Suddenly, as he spoke these words, the wind arose and began to blow fiercely. The sky became dark, and torrents of rain soon followed. This caused great confusion to all present, and each ran back to the house without finishing the ceremony of prayers. None of them were prepared for the storm, and all got drenched with the rain. From this the rain continued to pour down, and the surface of the sea became as it were tapestried with white, over which the lightning darted and the thunder rolled. It seemed as if thunderbolts were crashing overhead, and the force of the rain appeared to penetrate the earth. Everyone was frightened, for they thought the end of the world was near.

Genji occupied his time in quietly reading his Buddhist Bible. In the evening, the thunder became less loud, though the wind still blew not less violently than in the daytime. Everyone in the residence said that they had heard of what is termed a flood-tide, which often caused a great deal of damage, but they had never witnessed such a scene as they had that day. Genji dropped off into a slumber, when indistinctly the resemblance of a human figure came to him and said, "You are requested to come to the palace, why don't you come?"

Genji was startled by the words, and awoke. He thought that the king of the dragon palace[117] might have admired him, and was perhaps the author of this strange dream. These thoughts made him weary of remaining at Suma.

FOOTNOTES:

[106]When a person was exiled, he was generally deprived of his own title, or was degraded. Genji appears to have been deprived of his.

[107]A favorite phrase in Chinese poems describing the journey of exile.

[108]Suma is about sixty miles from Kiôto, the then capital.

[109]A musical instrument—often called a *koto.*

[110]When Sugawara, before referred to, arrived at Akashi, on his way to exile, the village postmaster expressed his surprise. Thereupon Sugawara gave him a stanza, which he composed:

"Oh, master, be not surprised to seeThis change in my estate, for soOnce to bloom, and once to fadeIs spring and autumn's usual lot."

[111]In Chinese history it is recounted that a certain artful intriguer made a fool of his Sovereign by bringing a deer to the Court and presenting it before the Emperor, declaring it to be a horse. All the courtiers, induced by his great influence, agreed with him in calling it a horse, to the Emperor's great astonishment and bewilderment.

[112]The coast along by Suma is celebrated for Chidori, a small sea-bird that always flies in large flocks. Their cries are considered very plaintive, and are often spoken of by poets.

[113]Expressions used in a poem by Hak-rak-ten, describing a tasteful residence.

[114]Here Tô-no-Chiûjiô is compared to the bird.

[115]The third day of March is one of five festival days in China and Japan, when prayers for purification, or prayers intended to request the freeing one's self from the influence of fiends, are said on the banks of a river.

[116]In the Japanese mythology the number of gods who assemble at their councils is stated to have been eight millions. This is an expression which is used to signify a large number rather than an exact one.

[117]In Japanese mythology we have a story that there were two brothers, one of whom was always very lucky in fishing, and the other in hunting. One day, to vary their amusements, the former took his brother's bow and arrows and went to the mountain to hunt. The latter took the fishing-rod, and went to the sea, but unfortunately lost his brother's hook in the water. At this he was very miserable, and wandered abstractedly along the coast. The dragon god of the dragon palace, under the blue main, admired his beauty, and wishing him to marry his daughter, lured him into the dragon palace.

CHAPTER XIII

EXILE AT AKASHI

The storm and thunder still continued for some days, and the same strange dream visited Genji over and over again.

This made him miserable. To return to the capital was not yet to be thought of, as to do so before the imperial permission was given, would only be to increase his disgrace. On the other hand, to render himself obscure by seeking further retreat was also not to be thought of, as it might cause another rumor that he had been driven away by mere fear of the disturbed state of the ocean.

In the meantime, a messenger arrived from the capital with a letter from Violet. It was a letter of inquiry about himself. It was written in most affectionate terms, and stated that the weather there was extremely disagreeable, as rain was pouring down continuously, and that this made her especially gloomy in thinking of him. This letter gave Genji great pleasure.

The messenger was of the lowest class. At other times Genji would never have permitted such sort of people to approach him, but under the present circumstances of his life he was only too glad to put up with it. He summoned the man to his presence, and made him talk of all the latest news in the capital.

The messenger told him, in awkward terms, that in the capital these storms were considered to be a kind of heavenly warning, that a Nin-wô-ye[118] was going to be held; and that many nobles who had to go to Court were prevented from doing so by the storms, adding that he never remembered such violent storms before.

From the dawn of the next day the winds blew louder, the tide flowed higher, and the sound of the waves resounded with a deafening noise. The thunder rolled and the lightning flashed, while everyone was trembling in alarm, and were all, including Genji, offering up prayers and vows to the God of Sumiyoshi, whose temple was at no great distance, and also to other gods. Meanwhile a thunderbolt struck the corridor of Genji's residence and set fire to it. The Prince and his friends retired to a small house behind, which served as a kitchen. The sky was as if blackened with ink, and in that state of darkness the day ended. In the evening the wind gradually abated, the rain diminished to a thin shower, and even the stars began to blink out of the heavens.

This temporary retreat was now irksome, and they thought of returning to their dwelling quarters, but they saw nothing but ruins and confusion from the storm, so they remained where they were. Genji was occupied in prayer. The moon began to smile from above, the flow of the tide could be seen, and the rippling of the waves heard. He opened the rude wooden door, and contemplated the scene before him. He seemed to be alone in the world, having no one to participate in his feelings. He heard several fishermen talking in their peculiar dialect. Feeling much wearied by the events of the day, he soon retired, and resigned himself to slumber, reclining near one side of the room, in which there were none of the comforts of an ordinary bedchamber.

All at once his late father appeared before his eyes in the exact image of life, and said to him, "Why are you in so strange a place?" and taking his hand, continued, "Embark at once in a boat, as the God of Sumiyoshi[119] guides you, and leave this coast."

Genji was delighted at this, and replied, "Since I parted from you I have undergone many misfortunes, and I thought that I might be buried on this coast."

"It must not be thus," the phantom replied; "your being here is only a punishment for a trifling sin which you have committed. For my own part, when I was on the throne, I did no wrong, but I have somehow been involved in some trifling sin, and before I expiated it I left the world. Hurt, however, at beholding you oppressed with such hardships I came up here, plunging into the waves, and rising on the shore. I am much fatigued; but I have something I wish to tell the Emperor, so I must haste away," and he left Genji, who felt very much affected, and cried out, "Let me accompany you!" With this exclamation he awoke, and looked up, when he saw nothing but the moon's face shining through the windows, with the clouds reposing in the sky.

The image of his father still vividly remained before his eyes, and he could not realize that it was only a dream. He became suddenly sad, and was filled with regret that he did not talk a little more, even though it was only in a dream. He could not sleep any more this night, and dawn broke, when a small boat was seen approaching the coast, with a few persons in it.

A man from the boat came up to the residence of Genji. When he was asked who he was, he replied that the priest of Akashi (the former Governor) had come from Akashi in his boat, and that he wished to see Yoshikiyo, and to tell him the reason of his coming. Yoshikiyo was surprised, and said, "I have known him for years, but there was a slight reason why we were not the best of friends, and some time has now passed without correspondence. What makes him come?"

As to Genji, however, the arrival of the boat made him think of its coincidence with the subject of his dream, so he hurried Yoshikiyo to go and see the new comers. Thereupon the latter went to the boat, thinking as he went, "How could he come to this place amidst the storms which have been raging?"

The priest now told Yoshikiyo that in a dream which he had on the first day of the month, a strange being told him a strange thing, and, said he, "I thought it too credulous to believe in a dream, but the object appeared again, and told me that on the thirteenth of this month he will give me a supernatural sign, directing me also to prepare a boat, and as soon as the storm ceased, to sail out to this coast. Therefore, to test its truth I launched a boat, but strange to say, on this day the extraordinarily violent weather of rain, wind, and thunder occurred. I then thought that in China there had been several instances of people benefiting the country by believing in dreams, so though this may not exactly be the case with mine, yet I thought it my duty, at all events, to inform you of the fact. With these thoughts I started in the boat, when a slight miraculous breeze, as it were, blew, and drove me to this coast. I can have no doubt that this was divine direction. Perhaps there might have been some inspiration in this place, too; and I wish to trouble you to transmit this to the Prince."

Yoshikiyo then returned and faithfully told Genji all about his conversation with the priest. When Genji came to reflect, he thought that so many dreams having visited him must have some significance. It might only increase his disgrace if he were to despise such divine warnings merely from worldly considerations, and from fear of consequences. It would be better to resign himself to one more advanced in age, and more experienced than himself. An ancient sage says, that "resigning one's self makes one happier," besides, his father had also enjoined him in the dream to leave the coast of Suma, and there remained no further doubt for taking this step. He, therefore, gave this answer to the priest, that "coming into an unknown locality, plunged in solitude, receiving scarcely any visits from friends in the capital, the only thing I have to regard as friends of old times are the sun and the moon that pass over the boundless heavens. Under these circumstances, I shall be only too delighted to visit your part of the coast, and to find there such a suitable retreat."

This answer gave the priest great joy, and he pressed Genji to set out at once and come to him. The Prince did so with his usual four or five confidential attendants. The same wind which had miraculously blown the vessel of the priest to Suma now changed, and carried them with equal favor and speed back to Akashi. On their landing they entered a carriage waiting for them, and went to the mansion of the priest.

The scenery around the coast was no less novel than that of Suma, the only difference being that there were more people there. The building was grand, and there was also a grand Buddha-hall adjoining for the service of the priest. The plantations of trees, the shrubberies, the rock-work, and the mimic lakes in the garden were so beautifully arranged as to exceed the power of an artist to depict, while the style of the dwelling was so tasteful that it was in no way inferior to any in the capital.

The wife and the daughter of the priest were not residing here, but were at another mansion on the hill-side, where they had removed from fear of the recent high tides.

Genji now took up his quarters with the priest in this seaside mansion. The first thing he did when he felt a little settled was to write to the capital, and tell his friends of his change of residence. The priest was about sixty years old, and was very sincere in his religious service. The only subject of anxiety which he felt was, as we have already mentioned, the welfare of his daughter. When Genji became thoroughly settled he often joined the priest, and spent hours in conversing with him. The latter, from his age and experience, was full of information and anecdotes, many of which were quite new to Genji, but the narration of them seemed always to turn upon his daughter.

April had now come. The trees began to be clothed with a thick shade of leaves, which had a peculiar novelty of appearance, differing from that of the flowers of spring, or the bright dyes of autumn. The Kuina (a particular bird of summer) commenced their fluttering. The furniture and dresses were changed for those more suitable to the time of year. The comfort of the house was most agreeable. It was on one of these evenings that the surface of the broad ocean spread before the eye was unshadowed by the clouds, and the Isle of Awaji floated like foam on its face, just as it appeared to do at Suma. Genji took out his favorite *kin*, on which he had not practised for some time, and was playing an air called "Kôriô," when the priest joined him, having left for awhile his devotions, and said that his music recalled to his mind the old days and the capital which he had quitted so long. He sent for a *biwa* (mandolin)[120] and a *soh-koto* from the hill-side mansion, and, after the fashion of a blind singer of ballads to the *biwa*, played two or three airs.

He then handed the *soh-koto* to Genji, who also played a few tunes, saying, as he did so, in a casual manner, "This sounds best when played upon by some fair hand." The priest smiled, and rejoined: "What better hand than yours need we wish to hear playing; for my part, my poor skill has been transmitted to me, through three generations, from the royal hand of the Emperor Yenghi, though I now belong to the past; but, occasionally, when my loneliness oppresses me, I indulge in my old amusement, and there is one who, listening to my strains, has learnt to imitate them so well that they resemble those of the Emperor Yenghi himself. I shall be very happy, if you desire, to find an opportunity for you to hear them."

Genji at once laid aside the instrument, saying: "Ah, how bold! I did not know I was among proficients," and continued, "From olden time the *soh-koto* was peculiarly adopted by female musicians. The fifth daughter of the Emperor Saga, from whom she had received the secret, was a celebrated performer, but no one of equal skill succeeded her. Of course there are several players, but these merely strike or strum on the instrument; but in this retreat there is a skilful hand. How delightful it will be."

"If you desire to hear, there is no difficulty. I will introduce her to you. She also plays the *biwa* very well. The *biwa* has been considered from olden time very difficult to master, and I am proud of her doing so."

In this manner the priest led the conversation to his own daughter, while fruit and *sake* were brought in for refreshment. He then went on talking of his life since he first came to the coast of Akashi, and of his devotion to religion, for the sake of future happiness, and also out of solicitude for his daughter. He continued: "Although I feel rather awkward in saying it, I am almost inclined to think your coming to this remote vicinity has something providential in it, as an answer, as it were, to our earnest prayers, and it may give you some consolation and pleasure. The reason why I think so is this—it is nearly eighteen years since we began to pray for the blessing of the God Sumiyoshi on our daughter, and we have sent her twice a year, in spring and autumn, to his temple. At the 'six-time' service,[121] also, the prayers for my own repose on the lotus flower,[122] are only secondary to those which I put up for the happiness of my daughter. My father, as you may know, held a good office in the capital, but I am now a plain countryman, and if I leave matters in their present state, the status of my family will soon become lower and lower. Fortunately this girl was promising from her childhood, and my desire was to present her to some distinguished personage in the capital, not without disappointment to many suitors, and I have often told her that if my desire is not fulfilled she had better throw herself into the sea."

Such was the tedious discourse which the priest held on the subject of his family affairs; yet it is not surprising that it awakened an interest in the susceptible mind of Genji for the fair maiden thus described as so promising. The priest at last, in spite of the shyness and reserve of the daughter, and the unwillingness of the mother, conducted Genji to the hill-side mansion, and introduced him to the maiden. In the course of time they gradually became more than mere acquaintances to each other. For some time Genji often found himself at the hill-side mansion, and her society appeared to afford him greater pleasure than anything else, but this did not quite meet with the approval of his conscience, and the girl in the mansion at Nijio returned to his thoughts. If this flirtation of his should become known to her, he thought, it perhaps would be very annoying to her. True, she was not much given to be jealous, but he well remembered the occasional complaints she had now and then made to him while in the capital. These feelings induced him to write more frequently and more minutely to her, and he soon began to frequent the hill-side mansion less often. His leisure hours were spent in sketching, as he used to do in Suma, and writing short poetic effusions explanatory of the scenery. This was also going on in the mansion at Nijio, where Violet passed the long hours away in painting different pictures, and also in writing, in the form of a diary, what she saw and did. What will be the issue of all these things?

Now, since the spring of the year there had been several heavenly warnings in the capital, and things in general were somewhat unsettled. On the evening of the thirteenth of March, when the rain and wind had raged, the late Emperor appeared in a dream to his son the Emperor, in front of the palace, looking reproachfully upon him. The Emperor showed every token of submission and respect when the dead Emperor told him of many things, all of which concerned Genji's interests. The Emperor became alarmed, and when he awoke he told his mother all about his dream. She, however, told him that on such occasions, when the storm rages, and the sky is obscured by the disturbance of the elements, all things, especially on which our thoughts have been long occupied, appear to us in a dream in a disturbed sleep; and she continued, "I further counsel you not to be too hastily alarmed by such trifles." From this time he began to suffer from sore eyes, which may have resulted from the angry glances of his father's spirit. About the same time the father of the Empress-mother died. His death was by no means premature; but yet, when such events take place repeatedly, it causes the mind to imagine there is something more than natural going on, and this made the Empress-mother feel a little indisposed.

The Emperor then constantly told her that if Genji were left in his present condition it might induce evil, and, therefore, it would be better to recall him, and restore his titles and honors to him. She obstinately opposed these ideas, saying, "If a person who proved to be guilty, and has retired from the capital, were to be recalled before the expiration of at least three years, it would naturally show the weakness of authority."

She gained her point, and thus the days were spent and the year changed.

The Emperor still continually suffered from indisposition, and the unsettled state of things remained the same as before. A prince had been born to him, who was now about two years old, and he began to think of abdicating the throne in favor of the Heir-apparent, the child of the Princess Wistaria. When he looked around to see who would best minister public affairs, he came to think that the disgrace of Genji was a matter not to be allowed to continue, and at last, contrary to the advice of his mother, he issued a public permission for Genji's return to the capital, which was repeated at the end of July. Genji therefore prepared to come back. Before, however, he started, a month passed away, which time was mostly spent in the society of the lady of the hill-side mansion. The expected journey of Genji was now auspicious, even to him, and ought also to have been so to the family of the priest, but parting has always something painful in its nature. This was more so because the girl had by this time the witness of their love in her bosom, but he told her that he would send for her when his position was assured in the capital.

Towards the middle of August everything was in readiness, and Genji started on his journey homeward. He went to Naniwa, where he had the ceremony of Horai performed. To the temple of Sumiyoshi he sent a messenger to say that the haste of his journey prevented him coming at this time, but that he would fulfil his vows as soon as circumstances would permit. From Naniwa he proceeded to the capital, and returned once more, after an absence of nearly three years, to his mansion at Nijiô. The joy and excitement of the inmates of the mansion were unbounded, and the development of Violet charmed his eyes. His delight was great and the pleasure of his mind was of the most agreeable nature; still, from time to time, in the midst of this very pleasure, the recollection of the maiden whom he had left at Akashi occurred to his thoughts. But this kind of perturbation was only the result of what had arisen from the very nature of Genji's character.

Before the lapse of many days all his titles and honors were restored to him, and he was soon created an extra Vice-Dainagon.

All those who had lost dignities or office on account of Genji's complications were also restored to them. It seemed to these like a sudden and unexpected return of spring to the leafless tree.

In the course of a few days Genji was invited by the Emperor to come and see him. The latter had scarcely recovered from his indisposition, and was still looking weak and thin. When Genji appeared before him, he manifested great pleasure, and they conversed together in a friendly way till the evening.

FOOTNOTES:

[118]A religious feast in the Imperial Palace, in which Nin-wô-kiô, one of the Buddhist Bibles, was read, an event which rarely took place. Its object was to tranquillize the country.

[119]The god of the sea.

[120]The "biwa," more than any other instrument, is played by blind performers, who accompany it with ballads.

[121]The services performed by rigid priests were six times daily—namely, at early morn, mid-day, sunset, early evening, midnight, and after midnight.

[122]The Buddhist idea that when we get into Paradise we take our seat upon the lotus flower.

CHAPTER XIV

THE BEACON

Genji well remembered the dream which he had dreamt at Suma, and in which his father, the late ex-Emperor, had made a faint allusion to his fallen state. He was always thinking of having solemn service performed for him, which might prove to be a remedy for evils.

He was now in the capital, and at liberty to do anything he wished. In October, therefore, he ordered the grand ceremony of Mihakkô to be performed for the repose of the dead. Meanwhile the respect of the public towards Genji had now returned to its former state, and he himself had become a distinguished personage in the capital. The Empress-mother, though indisposed, regretted she had not ruined Genji altogether; while the Emperor, who had not forgotten the injunction of the late ex-Emperor, felt satisfied with his recent disposition towards his half-brother, which he believed to be an act of goodness.

This he felt the more, because he noticed the improvement in his health continued from day to day, and he experienced a sensation of fresh vigor. He did not, however, believe he should be long on the throne, and when he found himself lonely, he often sent for Genji, and spent hours conversing with him, without any reserve, on public affairs.

In February of the next year the ceremony of the "Gembuk" of the Heir-apparent, who was eleven years of age, was performed.

At the end of the same month the Emperor abdicated the throne in favor of the Heir-apparent, and his own son was made the Heir-apparent to the new Emperor.

The suddenness of these changes struck the Empress-mother with surprise, but she was told by her son that his abdication had been occasioned by his desire to enjoy quiet and repose.

The new reign opened with several changes in public affairs. Genji had been made Naidaijin. He filled this extra office of Daijin because there was no vacancy either in the Sadaijin or the Udaijin. He was to take an active part in the administration, but as he was not yet disposed to engage in the busy cares of official life, the ex-Sadaijin, his father-in-law, was solicited to become the regent for the young Emperor. He at first declined to accept the office, on the ground that he was advanced in age, that he had already retired from official life, and that the decline of his life left him insufficient energy. There was, however, an example in a foreign State, where some wise councillors, who resigned and had retired into the far-off mountains when their country was in a disturbed state, came forth from their retreat, with their snow-crowned heads, and took part in the administration of affairs. Nor was it an unusual thing for a statesman who had retired from political scenes to assume again a place under another government.

So the ex-Sadaijin did not persist in his refusal, but finally accepted the post of Dajiôdaijin (the Premier). He was now sixty-three years of age. His former retirement had taken place more on account of his disgust with the world than from his indisposition, and hence, when he accepted his new post, he at once showed how capable he was of being a responsible Minister. Tô-no-Chiûjiô, his eldest son, was also made the Gon-Chiûnagon. His daughter by his wife, the fourth daughter of Udaijin, was now twelve years old, and was shortly expected to be presented at Court; while his son, who had sung the "high sand" at a summer-day reunion at Genji's mansion, received a title. The young Genji too, the son of the late Lady Aoi, was admitted to the Court of the Emperor and of the Heir-apparent.

The attendants who faithfully served the young Genji, and those in the mansion at Nijiô, had all received a satisfactory token of appreciation from Genji, who now began to have a mansion repaired, which was situated to the east of the one in which he resided, and which had formerly belonged to his father. This he did with a notion of placing there some of his intimate friends, such as the younger one of the ladies in the "Villa of Falling Flowers."

Now the young maiden also, whom Genji had left behind at Akashi, and who had been in delicate health, did not pass away from his thoughts. He despatched a messenger there on the first of March, as he deemed the happy event would take place about that time. When the messenger returned, he reported that she was safely delivered of a girl on the sixteenth of the month.

He remembered the prediction of an astrologer who had told him that an Emperor would be born to him, and another son who would eventually become a Dajiôdaijin. He also remembered that a daughter, who would be afterwards an Empress, would be also born to him, by a lady inferior to the mothers of the other two children. When he reflected on this prediction and on the series of events, he began thinking of the remarkable coincidences they betrayed; and as he thought of sending for her, as soon as the condition of the young mother's health would admit, he hurried forward the repairs of the eastern mansion. He also thought that as there might not be a suitable nurse at Akashi for the child, he ought to send one from the capital. Fortunately there was a lady there who had lately been delivered of a child. Her mother, who had waited at Court when the late ex-Emperor lived, and her father, who had been some time Court Chamberlain, were both dead. She was now in miserable circumstances. Genji sounded her, through a certain channel, whether she would not be willing to be useful to him. This offer on his part she accepted without much hesitation, and was despatched with a confidential servant to attend on the new-born child. He also sent with her a sword and other presents. She left the capital in a carriage, and proceeded by boat to the province of Settsu, and thence on horseback to Akashi.

When she arrived the priest was intensely delighted, and the young mother, who had been gradually improving in health, felt great consolation. The child was very healthy, and the nurse at once began to discharge her duties most faithfully.

Hitherto Genji did not confide the story of his relations with the maiden of Akashi to Violet, but he thought he had better do so, as the matter might naturally reach her ears. He now, therefore, informed her of all the circumstances, and of the birth of the child, saying, "If you feel any unpleasantness about the matter, I cannot blame you in any way. It was not the blessing which I desired. How greatly do I regret that in the quarter where I wished to see the heavenly gift, there is none, but see it in another, where there was no expectation. The child is merely a girl too, and I almost think that I need pay no further attention. But this would make me heartless towards my undoubted offspring. I shall send for it and show it to you, and hope you will be generous to her. Can you assure me you will be so?" At these words Violet's face became red as crimson, but she did not lose her temper, and quietly replied:

"Your saying this only makes me contemptible to myself, as I think my generosity may not yet be fully understood; but I should like to know when and where I could have learnt to be ungenerous."

"These words sound too hard to me," said he. "How can you be so cruel to me? Pray don't attribute any blame to me; I never thought of it. How miserable am I!" And he began to drop tears when he came to reflect how faithful she had been all the time, and how affectionate, and also how regular had been her correspondence. He felt sorry for her, and continued, "In my anxious thoughts about this child, I have some intentions which may be agreeable to you also, only I will not tell you too hastily, since, if I do so now, they might not be taken in a favorable light. The attractions of the mother seem only to have arisen from the position in which she was placed. You must not think of the matter too seriously." He then briefly sketched her character and her skill in music. But on the part of Violet she could not but think that it was cruel to her to give away part of his heart, while her thoughts were with no one but him, and she was quite cast down for some time.

Genji tried to console her. He took up a *kin* and asked her to play and sing with him; but she did not touch it, saying that she could not play it so well as the maiden of Akashi. This very manner of her mild jealousy made her more captivating to him, and without further remarks the subject was dropped.

The fifth of May was the fiftieth day of the birth of the child, so Genji sent a messenger to Akashi a few days before the time when he would be expected. At Akashi the feast for the occasion was arranged with great pains, and the arrival of Genji's messenger was most opportune.

Let us now relate something about the Princess Wistaria.—Though she had become a nun, her title of ex-Empress had never been lost;

and now the change in the reigning sovereign gave her fresh honors. She had been recognized as equivalent to an Empress-regnant who had abdicated. A liberal allowance was granted to her, and a becoming household was established for her private use. She, however, still continued her devotion to religion, now and then coming to Court to see her son, where she was received with all cordiality; so that her rival, the mother of the ex-Emperor, whose influence was overwhelming till lately, now began to feel like one to whom the world had become irksome.

In the meantime, public affairs entirely changed their aspects, and the world seemed at this time to have been divided between the Dajiôdaijin and his son-in-law, Genji, by whose influence all things in public were swayed.

In August, of this year, the daughter of Gon-Chiûnagon (formerly Tô-no-Chiûjiô) was introduced at Court. She took up her abode in the Kokiden, which had been formerly occupied by her maternal aunt, and she was also styled from this time the Niogo of Kokiden. Prince Hiôb-Kiô had also the intention of introducing his second daughter at Court, but Genji took no interest in this. What will he eventually do about this matter?

In the same autumn Genji went to the Temple of Sumiyoshi to fulfil his vows. His party consisted of many young nobles and Court retainers, besides his own private attendants.

By a coincidence the maiden of Akashi, who had been prevented from coming to the Temple since the last year, happened to arrive there on the same day. Her party travelled in a boat, and when it reached the beach they saw the procession of Genji's party crossing before them. They did not know what procession it was, and asked the bystanders about it, who, in return, asked them sarcastically,

"Can there be anyone who does not know of the coming of Naidaijin, the Prince Genji, here to-day to fulfil his vows?"

Most of the young nobles were on horseback, with beautifully made saddles; and others, including Ukon-no-Jiô, Yoshikiyo, and Koremitz, in fine uniforms of different colors (blue, green, or scarlet), according to their different ranks, formed the procession, contrasting with the hue of the range of pine-trees on both sides of the road.

Genji was in a carriage, which was followed by ten boy pages, granted by the Court in the same way as a late Sadaijin, Kawara, had been honored. They were dressed in admirable taste, and their hair was twisted up in the form of a double knot, with ribbons of gorgeous purple. The young Genji was also in the procession on horseback, and followed the carriage.

The maiden of Akashi witnessed the procession, but she avoided making herself known. She thought she had better not go up to the Temple on that day; but she could not sail back to Akashi, so she had her boat moored in the bay of Naniwa for the night. As to Genji, he knew nothing of the maiden being a spectator of the procession, and spent the whole night in the Temple with his party in performing services which might please the God.

It was then that he was informed by Koremitz that he had seen the maiden of Akashi in a boat. On the morrow Genji and his party set off for their homes. As they proceeded Genji hummed,

"Ima hata onaji Naniwa nal,"[123]

and he stopped, while contemplating the bay. Koremitz, who stood beside him, and divined what he was thinking about, took out a small pen from his pocket and presented it to Genji, who took it and wrote the following on a piece of paper, which he sent to the maiden by one of his attendants who knew her whereabouts:—

"Divinely led by love's bright flame,To this lone temple's shrine we come;And as yon beacon meets our eye,To dream, perchance, of days gone by."

A few words more. The change of the ruler had brought a change of the Saigû; and the Lady of Rokjiô, with her daughter, returned to the capital. Her health, however, began to fail, and she became a nun, and after some time died. Before her death Genji visited her, and with her last breath she consigned her daughter to his care. Genji was thinking, therefore, of introducing her at Court at some future time.

FOOTNOTES:

[123]A line of an old ode about the beacon in the bay of Naniwa, at the same time expressing the desire of meeting with a loved one. It is impossible to translate this ode literally, as in the original there is a play upon words, the word beacon (in Japanese) also meaning "enthusiastic endeavor." The word "myo-tzkushi" (= beacon) more properly means "water-marker" though disused in the modern Japanese. In the translation a little liberty has been taken.

CHAPTER XV

OVERGROWN MUGWORT

When Genji was an exile on the sea-coast, many people had been longing for his return. Among these was the Princess Hitachi. She was, as we have seen, the survivor of his Royal father, and the kindness which she had received from Genji was to her like the reflection of the broad starlit sky in a basin of water. After Genji left the capital, however, no correspondence ever passed between them. Several of her servants left her, and her residence became more lonely than ever. A fox might have found a covert in the overgrown shrubbery, and the cry of the owl might have been heard among the thick branches. One might imagine some mysterious "tree-spirit" to reign there. Nevertheless, such grounds as these, surrounded with lofty trees, are more tempting to those who desire to have a stylish dwelling. Hence there were several Duriôs (local governors) who had become rich, and having returned from different provinces, sounded the Princess to see if she were inclined to part with her residence; but this she always refused to do, saying that, however unfortunate she might be, she was not able to give up a mansion inherited from her parents.

The mansion contained also a store of rare and antique articles. Several fashionable persons endeavored to induce the Princess to part with them; but such people appeared only contemptible to her, as she looked upon them as proposing such a thing solely because they knew she was poor. Her attendants sometimes suggested to her that it was by no means an uncommon occurrence for one to dispose of such articles when destiny necessitated the sacrifice; but her reply was that these things had been handed down to her only that she might make use of them, and that she would be violating the wishes of the dead if she consented to part with them, allowing them to become the ornament of the dwellings of some lowborn upstarts.

Scarcely anyone paid a visit to her dwelling, her only occasional visitor being her brother, a priest, who came to see her when he came to the capital, but he was a man of eccentric character, and was not very flourishing in his circumstances.

Such being the state of affairs with the Princess Hitachi, the grounds of her mansion became more and more desolate and wild, the mugwort growing so tall that it reached the veranda. The surrounding walls of massive earth broke down here and there and crumbled away, being trampled over by wandering cattle. In spring and summer boys would sometimes play there. In the autumn a gale blew down a corridor, and carried away part of the shingle roof. Only one blessing remained there—no thief intruded into the enclosure, as no temptation was offered to them for their attack.

But never did the Princess lose her accustomed reserve, which her parents had instilled into her mind. Society for her had no attractions. She solaced the hours of her loneliness by looking over ancient story-books and poems, which were stored in the old bookshelves, such as the Karamori, Hakoya-no-toji, or Kakya-hime. These, with their illustrations, were her chief resources.

Now a sister of the Princess's mother had married a Duriô, and had already borne him a daughter. This marriage had been considered an unequal match by the father of the Princess, and for this reason she was not very friendly with the family. Jijiû, however, who was a daughter of the Princess's nurse, and who still remained with the

Princess, used to go to her. This aunt was influenced by a secret feeling of spite, and when Jijiû visited her she often whispered to her many things which did not become her as a lady. It seems to me that where a lady of ordinary degree is elevated to a higher position, she often acquires a refinement like one originally belonging to it; but there are other women, who when degraded from their rank spoil their taste and habits just like the lady in question. She fondly hoped to revenge herself for having been formerly looked down upon, by showing an apparent kindness to the Princess Hitachi, and by wishing to take her into her home, and make her wait upon her daughters. With this view she[204] told Jijiu to tell her mistress to come to her, and Jijiu did so; but the Princess did not comply with this request.

In the meantime the lady's husband was appointed Daini (Senior Secretary to the Lord-Lieutenant), and they were to go down to Tzkushi (modern Kiusiu). She wished to take the Princess with her, and told her that she felt sorry to go to such a far-off locality, leaving her in her present circumstances; but the latter still unhesitatingly replied in the negative, and declined the offer; whereupon her aunt tauntingly remarked that she was too proud, and that, however exalted she might think herself, no one, not even Genji, would show her any further attention.

About this time Genji returned, but for some while she heard nothing from him, and only the public rejoicing of many people, and the news about him from the outside world reached her ears. This gave her aunt a further opportunity of repeating the same taunts. She said, "See now who cares for you in your present circumstances. It is not praiseworthy to display such self-importance as you did in the lifetime of your father." And again she pressed her to go with her, but the Princess still clung to the hope that the time would come when Genji would remember her and renew his kindness.

Winter came! One day, quite unexpectedly, the aunt arrived at the mansion, bringing as a present a dress for the Princess. Her carriage dashed into the garden in a most pompous style, and drove right up to the southern front of the building. Jijiu went to meet her, and conducted her into the Princess's apartment.

"I must soon be leaving the capital," said the visitor. "It is not my wish to leave you behind, but you would not listen to me, and now there is no help. But this one, this Jijiu at least, I wish to take with me. I have come to-day to fetch her. I cannot understand how you can be content with your present condition."

Here she manifested a certain sadness, but her delight at her husband's promotion was unmistakable, and she continued:—

"When your father was alive, I was looked down upon by him, which caused a coolness between us. But nevertheless I at no time entertained any ill-will towards you, only you were much favored by Prince Genji, as I heard, which made me ab stain from visiting you often; but fortune is fickle, for those in a humble position often enjoy comfort, and those that are higher in station are not quite so well circumstanced. I do really feel sorry to leave you behind."

The Princess said very little, but her answer was, "I really thank you for your kind attention, but I do not think I am now fit to move about in the world. I shall be quite happy to bury myself under this roof."

"Well, you may think so, but it is simply foolish to abandon one's self, and to bury one's life under such a mass of dilapidation. Had Prince Genji been kind enough to repair the place, it might have become transformed into a golden palace, and how joyous would it not be? but this you cannot expect. As far as I am informed the daughter of Prince Hiob-Kio is the only favorite of the Prince, and no one else shares his attention, all his old favorites being now abandoned. How, then, can you expect him to say that, because you have been faithful to him, he will therefore come to you again?"

These words touched the Princess, but she gave no vent to her feelings. The visitor, therefore, hurried Jijiu to get ready, saying that they must leave before the dusk.

"When I hear what the lady says," said Jijiu, "it sounds to me very reasonable; but when I see how anxious the Princess is, that also seems natural. Thus I am puzzled between the two. Let me, however, say this, I will only see the lady off to-day."

Nevertheless, the Princess foresaw that Jijiu was going to leave her, and she thought of giving her some souvenir. Her own dress was not to be thought of, as it was too old; fortunately she had a long tress of false hair, about nine feet long, made of the hair which had fallen from her own head. This she put into an old casket, and gave it to Jijiu, with a jar of rare perfume.

Jijiu had been an attendant on the Princess for a very long time, besides, her mother (the nurse), before she died, told the Princess and her daughter that she hoped they might be long together; so the parting with Jijiu was very trying to the Princess who said to her that though she could not blame her for leaving, she still felt sorry to lose her. To this Jijiu replied, that she never forgot the wishes of her mother, and was only too happy to share joy and sorrow with the Princess; yet she was sorry to say that circumstances obliged her to leave her for some time; but before she could say much, she was hurried away by the visitor.

It was one evening in April of the following year that Genji happened to be going to the villa of "the falling flowers," and passed by the mansion of the Princess. There was in the garden a large pine-tree, from whose branches the beautiful clusters of a wistaria hung in rich profusion. A sigh of the evening breeze shook them as they hung in the silver moonlight, and scattered their rich fragrance towards the wayfarer. There was also a weeping willow close by, whose pensile tresses of new verdure touched the half-broken walls of earth underneath.

When Genji beheld this beautiful scene from his carriage, he at once remembered it was a place he had seen before. He stopped his carriage, and said to Koremitz, who was with him as usual—

"Is this not the mansion of the Princess Hitachi?"

"Yes, it is," replied Koremitz.

"Do ask if she is still here," said Genji; "this is a good chance; I will see her if she is at home—ask!"

Koremitz entered, and proceeding to the door, called out. An old woman from the inside demanded to know who he was. Koremitz announced himself, and asked if Jijiû was within. The old women replied that she was not, but that she herself was the same as Jijiû.

Koremitz recognized her as an aunt of the latter. He then asked her about the Princess, and told her of Genji's intention. To his inquiries he soon obtained a satisfactory answer, and duly reported it to Genji, who now felt a pang of remorse for his long neglect of one so badly circumstanced. He descended from his carriage, but the pathway was all but overgrown with tall mugwort, which was wet with a passing shower; so Koremitz whisked them with his whip, and led him in.

Inside, meanwhile, the Princess, though she felt very pleased, experienced a feeling of shyness. Her aunt, it will be remembered, had presented her with a suitable dress, which she had hitherto had no pleasure in wearing, and had kept it in a box which had originally contained perfume. She now took this out and put it on. Genji was presently shown into the room.

"It is a long time since I saw you last," said Genji, "but still I have never forgotten you, only I heard nothing from you; so I waited till now, and here I find myself once more."

The Princess, as usual, said very little, only thanking him for his visit. He then addressed her in many kind and affectionate words, many of which he might not really have meant, and after a considerable stay he at last took his departure.

This was about the time of the feast in the Temple of Kamo, and Genji received several presents under various pretexts. He distributed these presents among his friends, such as those in the villa of "the falling flowers," and to the Princess. He also sent his servant to the mansion of the latter to cut down the rampant mugwort, and he restored the grounds to proper order. Moreover, he had a wooden enclosure placed all round the garden.

So far as the world hitherto knew about Genji, he was supposed only to cast his eyes on extraordinary and pre-eminent beauties; but we see in him a very different character in the present instance. He showed so much kindness to the Princess Hitachi, who was by no means distinguished for her beauty, and who still bore a mark on her nose which might remind one of a well-ripened fruit carried by mountaineers. How was this? it might have been preordained to be so.

The Princess continued to live in the mansion for two years, and then she removed to a part of a newly built "eastern mansion" belonging to Genji, where she lived happily under the kind care of the Prince, though he had much difficulty in coming often to see her. I would fain describe the astonishment of her aunt when she returned from the Western Island and saw the Princess's happy condition, and how Jijiu regretted having left her too hastily; but my head is aching and my fingers are tired, so I shall wait for some future opportunity when I may again take up the thread of my story.

CHAPTER XVI

BARRIER HOUSE

We left beautiful Cicada at the time when she quitted the capital with her husband. Now this husband Iyo-no-Kami, had been promoted to the governorship of Hitachi, in the year which followed that of the demise of the late ex-Emperor, and Cicada accompanied him to the province. It was a year after Genji's return that they came back to the capital. On the day when they had to pass the barrier house of Ausaka (meeting-path) on their homeward way, Hitachi's sons, the eldest known to us as Ki-no-Kami, now became Kawachi-no-Kami, and others went from the city to meet them. It so happened that Genji was to pay his visit to the Temple of Ishiyama on this very day. This became known to Hitachi, who, thinking it would be embarrassing if they met with his procession on the road, determined to start very early; but, somehow or another, time passed on, and when they came to the lake coast of Uchiide (modern Otz, a place along Lake Biwa), the sun had risen high, and this was the moment when Genji was crossing the Awata Road. In the course of a few hours the outriders of Genji's cortège came in sight; so that Hitachi's party left their several carriages, and seated themselves under the shade of the cedars on the hill-side of Ausaka, in order to avoid encountering Genji and his procession. It was the last day of September. All the herbage was fading under the influence of the coming winter, and many tinted autumn leaves displayed their different hues over the hills and fields. The scene was in every way pleasing to the eyes of the spectators. The number of the carriages of Hitachi's party was about ten in all, and the style and appearance of the party showed no traces of rusticity of taste. It might have been imagined that the party of the Saigû journeying towards or from Ise, might be something similar to this one.

Genji soon caught sight of them, and became aware that it was Hitachi. He therefore sent for Cicada's brother—whom we know as Kokimi, and who had now been made Uyemon-no-Ske—from the party, and told him that he hoped his attention in coming there to meet them would not be considered unfavorable. This Kokimi, as we know, had received much kindness from Genji up to the time of his becoming a man; but when Genji had to quit the capital he left him and joined his brother-in-law in his official province. This was not viewed as very satisfactory; but Genji manifested no bad feeling to him, and treated him still as one of his household attendants. Ukon-no-Jiô, a brother-in-law of Cicada, on the other hand, had faithfully followed Genji to his exile, and after their return he was more than ever favored by Genji. This state of things made many feel for the bad taste of the ordinary weakness of the world, exhibited by the faithfully following of one when circumstances are flourishing, and deserting him in the time of adversity. Kokimi himself was one of those who fully realized these feelings, and was pained by them. When Genji finished his visit to the Temple, and was coming back, Kokimi once more came from the capital to meet him. Through him Genji sent a letter to his sister, asking her if she had recognized him when he passed at Ausaka, adding the following verse:—

"As onward we our way did take,On Meeting-Path, both I and you,We met not, for by the saltless lake,No *milme*[124] by its waters grew."

In handing the letter to Kokimi, Genji said, "Give this to your sister; it is a long time since I heard anything from her, still the past seems to me only like yesterday. But do you disapprove of my sending this?" Kokimi replied in a few words, and took the letter back to his sister, and told her, when he gave it, that she might easily give him some sort of answer. She did indeed disapprove of treating the matter in any way more seriously than she had formerly done, yet she wrote the following:—

"By Barrier-House—oh, name unkind,That bars the path of friendly greeting; We passed along with yearning mind,But passed, alas! without a meeting."

After this time some other correspondence now and then passed between them. As time rolled on the health of her aged husband visibly declined; and after fervently enjoining his sons to be kind and attentive to her, in due time he breathed his last.

For some time they were kind and attentive to her, as their father had requested, and there was nothing unsatisfactory in their behavior towards her, yet many things which were not altogether pleasant gradually presented themselves to her, and so it is always in life. Finally Cicada, telling her intentions to no one beforehand, became a nun.

FOOTNOTES:

[124]The name of a seaweed, but also meaning the eyes that meet, and hence the twofold sense of the word.

CHAPTER XVII

COMPETITIVE SHOW OF PICTURES

T he introduction of the late Saigû, the daughter of the Lady of Rokjiô, at Court, was now arranged to take place, with the approval of the Empress-mother (the Princess Wistaria). All the arrangements and preparations were made, though not quite openly, under the eye of Genji, who took a parental interest in her. It may be remembered that the ex-Emperor was once struck by her charms, on the eve of her departure for Ise; and though he never encouraged this fancy to become anything more than an ordinary partiality, he took no small interest in all that concerned her welfare.

When the day of introduction arrived, he made her several beautiful presents, such as a comb-box, a dressing-table, and a casket containing rare perfumes. At her residence all her female attendants, and some others, assembled, who made every preparation with the utmost pains.

In the Palace, the Empress-mother was with her Royal son on this day. He was still a mere boy, and scarcely understood what was going on; but he was now fully informed on the subject by his mother, and was told that a very interesting lady was going to reside in the Palace to attend on him, and that he must be good and kind to her. The presentation took place late in the evening, and henceforth she was called the Niogo of the Ume-Tsubo (plum-chamber), from the name of her apartment.

She was a charming lady, and the Emperor was not without a certain liking for her; yet Lady Kokiden, the daughter of Gon-

Chiûnagon (Tô-no-Chiûjiô), who had been introduced some time previously, and consequently was an acquaintance of an older date, was much more frequently preferred by him to the other for society in daily amusement. When Gon-Chiûnagon introduced his daughter, he did not of course do so without hope of her further elevation; but now Lady Plum came to assume a position through Genji's influence, as if to compete with his daughter for the royal favor; and it was by no means glad tidings for him. It may be here mentioned that Prince Hiob-Kio had also, as we have already seen, an intention of introducing one of his daughters at Court; but this hope was doomed to disappointment by the establishing of the two ladies already introduced, and he was induced to defer his intention, at least for the present.

The Emperor was very fond of pictures, and painted with considerable ability. Lady Plum, too, as it happened, possessed the same taste as the Emperor, and used often to amuse herself by painting. If, therefore, he liked ordinary courtiers who exhibited a taste for painting, it was no matter of surprise that he liked to see the delicate hands of the lady occupied in carefully laying on colors. This similarity of taste gradually drew his attention to her, and led to frequent visits to the "plum-chamber." When Gon-Chiûnagon was informed of these circumstances, he took the matter into his own hands. He himself determined to excite a spirit of rivalry. He contrived means to counteract the influence of painting, and commissioned several famous artists of the times to execute some elaborate pictures. Most of these were subjects taken from old romances, as he conceived that these were always more attractive than mere fanciful pictures. He had also caused to be painted a representation of every month of the year, which would also be likely, he thought, to interest the Emperor. When these pictures were finished he took them to Court, and submitted them to his inspection; but he would not agree that he should take any of them to the plum-chamber; and they were all deposited in the chamber of his daughter.

Genji, when he heard of this, said of his brother-in-law, "He is young; he never could be behind others." He was, however, unable to pass the matter over unnoticed. He told the Emperor that he would present him with some old pictures, and returning to his mansion at Nijio he opened his picture cabinet, where numbers of old and new pictures were kept. From these, with the assistance of Violet, he made a selection of the best. But such pictures as illustrations of the "Long Regrets," or representations of "O-shio-kun," were reserved, because the terminations of these stories were not happy ones. He also took out of his cabinet the sketches which he had made while in Suma and Akashi, and showed them for the first time to Violet, who was a little angry at his not having shown them to her sooner.

It was about the tenth of February, and the face of Nature began to smile with the approach of spring, making the hearts and tempers of people more calm and cheerful; besides, it was just the time when the Court was unoccupied with the keeping of any festival. There could be no better chance than this for such an exhibition of pictures to attract the attention of people enjoying leisure. Genji, therefore, sent his collection of pictures to the Palace in behalf of the lady of the plum-chamber.

This soon created a sensation in the Palace. Most of the pictures that were in the possession of the lady of the plum-chamber were from old romances, and the pictures themselves were of ancient date, being rare, while those of Kokiden were more modern subjects and by living artists. Thus each of them had their special merits, so that it became difficult to say which were more excellent. Talking of these pictures became quite a fashionable subject of conversation of the courtiers of the day. The Imperial-mother happened to be at Court, and when she saw these pictures and heard different persons at Court discussing their relative merits, she suggested that they should divide themselves into two parties, right and left, and regularly to give their judgment. This was accordingly done: Hei-Naishi-no-Ske, Jijiû-no-Naishi, and Shiôshiô-no-Miôbu took the left, on the side of the lady of the plum-chamber; while Daini-no-Naishi-no-Ske, Chiûjiô-no-Miôbu, and Hiôye-no-Miôbu took the right, on the side of the Kokiden.

The first picture selected was the illustration of the "Bamboo Cutter,"[125] by the left, as it was the most appropriate to come first for the discussion of its merits, as being the parent of romance. To compete with this, that of "Toshikagè,"[126] from "The Empty Wood," was selected by the right. The left now stated their case, saying, "The bamboo—indeed, its story too—may be an old and commonly known thing, but the maiden Kakya, in keeping her purity unsullied in this world, is highly admirable; besides, it was an occurrence that belongs to a pre-historical period. No ordinary woman would ever be equal to her, and so this picture has an excellence." Thereupon the right argued in opposition to this, saying, "The sky, where the maiden Kakya has gone away, may indeed be high, but it is beyond human reach, so we may put it aside. When she made her appearance in this world she was, after all, a creature of bamboo; and, indeed, we may consider her even lower than ourselves. It may also be true that she threw a bright radiance over the inside of a cottage, but she never shone in the august society of a palace. Abe-no-oshi's[127] spending millions of money in order to get the so-called fire-proof rat, which, when obtained, was consumed in the flames in a moment, is simply ridiculous. Prince Kuramochi's[128] pretended jewel branch was simply a delusion. Besides, this picture is by Kose-no-Omi, with notes[129] by Tsurayuki. These are not very uncommon. The paper is Kamiya, only covered with Chinese satin. The outer cover is reddish purple, and the centre stick is purple Azedarach. These are very common ornaments. Now Toshikagè, though he had undergone a severe trial from the raging storm, and had been carried to a strange country, arrived at length at the country to which he was originally despatched, and from there returned to his native land, having achieved his object, and having made his ability recognized both at home and abroad. This picture is the life of this man, and it represents many scenes, not only of his country but of foreign ones, which cannot fail to be interesting. We therefore dare to place this one above the other in merit."

The ground of this picture was thick white tinted paper, the outer cover was green, and the centre stick jade. The picture was by Tsunenori, and the writing by Michikage. It was in the highest taste of the period.

The left made no more protestation against the right.

Next the romance of Ise by the left, and that of Shiô-Sammi by the right, were brought into competition. Here again the relative merit was very difficult to be decided at once. That of the right had apparently more charms than that of the other, since it beautifully represented the society of a more recent period.

Hei-Naishi, of the left, therefore said,

"If leaving the depths of Ise's night-sea,We follow the fancies of new-fashioned dreams,All the beauty and skill of the ancients will beSwept away by the current of art's modern streams.

Who would run down the fame of Narihira for the sake of the pretentious humbug of our own days?"

Then Daini-no-Naishi-no-Ske, of the right, replied,

"The noble mind that soars on high,Beyond the star-bespangled sky;Looks down with ease on depths that lieA thousand fathoms 'neath his eye."[130]

Upon this, the Empress-mother interceded. She said, that "The exalted nobility of Lord Hiôye[131] may not, indeed, be passed over without notice, yet the name of Narihira could not altogether be eclipsed by his.

Though too well-known to all may beThe lovely shore of Ise's sea;Its aged fisher's honored name,A tribute of respect may claim."

There were several more rolls to be exhibited, and the rival protestations on both sides became very warm, so that one roll occasioned considerable discussion.

While this was going on, Genji arrived on the scene. He suggested to them that if there was any competition at all it should be decided on a specially appointed day, in a more solemn manner, in the presence of the Emperor. This suggestion having been adopted, the discussion came to an end.

The day for this purpose was fixed. The ex-Emperor, who had been informed of this, presented several pictures to the lady of the plum-chamber. They were mostly illustrations of Court Festivals, on which there were explanatory remarks written by the Emperor Yenghi. Besides these, there was one which had been expressly executed at his own order by Kim-mochi. This was an illustration of the ceremony which took place at his palace on the departure of the lady for Ise, some time back, when she had gone there as the Saigû. It was also probable that some of his pictures came into the possession of her rival, the Lady Kokiden, through his mother (as the mother of the former was a sister of the latter).

When the day arrived every arrangement was made in the large saloon at the rear of the Palace, where the Imperial seat was placed at the top. The Court ladies of both parties—those of the lady of the plum-chamber, and those of the lady of Kokiden—were arranged respectively left and right, the left, or those of the lady of the plum-chamber, facing southwards, and those of the right, northwards. All the courtiers also took the places allotted to them. Here the pictures were brought. The box, containing those of the left was of purple Azedarach. The stand on which the box was placed was of safran, and over this was thrown a cover of Chinese brocade with a mauve ground. The seat underneath was of Chinese colored silk. Six young girls brought all this in, and arranged it all in order. Their Kazami (outer dress) was of red and cherry color, with tunics of Wistaria lining (light purple outside, and light green within).

The box which contained the pictures of the right was of "Jin" wood, the stand of light colored "Jin," the cover of Corean silk with a green ground. The legs of the stand, which were trellised round with a silken cord, showed modern and artistic taste. The Kazami of the young girls was of willow lining (white outside and green within), and their tunics were of Kerria japonica lining (or yellow outside and light red within). Both Genji and Gon-Chiûnagon were present, by the Emperor's special invitation, as also the Prince Lord-Lieutenant of Tzkushi who loved pictures above all things, and he was consequently chosen umpire for this day's competition. Many of the pictures were highly admirable, and it was most difficult to make any preference between them. For instance, if there was produced by one party a roll of "The Season," which was the masterpiece of some old master, on selected subjects; there was produced also, by the other party, a roll of sketches on paper, which were scarcely inferior to, and more ornamented with flourishing than the ancient works, in spite of the necessary limitation of space which generally makes the wide expanse of scenery almost too difficult to express. Thus the disputes on both sides were very warm.

Meanwhile the Imperial-mother (the Princess Wistaria) also came into the saloon, pushing aside the sliding screen of the breakfast chamber. The criticisms still continued, in which Genji made, now and then, suggestive remarks. Before all was finished the shades of evening began to fall on them. There remained, on the right, one more roll, when the roll of "Suma" was produced on the left. It made Gon-Chiûnagon slightly embarrassed. The last roll of the right was, of course, a selected one, but it had several disadvantages in comparison with that of "Suma." The sketches on this roll had been done by Genji, with great pains and time. They were illustrations of different bays and shores. They were most skilfully executed, and carried away the minds of the spectators to the actual spots. On them illustrative remarks were written, sometimes in the shape of a diary, occasionally mingled with poetical effusions in style both grave and easy. These made a great impression on the Emperor, and on everyone present; and finally, owing to this roll, the left was decided to have won the victory.

Then followed the partaking of refreshments, as was usual on such occasions. In the course of conversation, Genji remarked to the Lord-Lieutenant, "From my boyhood I paid much attention to reading and writing, and perhaps my father noticed that I had benefited by these pursuits. He observed that 'few very clever men enjoyed worldly happiness and long life'; perhaps because ability and knowledge are too highly valued in the world to admit of other blessings. True it is, that even a man whose high birth assures him a certain success in life, ought not to be devoid of learning, but I advise you to moderate your exertions. After this time, he took more pains in instructing me in the ways and manners of men of high position than in the minute details of science. For these reasons, though on the one hand I was not quite clumsy, I cannot, on the other, say in what particular subject I am well versed and efficient. Drawing, however, was a favorite object of my taste and ambition, and I also desired to execute a work to the full extent of my ideas. In the meantime, I enjoyed quiet leisure by the sea-shore, and as I contemplated the wide expanse of scenery, my conception seemed to enlarge as I gazed upon it. This made me take up my brush, but not a few parts of the work have fallen short of those conceptions. Therefore, I thought them altogether unworthy to be shown expressly, though I have now boldly submitted them to your inspection on this good opportunity."

"Nothing can be well learned that is not agreeable to one's natural taste," replied the Lord-Lieutenant. "It is true, but every art has its special instructor, and by this means their methods can be copied by their pupils, though there may be differences in skill and perfection. Among arts, however, nothing betrays one's tastes and nature more than work of pen or brush (writing and painting), and playing the game of Go. Of course men of low origin, and of little accomplishment, often happen to excel in these arts, but not so frequently as persons of position. Under the auspicious care of the late Emperor, what prince or princess could have failed to attain the knowledge of such arts? a care which was directed towards yourself especially. I will not speak of literature and learning too. Your accomplishments comprised the *kin*, next the flute, the mandolin, and *soh-koto*—this we all knew, and so, too, the late Emperor said: your painting, however, has been hitherto thought to be mere amusement, but we now have seen your sketches executed with a skill not unequal to the ancient famous draughtsmen in black ink."

It was about the twentieth of the month, and the evening moon appeared in the sky, while they were thus conversing. Her radiance was too weak to make the ground near them bright, but afar-off the sky became palely white. Several musical instruments were sent for from the guardian of the library. Genji played a *kin*, Gon-Chiûnagon a *wagon*, the Lord-Lieutenant a *soh-koto*, and Shiôshiô-no-Miôbu a mandolin. The *hiôshi* (beating time to music) was undertaken by a courtier. As this went on, the darkness of night began to diminish, and the hues of the flowers in the garden, and the countenance of each of the party, became gradually visible, while the birds themselves began to chirp in the trees. It was a pleasant dawn. Several presents were made to the company by the Imperial-mother, and to the Lord-Lieutenant a robe was given in addition, as an acknowledgment of his services as judge in the competition. And so the party broke up. The roll of "Suma" was left, as was requested, in the hands of the Imperial-mother. Genji had some more rolls of the same series, but they were reserved for some future occasion.

During the reign of this Emperor every care was taken on the occasion of all Court Festivals, so that future generations should hold that such and such precedents took their origin in this reign. Hence a meeting even such as above described, which was only private in its nature, was carried out in a manner as pleasant and enlightened as possible.

As to Genji, he thought he had obtained a position too exalted, and an influence too great. There were, indeed, several instances of public men surprised by misfortune, who, in premature age, obtained high position and vast influence. He thought of these examples, and though he had hitherto enjoyed his position and authority, as if he regarded them as a compensation for his former fall, he began, as the Emperor was now becoming older, to retire gradually from public life, so as to prepare his mind and thoughts, and devote himself to the attainment of happiness in the world to come, and also for the prolongation of life. For these reasons he ordered a chapel to be built for himself on a mountain side, where he might retire. In the meantime he had the ambition to see his children satisfactorily brought out into the world—an ambition which restrained him from carrying out his wishes of retiring.

It is not easy to understand or define the exact state of his mind at this period.

FOOTNOTES:

[125]A short romance, supposed to be the oldest work of the kind ever written in Japan, as the authoress states. The story is, that once upon a time there was an aged man whose occupation was to cut bamboo. One day he found a knot in a bamboo cane which was radiant and shining, and upon cutting it he found in it a little girl who was named Kakya-hime. He took her home and brought her up. She grew a remarkable beauty. She had many suitors, but she refused to listen to their addresses, and kept her maiden reputation unsullied. Finally, in leaving this world, she ascended into the moon, from which she professed to have originally come down.

[126]This is another old romance, and Toshikagè is its principal hero. When twelve or thirteen years of age he was sent to China, but the ship in which he was, being driven by a hurricane to Persia, he met there with a mystic stranger, from whom he learned secrets of the "Kin;" from thence he reached China, and afterwards returned to Japan.

[127]This man was one of the maiden's suitors. He was told by her that if he could get for her the skin of the fire-proof rat she might possibly accept his hand. With this object he gave a vast sum of money to a Chinese merchant, who brought him what he professed to be the skin of the fire-proof rat, but when it was put to the test, it burnt away, and he lost his suit.

[128]This Prince was another suitor of the maiden. His task was to find a sacred island called Horai, and to get a branch of a jewelled tree which grew in this island. He pretended to have embarked for this purpose, but really concealed himself in an obscure place. He had an artificial branch made by some goldsmith; but, of course, this deception was at once detected.

[129]Japanese pictures usually have explanatory notes written on them.

[130]It seems that this stanza alludes to some incident in the Shiô-Sammi, at the same time praising the picture.

[131]This seems to be the name of the hero in the story alluded to above.

End of the book.